W9-DBE-807

American Political Parties
and Constitutional Politics

The Ashbrook Series on Constitutional Politics

Sponsored by the John M. Ashbrook Center for Public Affairs at Ashland University

General Editors: Peter W. Schramm and Bradford P. Wilson

American Political Parties and Constitutional Politics

Separation of Powers and Good Government: Congress and the Presidency

The American Judiciary and Constitutional Politics

American Political Parties and Constitutional Politics

Edited by

Peter W. Schramm
and Bradford P. Wilson

ROWMAN & LITTLEFIELD PUBLISHERS, INC.

TECHNICAL COLLEGE OF THE LOWCOUNTRY
LEARNING RESOURCES CENTER
POST OFFICE BOX 1288
BEAUFORT, SOUTH CAROLINA 29901-1288

ROWMAN & LITTLEFIELD PUBLISHERS, INC.

Published in the United States of America
by Rowman & Littlefield Publishers, Inc.
4720 Boston Way, Lanham, Maryland 20706

British Cataloging in Publication Information Available

Library of Congress Cataloging-in-Publication Data

American political parties and constitutional politics / edited by
Peter W. Schramm, Bradford P. Wilson.
p.   cm. — (Ashbrook series in constitutional politics)
Based on a conference held Nov. 10, 1990 at Ashland University,
sponsored by the John M. Ashbrook Center for Public Affairs.
Includes bibliographical references and index.
1. Political parties—United States—History—Congresses.   2. United
States—Constitutional history—Congresses.   I. Schramm, Peter W.
II. Wilson, Bradford P.   III. Series.
JK2261.A54   1993
324.273'09—dc20   92-43099 CIP

ISBN 0-8476-7819-9 (cloth : alk. paper)
ISBN 0-8476-7820-2 (pbk. : alk. paper)

Printed in the United States of America

∞ TM The paper used in this publication meets the minimum requirements of
American National Standard for Information Sciences—Permanence of
Paper for Printed Library Materials, ANSI Z39.48–1984.

CONTENTS

PREFACE

THE AMERICAN CONSTITUTION'S PARTISANSHIP FOR REPUBLICAN government is a theme running through this volume. American political parties have been a very important, albeit informal, part of our politics in trying to secure this constitutional end.

Political parties at their best have acknowledged that their work is made possible and in crucial ways guided by the Constitution. They have therefore admitted the Constitution's supremacy and have understood that their purposes must be tailored to perpetuating and improving the Constitution's work. As Harvey Mansfield, Jr., states in this volume, "A constitution is a means by which a democratic people holds itself formally responsible for its government; and parties, which are informal or less formal, can help or hinder the quality of the people's choice." If political parties do not further the Constitution's work, if they are not channels forcing ambitious citizens to compete with one another in the service of constitutional ends, the American people do not experience the full benefits of constitutional government. Perhaps what suffers most when parties fail is the quality of deliberation through which policy is chosen and consent is given.

Much has been written in recent decades on the decline of American political parties. Analyses of the history, functions, and current status of American parties from the perspective of the concerned constitutionalist, however, have been in little evidence. The Constitution is no longer in the forefront of political debate, except for the single issue inserted by the Supreme Court's abortion decisions. In contrast to party rivalries of past generations, today's contests are eerily silent on the Constitution and its ends. Perhaps the decline of political parties is connected with the decline of constitutional rhetoric: by not arguing the sense in which their own work is the work of the Constitution, parties diminish their importance and lose the respect that accompanies service to constitutional ends. The Perot phenomenon illustrates the degree to which parties, and discussion of the constitutional dimension of American politics, have fallen into disrepute.

We think that the thoughtful essays in this volume lead us to a renewed, and deeper, understanding of political parties and, in a small way, point us in the direction of political wisdom and courage on behalf of the Constitution. We offer it to the reader with this hope and this expectation.

This volume stems from a conference on The Future of Political Parties, sponsored by the John M. Ashbrook Center for Public Affairs at Ashland University on November 10, 1990. In addition to the participants writing for this volume, the conference included William B. Allen, Frank J. Fahrenkopf, Jr., Charles Manatt, F. Clifton White, and John C. White. We would like to thank Julie Ann Kessler for her thoughtful and spirited editorial suggestions and assistance. We are grateful to the Lynde and Harry Bradley Foundation for generously supporting the conference and this book.

Peter W. Schramm

Bradford P. Wilson

October 5, 1992
Ashland, Ohio

POLITICAL PARTIES AND AMERICAN CONSTITUTIONALISM

Harvey C. Mansfield, Jr.

THE FIRST THING TO SAY ABOUT POLITICAL PARTIES IS SOMETHING obvious—that they are not mentioned in the Constitution. That is the case not only in America, but in free countries generally; only the constitutions of one party states will occasionally provide status for the ruling party. Parties are informal associations like committees in Congress, which are also not mentioned in the Constitution. What does it mean, why does it matter, that parties are informal and extra-constitutional?

At first sight, it is very strange that parties should be excluded from the Constitution because it is easy to see, and everyone admits, that politics is essentially partisan. "A political issue" means a controversial one, in which two or more groups dispute as to what is the right thing to do. Such dispute is very likely, even inevitable, because people form different opinions and have opposing interests on matters that concern them. On such matters people do not sit back, content with their speculations as if they were books in a private library; they want to see their opinions put into practice. They want to rule—if not themselves (because of the trouble involved), then through others ruling in their name. Parties perform the function of carrying controversial opinions into practice. They organize; and they do so by combining and dividing. Combining is not enough, because people more often form opinions against something they do not like than in favor of something they approve. So one can say that people combine in parties and that they divide into parties; it's the same action. Then, given the essential partisanship of politics, why are parties not in the Constitution?

The answer is that the American Constitution is not the same as the American political system. The Constitution was made by the Framers in 1787; the "system" was invented by political scientists

1

two generations ago. Understood as a system, one could include everything relating to the way Americans rule themselves—the political structure of the country. One could call the system a "constitution" in the Aristotelian sense of everything pertaining to rule (*politeia*) except that the political scientists who speak of "system" have in mind a more democratic interaction than ruling. In the sense of "system," every country has a constitution. But the American Constitution is different: it is normative or formal, and therefore makes a distinction between constitutional and unconstitutional behavior. Some countries have a formal constitution and are known as constitutional, the American being a constitutional democracy; others are nonconstitutional in this sense. To have a formal Constitution a country must adopt it formally, usually at one time—though Britain's constitution, often considered informal, consists of a mixture of formal documents (for example, the law setting a five-year term for parliaments) and conventions given formal respect (that the Queen will choose the leader of a majority in Parliament as prime minister).

Besides having been formally adopted when it was ratified in 1787–88, the American Constitution confines itself to formal statements of the powers and terms of its offices, not prescribing how they are to be exercised. Very general purposes are stated in the preamble, but they do not give specific guidance and hardly distinguish one free government from another. Thus the Constitution leaves open the direction that policies ought to take; it does not tell the American people how it ought to live (or the American people does not tell itself how to live in the Constitution); it is more form than content. Such a Constitution of formal powers is appropriate for a government based on the "rights of man" in the Declaration of Independence, for the rights of the people, like the powers of government, are not specified as to their exercise.

Parties, then appear to be necessary parts of the constitution in the informal sense, but also necessarily not part of the formal Constitution. If they were mentioned in the Constitution, the Constitution would have been, or would have become, a partisan document. Or, if parties had been mentioned—perhaps as instruments of election—they would have had to be described formally, not named or described specifically. We conclude from this reasoning that the Constitution stands above parties. That point may seem obvious too, but on reflection, is it not questionable? If politics is essentially partisan—and it certainly appears to be—what kind of magic permits the Constitution to rise above politics? Were not the Framers of the Constitution members of a party, the Federalists? And party conflict came to American politics so soon after the adoption of the Constitution, during George Washington's first term as president, that it seems impossible to regard the Constitution with awe, as if it were something almost divine, elevated above partisan interpretation.

Let us return to the comparison between parties and Congressional committees, both being necessary to the Constitution yet not mentioned in it. The reason why they are not mentioned is not that the Framers did not have time for detail, but because there is something essentially informal about both. It is often said that the "real work of Congress gets done in committees"—meaning that the task of deliberation, bargaining and compromise must necessarily take place out of public view where members are free to consider possibilities they would not want to argue publicly. Of course committees are partly formal institutions as well, with public meetings and open hearings. But at some point members close the doors for an "executive session" in secret, or they leave for the corridors, seeking privacy in a crowd.

In the same way it used to be said that parties did the real work of American politics by organizing the majorities necessary to fill offices and adopt policies. If this would be said less today it is because parties are thought to be in decline. One reason given for the decline is the prolonged attempt at party reform, beginning with the McGovern-Fraser reforms of 1970, having the tendency to make informal activities of the parties more formal.[1] Substituting nomination of presidential candidates in primaries for choice managed by unelected party notables in a party convention was the most salient instance of formalizing reform. So the decline of the parties seems to be associated with intolerance for informal politicking, which has the appearance of undemocratic manipulation. Parties, like congressional committees, may be more or less formalized, but both are nourished by the need to act informally in politics.

To act informally is to prepare a formal action that takes place later in public. At some point anything agreed on in private must, if it is to take effect, become public; every informal activity in politics points toward a formal one. But here the difference between parties and committees appears. Committees prepare the actions of Congress without ever challenging the authority of Congress; they use, they depend on, Congress' authority. They are parts of a greater whole. Parties, however, are "parts" in a different sense— parts that can become a whole. To extreme partisans the party can seem greater and more attractive than their country. Parties raise a question of loyalty not seen in other informal institutions or

[1] See Nelson W. Polsby, *Consequences of Party Reform* (New York: Oxford University Press, 1983).

associations. In our time we have witnessed the questionable loyalty of Communist partisans in liberal democracies, but the problem is inherent in every party. Even moderate partisans may find partisan advantage in a misfortune for their country if the blame can be fixed on the other party.

Thus we should be surprised at the general agreement today that parties, though not mentioned in the Constitution, are necessary to the working of the Constitution. Despite the possibility of divided loyalties, parties are now accepted as legitimate, even respectable instruments of free government. But it was not always so. Only in late eighteenth century Britain and in nineteenth century America did opinion turn favorable to parties. Before that time most accepted some version of the "mixed regime" characteristic of Aristotelian political science. In this view each of the simple regimes—monarchy, aristocracy, democracy—was a party seeking to rule the whole; and the remedy for such partisanship was a regime mixing all three parties for the common good. Here the regime or constitution is the same as party rule; even the mixed regime is a mixture of parties. So in the Aristotelian picture parties are not extra-constitutional at all; the danger from them lies in their narrowness, not in the claim to sovereignty that is inherent in partisanship. The Aristotelians accepted the partisan impulse but attempted to educate and perfect it.

A more modern approach, still hostile to party government, dates from the political science of Thomas Hobbes. It tries to create an impartial sovereign above or distinct from the parties in society. That sovereign can carry out several diverse or alternative policies in regard to parties: suppress them; construct a homogeneous people unlikely to divide into parties (these are strategies of Jean-Jacques Rousseau); provide economic opportunity as a channel for partisan passion away from politics; allow free speech and free association but frown on organized parties; tolerate but not encourage parties. In eighteenth century England political opinion permitted opposition but disapproved "formed opposition" even in Parliament of potential cabinet members who in parties might attempt to limit, or coerce, the choice of the king. Edmund Burke wrote his *Thoughts on the Cause of the Present Discontents* (1770), the first argument in political science for the respectability of party, to correct the prevailing opinion hostile to parties.[2] In

<hr />

[2]Edmund Burke, *Thoughts on the Cause of the Present Discontents*, *Works* (Bohn Library), I 306–81. Harvey C. Mansfield, Jr., *Statesmanship and Party Government: A Study of Burke and Bolingbroke* (Chicago, Ill.: University of Chicago Press, 1965), Ch. 1.

America that hostile opinion can be found in *Federalist* No. 10 (1787), in which James Madison makes his celebrated argument in favor of a republic with a multitude of sects and interests. Being a republic, America would of course be governed by a majority of the people, but to be moderate and to avoid the tyranny of majority faction, the majority should be composed of temporary, shifting coalitions rather than be fixed in parties organized for a long life. Even the first American party, the Jeffersonian Republicans, presented itself as an emergency device to counter the centralizing policies of the Federalists. Theirs was the one true party to revive the principles of the American Revolution, not one of two or several parties equally respectable. As soon as the Jeffersonians achieved victory in the election of 1800 they hoped to be able to disband; and in fact during the "Era of Good Feelings" in the administrations of James Madison and James Monroe the Federalist party and the Republicans decayed. The first substantial statement in America justifying party government was made by Martin Van Buren, who has been called the "true founder of the American party system."[3] His *Inquiry into the Origin and Course of Political Parties in the United States* (written in the 1850s and published posthumously in 1867) criticized the one-party utopianism of the Jeffersonian Republicans. Republicanism, he argued, will always have its opponents in those who want to live by their wits instead of by the sweat of their brow, and it is better to organize both sides so that the distinction between them is not obscured and the anti-republicans cannot hide among the ranks of the republicans. When parties recognize differences of principle that are bound to recur instead of attempting to re-establish revolutionary unity like the Jeffersonians, they bring principled behavior within the reach of ordinary politicians, do not require the services of heroes, and offer less opportunity to demagogues who pretend to be heroes.

Parties, then, are as old as politics; party government appeared recently. Party government requires that two or more parties be held not only tolerable but also respectable. Some parties, of course, might still be considered subversive, but it must be supposed that within limits, a free society can tolerate and will find

[3]See Dean McSweeney and John Zvesper, *American Political Parties: the Formation, Decline and Reform of the American Party System* (London: Routledge, 1991), 47–52; James W. Ceaser, *Presidential Selection* (Princeton: Princeton University Press, 1979), ch. 3, and "Political Change and Party Reform," in Robert A. Goldwin, ed., *Political Parties in the Eighties* (Washington, D.C.: American Enterprise Institute, 1980); Donald V. Weatherman, "From Factions to Parties," in Thomas B. Silver and Peter W. Schramm, eds., *Natural Right and Political Right* (Durham, N.C.: Carolina Academic Press, 1984), 401–13.

useful a permanent and public division of its citizens. And the division is not like that between the nobles and the plebeians in Rome, that is, between respectable people and riff-raff, but respectable citizens will be found in both (or more) parties. Respectability for parties in party government is not the same as formal recognition in the Constitution, because the Constitution still remains somehow above parties—but it is surely a step in that direction. The main historical condition for the establishment of party government is the disappearance of what Edmund Burke calls the "great parties" of the seventeenth century.[4] These were the religious parties, Protestant and Catholic, that fought bloody civil wars in Britain and Europe over the question of which religion would dominate society. After the religious question was settled, as in Britain, by a policy of toleration, it became possible when the stakes were less—after the pursuit of happiness replaced the salvation of one's soul as the end of politics.

Nonetheless, precisely because no one today challenges the respectability of parties, the arguments against them must not be forgotten. Although we take the point for granted, party government in a free society was at first considered a matter of choice. Whether it is in fact inevitable, as political scientists today tend to assume, would have to be decided by a careful and imaginative study of political history. But it is simple good sense to remember that parties can dangerously divide a free country; they can make compromise difficult by organizing moderates under the domination of extremists and by fixing opinion into opposed categories equipped with slogans designed to raise heat rather than convince. Or, on the contrary, parties may spread corruption in quiet times by making a market in private deals and paving the way for mediocre politicians (or worse) to rise. The necessity of combining into parties, it can be argued, detracts from the independence of mind required of both politicians and citizens in a free country. The appeal of that argument can be seen in the universal desire to be known as an independent not vulnerable to pressure to conform to the "party line." And the qualifier "partisan" used in such phrases as "partisan choice," "partisan debate," "partisan inquiry," is usually not approving. Whether on the whole for good or ill— but still for understandable reasons—parties at best always operate in an atmosphere of latent distrust.

In the brief survey above we have seen a tendency toward greater acceptance of parties together with a continuing refusal to

---

[4]Burke, *Thoughts on the Cause of the Present Discontents*, I 308; Mansfield, *Statesmanship and Party Government*, 42–45, 245.

adopt them in the Constitution. Parties are now respectable, but they remain extra-constitutional. They are respectable because the arguments in their favor have overcome arguments against them, not because we have merely become accustomed to them over time. It is true that the Supreme Court in recent years has taken notice of parties, and that parties have been accorded status in constitutional law. To put an end to the notorious "white primaries" practiced in the South until the 1940s, the Court pronounced political parties to be instruments of state action, and their primaries liable to the Court's review.[5] In the South at that time the Democratic party was so dominant that the winner of its primary—the informal election—was sure to win the formal election. While allowing blacks to vote in the formal elections, some Democrats attempted to exclude them from the effective, informal elections on the grounds that the Democratic party was in the nature of a private club entitled to exclude whomever it pleased. To attack that position, the Court formalized a previously informal practice, so that it could hold the state responsible for the actions of the Democratic party. Indeed, to formalize the informal has been a general strategy of reform adopted in the interest of blacks. More generally, one could say that the aim was to make the American way of life more democratic. Once the offensive practice has been identified as part of, or connected to, the government, it can be reformed in accordance with the dictates of the Constitution.

There is a limit, however, to the use of that strategy. The limit is the very nature of American (i.e., liberal) constitutionalism, which requires a distinction to be maintained between formal and informal, constitutional and extra-constitutional. As more and more private activities are brought within reach of reform by government, the range of privacy shrinks and the Constitution is stretched to specify all the informal, extra-constitutional arrangements that cause it to work as it does. Then the Constitution loses its formal character and comes to signify the American "system" as described by political scientists today (or even the constitution in the Aristotelian sense). When this happens, the freedom of a liberal constitution is lost, at least in principle, because the Constitution then seems to *command* that the people perform the private, voluntary activities that make it work.[6] The danger is general

---

[5]*Smith* v. *Allwright*, 321 U.S. 649 (1944), is the leading case in a series known as the "white primary cases."

[6]The danger cannot be remedied by supposing that there is a constitutional right to privacy because in that case privacy would be *given* by the Constitution instead of being the *basis* of the Constitution.

because it includes both the economic liberties that conservatives want to protect and the intellectual liberties dear to liberals—but also because it concerns the political parties by which all tendencies make their weight felt. Political parties must remain outside a liberal constitution if politics is to be a free, voluntary activity with its source in the people. The formality of the American Constitution is necessary to the freedom it permits and the responsible voluntarism it invites.

Let us then consider political parties as voluntary associations outside of the Constitution that help to make it work as it does. Two constitutional locations of party activity may be identified: within the government in regard to separation of powers and outside the government in elections. These have been the two central battlegrounds of American political history and also the two essential topics of American political science, for they show the Constitution not merely on paper but also in action.

In regard to separation of powers the Constitution provides for a formal distancing of the three branches of government, each of which has a separate article in the Constitution stating definite powers (most definite in the case of Congress). More generally, it is implied that legislating, executing and judging are different sorts of power, and that the differences supply the reasonable grounds for separating them. But it is also emphasized in *Federalist* Nos. 47 and 48 that the branches are involved with one another by the terms of the Constitution, so that being separated does not mean being isolated or independent. Although all can take initiatives on their own, none can accomplish an action without the possibility of interference while doing it or a calling to account afterwards. Even the emergency powers of the executive, though unimpeded, are subject to criticism and ultimately to the possibility of impeachment. Thus the three separate branches must necessarily cooperate in any action. Here parties come in, because partisan ties across the branches facilitate cooperation among the like-minded (as well as division between those of unlike minds). As we have seen, it was not inevitable that permanent parties, rather than, or in addition to, temporary alliances, perform the task of facilitating cooperation; but that is what we have.

Montesquieu, regarded as the authoritative theorist on separation of powers by the American Founders, expected that in a free constitution (he had Britain's in mind) parties would form around the legislative and executive branches. He thought such parties would change easily because any partisan sentiment would find one branch or the other more convenient in changing circumstances.[7] That tendency has been compounded in America by the availability of a written document that enables, and requires, a party to offer a constitutional interpretation on behalf of the branch it favors—that is, controls or hopes to control. Thus in the last fifty years of American politics we have gazed at the spectacle, all the more ridiculous because the partisans are so serious, of Republicans defending the powers of Congress under the presidency of Franklin Roosevelt and the prerogatives of the executive under Ronald Reagan, and of Democrats performing the same acrobatic maneuver in reverse.

In view of such exchanges of position, it might seem that the Constitution has little effect on partisan sentiment or activity and merely serves as a convenient tool with which to defend one's own forces and attack the other side. Certainly the Constitution lends itself to partisan interpretation. But given the inevitable partisanship of politics that we have discussed, is that a bad thing? Part of the freedom given structure by the Constitution is the freedom to interpret the Constitution—to emphasize the powers of one's own party are of little account or ought to be exercised with deference to the first. Such partisan shaping avoids a frontal and total criticism of the Constitution as the creation of a single party. And in shaping the Constitution to its will, each party finds itself compelled to admit a role for the other branches, however minimized, and to acknowledge the Constitution as a whole, even if distorted. Thus the Constitution yields something to partisan tempers but gets in return a concession from them and loyalty to the whole. It is easier for Democrats, for example, to concede the necessity of an executive, even though Republican, than to accept directly a tenet of the other party's doctrine. The Constitution entices parties into *its* system just as much as parties use it for *their* purposes.

The situation of a non-partisan Constitution and its partisan interpretations might be compared to a genus and its species. Just as one never actually sees a dog in its generic definition—a four legged barking creature that wags its tail—but always sees a specific dog—an Airedale, a Great Dane or whatever—so, in politics at least, one only hears of a partisan Constitution being used by a party for its purposes. But the inevitability of partisan interpretation does not mean that the non-partisan Constitution (or the generic dog) does not exist. It exists even though it cannot be found in politics without a partisan bias. For a partisan Constitution has to be a recognizable version of the non-partisan Constitution, as

---

[7]Montesquieu, *Spirit of the Laws*, XIX 27.

an Airedale is his owner's version of a dog. The non-partisan Constitution is available without distortion only to those who stay out of politics in order to think. But it has an effect in politics by controlling the degree of distortion.

After this explanation of the Constitution's flexibility, deriving from a non-partisan Constitution hidden away in thought, I must nonetheless report that one big thinker in American political history denied that the Constitution was either flexible or non-partisan. This was Woodrow Wilson, the first American president to criticize the American Constitution. Not content to offer a partisan constitutional position, Wilson took aim at the Constitution as a whole, and especially at the separation of powers, which he considered to be a mechanical construction of eighteenth century Newtonian science. The Constitution was not non-partisan, Wilson believed, because it was embedded in the obsolete science of a bygone era. Every generation needs a new inspiration for the Constitution, and Wilson's time needed a Darwinian, evolutionary view to replace the static mechanics of the Founders.[8] At the same time the Founders were coming under attack by Wilson's fellow progressives, J. Allen Smith and Charles Beard, as property-holders who had made a partisan Constitution to suit their economic interests, and thus to sustain the status quo. From Wilson's historicist viewpoint, one could not become too indignant over the Founders' partisanship, however, because a non-partisan Constitution that looks beyond a particular political and historical situation to make a *founding* is in that view impossible. Progressives replaced the founding Constitution with what they called the "living Constitution" constantly evolving to meet the needs of the time. They assumed that the truths of human nature discussed in *The Federalist,* including the dangers of faction, were temporary, and as the basis of the Constitution they substituted for those truths an historical understanding of the trend of events which they believed was toward democratic progress. In our time the big thinkers reject the naivete of progress as well as the conservatism of human nature, and they look to Heideggerean authenticity rather than Darwinian evolutionism. Even the living Constitution

[8]See especially Woodrow Wilson, "The Nature of Democracy in the United States," a speech delivered on May 17. 1889; Ceaser, *Presidential Selection*, 188–207; Charles R. Kesler, "Woodrow Wilson and the Statesmanship of Progress," in Silver and Schramm, eds., *Natural Right and Political Right*, 103–129; Robert Eden, *Political Leadership and Nihilism: A Study of Weber and Nietzsche* (Gainesville, Fl.: University Presses of Florida, 1984).

has not kept up with the times, which now are thought to require new rights in response to new values with little or no regard for the structure of government in the Constitution.[9]

Wilson thought that the Constitution was inflexible because the mechanical action and counteraction of interests he conceived among the separated powers leads not to progress but to stalemate and deadlock. *The Federalist* presents no such mechanical conception of interests, but to Wilson's idealism interests were obstacles more than incentives to progress. To overcome the stalemate in American government, presidential leadership appealing directly to the people over the Congress was required. Political parties would be an instrument of the appeal, but their task would be to direct the people's will against the entrenched interests in Congress rather than to offer a constitutional interpretation of the president's power. Indeed it is the Constitution, with its checks and balances, that offers conservative interests defensible positions where they can entrench themselves. As the party of progress, Wilson's Democratic party assailed the machine Democrats and the Republicans as corrupt and illegitimate. Instead of a system of respectable constitutional parties, each with a defensible interpretation, Wilson promoted a single party critical of the Constitution and contemptuous of its rivals. If he had succeeded, he would perhaps have introduced a new inflexibility into American parties. As opposed to a system that slows reform by permitting partisan opposition and justifying partisan dispute, Wilson's progressivism would shut off debate by claiming that the "time has come" for a certain reform and by asserting that once passed, a reform could be questioned only by "reactionaries." The progressive outlook uses history to narrow, if not quite determine, the issues of partisanship.

The Wilsonian revolution in the use of parties within the government is still with us. It was developed further by Franklin Roosevelt's New Deal, which combined presidential leadership with executive administration in the same attempt to dampen party dispute and to evade the obstacles placed in the way of reform by the constitutional separation of powers. But progressivism has clearly not succeeded in ignoring—to say nothing of

---

[9]The *Chadha* case (1983), in which the Supreme Court upheld constitutional separation of powers against the legislative veto, shows that concern for constitutional propriety has not disappeared; Chief Justice Warren Burger stated the issue as one of constitutionalism versus efficiency. *Immigration and Naturalization Service* v. *Chadha*, 462 U.S. 919.

overthrowing—the Constitution it criticized. American politics is now characterized by partisan dispute between the constitutional branches, when the President and Congress argue against each other as they have always done, and also by appeals to the people in the manner of Wilson and Roosevelt, in order to put the pressure of the president's constituency on Congress. Jeffrey Tulis, who first described the pattern, calls it a "layered text" of constitutional and nonconstitutional disputes that continue despite their inconsistency of intent.[10] In recent years progressivism has been opposed with its own method of popular appeal by Ronald Reagan, so that the progressive outlook has been matched against a determined and confident conservatism that no longer seems reactionary. One result has been the continued decline of political parties as institutions, for several reasons including the popular standing of the presidency; but another result has been a revival of partisanship in which argument cannot be foreclosed merely by referring to the inevitability of progress. In the present conflict between progressive "entitlements" and conservative "opportunities" Democrats control Congress and Republicans the presidency for the foreseeable future (though not much of the future is ever foreseeable in politics); and so the constitutional partisanship between the branches has also intensified. Each party, in fact, has so little hope of gaining stronghold of the other side that it sees little reason for restraint in expanding the powers of its own branch.

In elections, parties help the people choose their government, but in a certain way: not by choosing the best individuals (i.e., best in the circumstances) but by grouping candidates according to their partisan dispositions or policies. The Electoral College was originally intended to select the best individuals, but that method failed in the election of 1800 and was changed soon after in the Twelfth Amendment (giving unacknowledged but real constitutional recognition to parties). That election gave rise to the long-term domination of Thomas Jefferson's Democratic-Republican party, ended only in 1860 by Abraham Lincoln's election, giving rise to another long-term domination. Such domination, featuring one majority party that usually wins and one principal minority party that usually loses, has been characteristic of American political history. Most elections follow the pattern, but certain ones—at the least, the elections of 1800, 1860, 1932—set the pattern; these

---

[10]Jeffrey K. Tulis, *The Rhetorical Presidency* (Princeton, N.J.: Princeton University Press, 1989), 17, 146–47.

are called "critical elections" by political scientists, who, following V.O. Key in 1955, have developed a literature and a theory about them.[11]

The pattern of critical elections and majority-party domination might be regarded, perhaps somewhat fancifully, as a kind of choosing by a democratic people. In order not to change its government whimsically, just for the sake of change, and also in order not to keep it in power for no good reason, it makes sense for a people to establish a long-term trend of policy in critical elections. This practice engages the ambition and the capacity of far-sighted leaders, such as Jefferson, Lincoln, and Roosevelt, and enables them to be useful to a democratic people in a role it could not perform for itself but can only choose them for. Within this long-term trend, variations are possible as experience and circumstances dictate; the domination of the majority party is neither absolute nor assured. So a certain flexibility is achieved along with the long-term determination. The Constitution supplies the formal structure of elections (in surprising detail) by which the people chooses its government. But the "party alignment" of majority and minority parties reveals the actual choice of the people over time by which one can judge how well they have chosen and whether they have kept the republic that the Founders gave them. Party alignment is an informal structure of choice, dependent on the formal structure but specifying what it cannot specify, the actual content of choice.[12] It is important to realize that not all constitutional choosing was done by the Founders or by the American people who ratified the Constitution in 1787–88. The wisdom of the Constitution must be judged by the quality of democratic choices made under the Constitution through American political history, just as the character of the people can be judged by its success in making the Constitution work well. A constitution is a means by which a democratic people holds itself formally responsible for its government; and parties, which are informal or less formal, can help or hinder the quality of the people's choice.

[11]McSweeney and Zvesper, *American Political Parties*, ch. 4; V.O. Key, "A Theory of Critical Elections," *Journal of Politics*, XVII (1955), 3–18; Harry V. Jaffa, "The Nature and Origin of the American Party System," in *Equality and Liberty* (New York: Oxford University Press, 1965); Walter Dean Burnham, *Critical Elections and the Mainsprings of American Politics* (New York: W.W. Norton, 1970); James L. Sundquist, *Dynamics of the Party System; Alignment and Realignment of Political Parties in the United States* (Washington, D.C.: Brookings Institution, 1973, rev. ed. 1983); Harvey C. Mansfield, Jr., *America's Constitutional Soul* (Baltimore, Md.: Johns Hopkins University Press, 1991), 25–27.

[12]Mansfield, *America's Constitutional Soul*, 56–59.

Two questions arise about party alignment, one immediate and the other long-term. Everyone wants to know, first, what has happened to party alignment since Reagan's election in 1980, for there appears to be, in contrast to previous experience, one majority party for the presidency and another for Congress. What explains the failure of the Reagan revolution to establish itself in Congress? One does not ask the question the other way round— why the Democrats seem to have lost control of the presidency— because strains and failures in the programs of the New Deal and its successors have become manifest. Nonetheless the American people have not, or not yet, chosen to reject the New Deal, preferring rather to elect its opponents to the presidency and its proponents to Congress. The American people seem to be suspended between the New Deal and the Reagan revolution, unwilling to choose between entitlements and opportunity and hopeful of having both. It is hard to say whether this is a failure to choose that will be resolved in a crisis or a kind of choice that will be maintained. A political situation that seems unreasonable and inconsistent to an observer can often last a long time and even make sense to the voters. Who knows at what point contradictory ideas—that of entitlement to a risk-free life and that of opportunity to take risks—become incompatible in practice? Who knows for sure that they are incompatible? As to the decline of parties that accompanies the failure of party realignment, it should be noted that the New Deal intended a decline of partisanship; it meant to put welfare entitlements "beyond politics," that is, beyond partisan dispute. Of course the Democratic party would take credit for having established them, and Republicans such as Richard Nixon could then compete only by raising benefits, not by challenging the idea. So the failure of American parties to realign in the 1980s is at least in part the result of a party realignment in the 1930s that was meant to stick.

The notion of party alignment and the theory of critical elections emphasize partisan differences and light up the drama of American political history. But a long-term, uninterrupted trend toward democratization, more powerful than party differences though less visible, can also be discerned. America has a constitutional democracy as opposed to a direct democracy. That distinction appears in *Federalist* No. 10 as the one between a republic and a democracy, and to the Framers, it was fundamental. A republic or constitutional democracy is government by the people but it keeps the government at a distance from the people, so that government, while remaining popular, will be as wise and moderate as possible. The distance between government and people might be called "constitutional space," and it is created by formal barriers to direct democracy, such as fixed terms of office that allow a constitutional official to continue through temporary periods of unpopularity. In great part, American political history consists in the lowering or overcoming of constitutional barriers to the people's will: the near abolition of the Electoral College, the direct election of Senators, the passage of the Fourteenth Amendment, the application of the Bill of Rights to the states, referenda and recall, direct primaries, survey polls, and television are examples. Some of them came by formal legislation, some not; some for good reason, some perhaps not. But whether for good or ill, all tend in the direction of more democracy.

Moreover, the trend toward more direct democracy has been led by the parties and by their great leaders in the critical elections: Jefferson, Lincoln, Roosevelt. All of these could or did claim that they were rescuing the Constitution by making it more democratic, but so far there does not appear to be an instance of an American statesman coming to the aid of the Constitution by deliberately making it *less* democratic. Certain democratizing reforms such as the McGovern-Fraser Democratic party reform and the two-term limitation on the presidency—one made by Democrats and the other by Republicans—are widely if not universally regarded as mistakes. Yet no one thinks they can be reversed. It seems that all the constitutional space was created at America's Founding, and that ever since it has been gradually encroached upon and taken away. The trend has been described by Tocqueville as the irresistible, irreversible power of the democratic revolution of modern times, and it is related to a famous distinction of his between great and small parties.[13] Great parties are those involving the difference between democrats and aristocrats; he calls the Federalists and the Jeffersonian Republicans great parties because they contended over the great question of whether the people's power should be restricted. Once that question was decided in favor of the Republicans, the parties following upon the decision are content to make democracy more democratic; they play for smaller stakes, and their leaders have lesser ambitions. When making these remarks in 1835, Tocqueville could not have had the greatness of Abraham Lincoln in view. But Lincoln too, savior of the union made by the Constitution, also made it more democratic. While ennobling democracy and making it more worthy of choice, he hardly made its progress seem less irreversible.

[13]Tocqueville, *Democracy in America*, I.2.2.

Parties today, I have argued, depend on the Constitution, but the Constitution has come to depend on them, on their methods of democratization, to sustain its constitutional space. The Constitution lives, so to speak, on its unrenewable capital, surviving by becoming ever less formal and ever more democratic. Strangely enough, as one sees in the example of Woodrow Wilson, the intellectuals—who might seem to have the most to lose from direct democracy and the most to gain from a Constitution that shelters their rights—lead the charge toward democratization. But Tocqueville saw this too. The very difficult task for a party today is to arrest the tendency of democracy to become more extreme and to recapture the constitutional sense of the American people.

POLITICAL PARTIES AND THE AMERICAN FOUNDING

Michael Allen Gillespie

IT HAS LONG BEEN HELD AS AN ESTABLISHED FACT THAT THE AMER-
ICAN Founders believed that parties were antithetical to republican
government. Such a view is not surprising. After all, the most famous essay in American political philosophy, Madison's *Federalist*
No. 10, characterizes parties as the mortal diseases of republican
government. On the basis of this claim and similar remarks made
by other Founders during the period of the formation and ratification of the Constitution a general opinion has arisen that the
Constitution is opposed to parties. The rise of parties in the years
following the ratification of the Constitution and their continuing
importance for most of the rest of our Constitutional history has
led some to conclude that the Constitutional system as originally
envisaged was insufficient because it did not make provisions for
parties. Others have concluded that parties themselves are suspect
because they were not originally part of the Constitutional system.
Both of these views have had many adherents throughout American political history and both have many supporters today.

The problems posed by parties, of course, were recognized
long before there was an American Constitution, indeed, long before there was an America. Aristotle discusses these problems at
length in his *Politics* in a way that set the framework for much of
the succeeding debate.[1] For Aristotle, parties or factions are essentially partial, the political instruments by which one or another
class gains power in the state and uses it to secure its interest and
to injure its political enemies. These classes and the parties that
arise out of them are universal because they rest on economic differences which are universal. Political parties are thus intrinsic to
political life and a source of continual internal conflict in all states.
If the rich rule, they tyrannize over the poor; if the poor rule they

[1] 1295a–1296b.

tyrannize over the rich. Reasonably decent government is thus only possible in Aristotle's view if the middle class rules or if there is a kind of mixed regime in which elements of all classes are present.

Machiavelli was the first modern thinker to deal explicitly with the problem of parties. In his *Prince* he suggests to absolute rulers that they can only secure their rule by allying themselves with the people against the nobles and thus eliminating the other notables as a political force.[2] In his *Discourses*, by contrast, he suggests that political freedom can only be maintained if there is a relative balance in the struggle between the rich and the poor.[3] It would perhaps not be altogether unfair to say that the civil wars of the Reformation period led many thinkers, the foremost of whom was Thomas Hobbes, to conclude that no such balance was possible and that only the absolute rule of a prince could provide a solution to political parties and the internecine conflict they seemed necessarily to engender. John Locke, the father of modern liberalism, thought that this conclusion was too pessimistic. He knew that all men were partial toward themselves and therefore partisan in their political activities but thought that a legal system based on natural right and administered by a representative government characterized by checks and balances would go a long way toward securing the rights not merely of those in power but of all individuals and groups.

Political parties and the suspicion of political parties are thus as old as political life and the attempt to find a solution to the problems they pose for politics has been a central concern of political philosophy since its ancient beginnings. On the surface the American Founders' view of parties lies very much within this tradition. However, we must avoid coming to the overhasty conclusion that this appearance corresponds to reality. The necessity of caution is indicated by the fact that the principal critics of party in the Constitutional period were also the organizers of the first parties. This fact alone is sufficient to alert us to the necessity of examining more carefully the supposed anti-party sentiment of the political thought of the American Founding. In what follows I will try to show that the idea of party was not nearly as anathema to the members of the Founding generation as is generally believed and that parties as such are therefore not antithetical to the Constitutional system they established. I will also try to show that the Founders did not betray their own principles in establishing the

[2]Ch. IX.
[3]Bk. I.

first parties. Thus, while parties were not recognized as positive elements in our political system until the time of Van Buren, I want to suggest that parties of a certain sort were accepted as an inevitable and in some cases as a salutary factor in political life already in the Founding period and that the Founders themselves left room for such parties within the Constitution they established.

The principal piece of evidence that is generally brought to bear in support of the view that the American Founders were bitter opponents of parties is Madison's famous argument against factions in *Federalist* No. 10.[4] Madison observes that,

Complaints are everywhere heard from our most considerate and virtuous citizens, equally the friends of public and private faith and of public and personal liberty, that our governments are too unstable, that the public good is disregarded in the conflicts of rival parties, and that measures are too often decided, not according to the rules of justice and the rights of the minor party, but by the superior force of an interested and overbearing majority.[5]

The principle cause of domestic turmoil in republics and in the American republic in particular is what Madison calls the "factious spirit." The principal cause of injustice is the factious spirit of the majority.

Madison uses the term "faction" to refer to a specific type of party. He remarks:

By a faction I understand a number of citizens whether amounting to a majority or a minority of the whole, who are united and actuated by some common impulse of passion, or of interest, adverse to the rights of others citizens, or to the permanent and aggregate interests of the community.[6]

What must be noted at the outset is that this condemnation of faction is not a blanket condemnation of all parties. A party is a faction only if it is opposed to the *rights* of other citizens or to the

---

[4]Madison developed the arguments that underlie his arguments in *Federalist* No. 10 over several years. See his "Vices of the Political System of the United States," April 1787 in *The Papers of James Madison*, ed. William T. Hutchinson et al. (Chicago: University of Chicago Press, 1962–), 9:354–57; his speech of 6 June 1787 in Max Farrand, ed., *The Records of the Federal Convention of 1787*, 4 vols. (New Haven: Yale University Press, 1966), 1:134–36; and his letter to Jefferson of 24 Oct. 1787, *Papers of James Madison*, 10:212–14.

[5]*The Federalist Papers*, ed., Clinton Rossiter (New York: New American Library, 1961), 77.

[6]Ibid., 78.

permanent and aggregate interest of the community. Thus, a party is not a faction, for example, if it is only opposed to the particular interests of other citizens or if it represents a political position that is in the interest of the rights and/or permanent interest of the community. Thus, the party that fomented and carried through the American Revolution was not a faction in Madison's restricted sense.[7] It aimed to secure the rights and the permanent and aggregate interest of the community. Moreover, insofar as parties are concerned only with conflicts over particular interests, as our modern parties in many instances are, they are also not factions.

In detailing the formation of parties, Madison follows a generally Aristotelian line. Parties in his view have many sources but the most lasting and universal of these are the differences in property. Parties for the most part thus arise from different means and capacities of acquiring property. While this notion of party has an Aristotelian beginning, Madison gives it an important modern twist that grows out of his recognition of the differences between ancient and modern economies. While one of the principal party divisions in his view is the Aristotelian distinction of creditors and debtors, there are other decisive economic differences that also produce party antagonism. Parties in his view form around the landed interest, the manufacturing interest, the mercantile interest, the moneyed interest, and many other lesser interests.[8] What is striking about this enumeration from the perspective of the traditional, Aristotelian notion of party is that all of these new parties that Madison points to are what we might characterize as middle class parties. Madison's argument thus takes a decisive step beyond Aristotle. Party division corresponds not merely to the social classes of the citizens but to the means by which they acquire property. This notion would have been alien to Aristotle. It focuses on the accumulation and not merely the possession of wealth. It thus assumes that the accumulation of wealth through work is a legitimate and indeed even an essential human activity. Finally, it recognizes that political divisions arise from these different ways of accumulating wealth. Madison thus has a different view of the origin and nature of property than Aristotle and a different view of its political importance. These differences in part are theoretical

[7]Such a party was authorized already in Locke's thought as necessary to the preservation of man's life, liberty, and property in the face of despotism and served as the basis for Jefferson's claim in the Declaration of Independence that a people that had hitherto been bound up with another people had a right to sever the political bonds that connected it to that people and establish a government of its own if that other people acted in a tyrannical fashion toward them.

[8]Ibid., 79.

but in part also are clearly the consequence of Madison's experience of a more differentiated economy than that known to the ancients.

While Madison argues in Aristotelian fashion that the parties of the rich and the poor or of creditors and debtors are universal, he argues that this distinction is not exhaustive, that other kinds of parties arise in "civilized" as opposed presumably to uncivilized nations because of the differentiation in the means of acquiring property. Madison's argument here echoes an argument about economic development and commercial society that is generally considered more characteristic of Hamilton.[9] Hamilton believed that the increasing importance of middle class parties was the result of the relative equality of condition that existed in the American republic. Under these relatively egalitarian conditions the political significance of the distinction of the rich and the poor was of diminishing importance. The rich and poor continued to exist but, with the increasing fluidity of wealth in an emerging capitalist economy, no one person or group of persons was permanently at one or the other extreme. Moreover, those who were momentarily poor would not be simply opposed to those who were momentarily rich in a more highly diversified economic system because their interests would in many instances be combined against the interests of the rich and the poor in other economic sectors. Thus, the interests of rich and poor farmers would often be opposed to those of rich and poor manufacturers. In a representative government, the rich in each sector will thus represent the economic interests of their poorer compatriots.[10]

While Madison may not have accepted the notion of representation that Hamilton presents here, he agrees that the middle class tends to predominate under the conditions of relative equality prevailing in America. As a result, the necessity for the unity of the middle class, hitherto imposed by the factious character of the

[9]Ibid. Hamilton clearly recognized a distinction of this kind and described it in detail in *Federalist* No. 8: "The industrious habits of the people of the present day, absorbed in the pursuits of gain and devoted to the improvements of agriculture and commerce, are incompatible with the condition of a nation of soldiers, which was the true condition of those [ancient] republics." Ibid., 69. Madison must have had a similar distinction in mind although it is not at all clear that he would entirely agree with Hamilton. Not only did they disagree in some respects about the political consequences of modern economic development but they also disagreed about the nature of the ancient world. Madison grew up within the tradition of civic republicanism that looked to the ancient republics as models of a virtuous republican life. Hamilton recognized that they were martial republics that were not suitable for emulation by modern commercial societies.

[10]See *Federalist* No. 35. Ibid., 214–17. Madison never articulated such an extreme theory of interest representation as the one Hamilton develops here.

upper and lower classes, is diminished. Thus, with the relative decline of the political importance of the distinction of the rich and the poor, the latent antagonisms of the middle class that were suppressed in the interest of unity in the face of the other two classes come to the fore. The differences between middle class parties, however, do not fall on the same continuum as the differences between traditional classes. These differences are not vertical differences in the amount of wealth and social prestige but horizontal differences between groups of approximately the same distribution of wealth and prestige each of which is characterized by a different means of acquiring property. These are in short the distinctions between different economic sectors of the middle class. The America that Madison sees here is thus not an agrarian but a commercial society.[11]

[11] For a fuller presentation of this argument, see Martin Diamond, "Democracy and The Federalist: A Reconsideration of the Framers' Intent," in Jack P. Greene, ed., *The Reinterpretation of the American Revolution 1763–1789* (New York: Harper & Row, 1968), 522–23. While this position is evident in a number of other places in Madison's thought, Madison himself often seems to contradict it. In general Madison is closer to the civic republican tradition most prominently represented by Jefferson with its vision of a nation of yeoman farmers than to the Hamiltonian vision of a commercial society presented here. As early as 1783 Madison openly expressed his opposition to the Hamiltonian vision of a nation unified by a commercial and financial elite. In the Virginia Ratifying Convention and in his later struggle against the Federalist Party he explicitly argues that the Constitution is the best instrument not to facilitate but *to delay* the development of such a commercial and manufacturing republic with all of its dehumanizing features. By securing the Union, the Constitution, in his view, guarantees the opening up of the Western lands for agricultural development. The opportunity afforded by this frontier for individual independence will draw the excess population away from the East and deprive the rising manufacturing sector of the cheap labor it needs to succeed. Beyond the mountains the real America will emerge and it will be an America that is for a long time predominantly agricultural.

There are several possible explanations for this apparent discrepancy in Madison's thought. His arguments in both cases may simply be rhetorical. The argument for a commercial republic would be as little effective in Virginia as the argument against the commercial republic would be in New York. It seems more likely that Madison had not yet thoroughly thought through the consequences of Hamilton's commercial republic when they wrote *The Federalist*, that these consequences first became apparent to him during the course of the ratification debate, that he saw them more fully in Hamilton's proposals of the early 1790s, and that he rejected them when he saw how little they had in common with the civic republicanism he prized. It should be noted, however, that the failure of the economic alternative that he recommended and that he believed was more compatible with his civic republicanism after 1807 led him and the Republicans generally back to more or less the position that he and Hamilton espoused in *The Federalist*. Moreover, even if we assume that Madison preferred an agrarian republic he clearly had real doubts that it could be sustained since even the land beyond the mountains in his

On one level Madison's argument thus seems to imply that Aristotle's solution to the problem of faction or party is insufficient because even where the middle class rules, or at least where the middle class rules in the absence of real upper and lower classes, antagonistic parties form that undermine political stability. This conclusion would be correct, however, only if Madison viewed traditional class parties and modern middle class or sectoral parties as equally antagonistic to the public good. Madison had ample opportunity to come to the opposite conclusion. Indeed, the whole history of party government in eighteenth century Britain is a testimony to such a conclusion.[12] Stable party government became possible in Britain precisely because the parties that came to form the government were parties of interest and not great parties, i.e., parties that pursued petty economic advantage and not parties that aimed at fundamental constitutional, social, or cultural change.[13] Hamilton clearly understood this fact and consciously sought to emulate the British example. Madison, more than Hamilton, had real doubts about the British case. Like many, if not most, of his fellow Americans he had been wedded to the early revolutionary condemnation of the corruption of the British system. It is not clear, however, that he believed that this corruption was concomitant with the existence of middle class parties. It is thus altogether conceivable that Madison believed that one could have the varying middle class parties of Britain without the corruption that was the result of the connection of the parties to the government's financial administration.

There are several hints in *Federalist* No. 10 that Madison envisages such a middle class society dominated by competing middle class parties in a future America. The first suggestion that Madison sees such a society is implicit in his argument that the problem of faction can in part be remedied by drawing into power men whose reason is relatively less corrupted by their passions and interests than that of most men. Such men in Madison's view

---

view would some day be filled up. Under such circumstances and with such wide climatological differences between the different parts of the republic a highly differentiated economic system would be likely. It is thus altogether possible that Madison had this continental republic in view when he wrote *Federalist* No. 10.

[12]If Madison had not grasped this point from his extensive reading, it is made time and time again in the Federal Convention. The applicability of this case to America and the desirability of such an application are also repeatedly discussed in the Convention.

[13]On this transformation of British parties see Harvey C. Mansfield, Jr., "Party Government and the Settlement of 1688," *American Political Science Review* 58, no.4 (1964):933–46.

require a certain degree of independence and this is probably most likely to be found among those who are independent farmers. The notion that such men can work some impartial or public good for the society as a whole, however, assumes that there is a permanent and aggregate interest of the community. Such an interest, however, is only possible if the results of politics are not always a zero sum game. If one group's gain is always another group's loss, then there is no aggregate good and no way in which reason can be anything but an instrument of the passions. There must thus be some basis for consensus, some basis for cooperation and mutual benefit. The capacity to transcend party spirit that Madison seeks to engender thus presupposes party differences that are not intrinsic to one's permanent place in society and that can therefore be transcended. Sectoral or middle class parties rest upon a consensus about such issues as the sanctity of rights in general and property rights in particular. Great parties do not. The upper class and the lower class for Aristotle can never reach a consensus because each profits only at the expense of the other. Middle class parties may find themselves at odds. A landed interest and a commercial interest, for example, may be deeply divided over the question of tariffs or trade policy generally as Americans were from the mid 1780s onward, but such questions can be resolved by compromise, first because they are not questions of principle and second because there are compromise positions that produce benefits for both parties.

A second and more explicit indication that Madison may have understood this distinction between traditional and middle class parties is his enumeration of the principal dangers of parties listed at end of *Federalist* No. 10. These include the possibility that a religious sect will degenerate into political faction, a rage for paper money and the abolition of debts, the agitation for an equal division of property, and "any other improper or wicked project."[14] What is striking about this list is that all of these are dangers of great parties, not of middle class parties. The danger of religious factionalism was well known to the Founders from the English experience. Indeed, part of the settlement of 1688 in England that brought the religious wars to a close was the elimination of religiously based parties by the exclusion of Catholicism under the Toleration Act. The extended republic in Madison's view obviates this danger by multiplying the number of religious sects as well as the number of economic interests.[15] The other dangers he lists are

[14]*Federalist Papers*, 84.
[15]On this point see *Federalist* No. 51. Ibid., 325.

the Aristotelian dangers brought about by the vertical division of the society into rich and poor. Madison has no doubt that these differences will threaten the political peace under all social arrangements, but he believes that this division will be less pronounced in America than in previous societies because of its relatively egalitarian character. Moreover, this division will in any case be neutralized to a large extent by the size and diversity of the extended republic. That is to say, the vertical distinctions that are universal in all societies will be offset by the horizontal distinctions characteristic of a "civilized," i.e., a middle class society, even if the society becomes less egalitarian in the future.

While the conflict of middle class parties has a variety of unfortunate and unsavory consequences, it is ultimately not a serious threat to the public peace and the Constitutional order. Thus, the argument in *Federalist* No. 10 is not an argument against interest based parties, at least as long as those interests are middle class interests and are the result of horizontal as opposed to vertical distinctions.

Madison's support for such middle class parties, however, was clearly qualified because of the manner in which even they distort our capacity for rational deliberation about the public good and thus undermine our capacity to do justice to our fellows. This problem in part is ameliorated by representation in general and representation in larger legislative districts in particular. While Madison believed that enlightened statesmen would not always be at the helm, he was more or less convinced that there was a better chance that more enlightened legislators would be elected in an extended as opposed to a small republic. Such legislators would be better able to rise above the party spirit that would inevitably spill over from the populace into the legislature. While Madison recognized that parties would form among the people, he believed that the constitutional system would help to check the development of parties in the legislature. However, he almost certainly did not believe that legislative parties would form first and then organize among the electorate.

These conclusions are generally borne out by the discussion of party in the rest of *The Federalist Papers*.[16] Madison and Hamilton

[16] There is some scholarly debate about the unity of the vision of the principal authors of *The Federalist*. On their essential unity see George W. Carey, "Publius—A Split Personality?" *Review of Politics* 17 (1984), 5–22; David F. Epstein, *The Political Theory of "The Federalist"* (Chicago: University of Chicago Press, 1984); and Gary Wills, *Explaining America: The Federalist* (Garden City: Doubleday, 1981). On their differences see Douglas Adair, "The Authorship of the Disputed Federalist Papers,"

were generally convinced that great parties and the factional animosity they engendered were inevitable in the states as they existed under the Articles of Confederation. The failure of the states to meet their federal obligations, the rage for paper money, the development of personalistic state parties, and the willingness of many state governments to violate their own constitutions were in their view ominous developments. What particularly concerned them and many other Federalists, however, were Shays Rebellion in Massachusetts and the more or less open class warfare in Rhode Island. Madison and Hamilton saw both of these events as evidence that civil unrest and indeed civil war were not far off. With these incidents firmly in mind they came to see faction inextricably linked to treason, sedition, and insurrection.[17] In hindsight their concerns may seem somewhat hyperbolic, but it would be a mistake to believe that their conclusions were simply the product of their own anxieties. In fact their views were the consequence of an extensive investigation of the experiences of many earlier republics. Madison and Hamilton thus came to see the events in Massachusetts and Rhode Island against the backdrop of Greek, Roman, and English history. Hamilton writes in *Federalist* No. 9 that

it is impossible to read the history of the petty republics of Greece and Italy without feeling sensations of horror and disgust at the distractions with which they were continually agitated, and at the rapid succession of revolutions by which they were kept in a state of perpetual vibration between the extremes of tyranny and anarchy.[18]

Again in *Federalist* No. 70 he notes that

every man the least conversant in Roman history knows how often that republic was obliged to take refuge in the absolute power of a single man, under the formidable title of dictator, as well against the intrigues of ambitious individuals who aspired to the tyranny, and the seditions of whole classes of the community whose conduct threatened the existence of all government, as against the invasions of external enemies who menaced the conquest and destruction of Rome.[19]

---

in *Fame and the Founding Fathers: Essays by Douglas Adair*, ed. Trevor Colbourn (New York: Norton, 1974), 55–60; Alpheus Thomas Mason, "The Federalist—A Split Personality," *American Historical Review* 57(1952):625–43; and Gottfried Dietze, *The Federalist: A Classic on Federalism and Free Government* (Baltimore: Johns Hopkins University Press, 1960), 150–51, 260–64, 267–71.

[17]See, for example, *Federalist Papers*, 54, 71–72, 99, 139–40, 324–25, 423, 443, 521.

[18]Ibid., 71.

[19]Ibid., 423.

In Hamilton's view it was precisely this danger that confronted the American states if they remained divided. He argues in *Federalist* No. 21 that

a successful faction may erect a tyranny on the ruins of order and law, while no succor could constitutionally be afforded by the Union to the friends and supporters of the government. The tempestuous situation from which Massachusetts has scarcely emerged evinces that dangers of this kind are not merely speculative. Who can determine what might have been the issue of her late convulsions if the malcontents had been headed by a Caesar or a Cromwell?[20]

Madison does not paint as grim a picture as Hamilton but he does contend in *Federalist* No. 14 that the union is necessary "as the proper antidote for the diseases of faction, which have proved fatal to other popular governments, and of which alarming symptoms have been betrayed by our own."[21] He is perhaps somewhat more sanguine than Hamilton that there is some good in the American people that will resist this slide into factionalism. Still the danger in his view cannot be discounted. Moreover, Shays Rebellion is not the only cause for concern; the deliberate policy of the Rhode Island government is an equal if not greater source of alarm. The rebels in Massachusetts were quickly suppressed by the legitimate government of the state; the elected "rebels" in Rhode Island ruled the state for years. Madison argues in *Federalist* No. 51 that

it can be little doubted that if the State of Rhode Island was separated from the Confederacy and left to itself, the insecurity of rights under the popular form of government within such narrow limits would be displayed by such reiterated oppressions of factious majorities that some power altogether independent of the people would soon be called for by the voice of the very factions whose misrule had proved the necessity of it.[22]

Madison and Hamilton clearly do not believe that such factions always lead to sedition and civil war but they are convinced, as Hamilton puts it in *Federalist* No. 65 that "the demon of faction will, at certain seasons, extend his sceptre over all numerous bodies of men."[23] Thus, all republics at one time or another face the

---

[20]Ibid., 139–40. See also *Federalist* No. 74 where Hamilton argues that this sedition embraced a large proportion of the community. Ibid., 448.

[21]Ibid., 99.

[22]Ibid., 325.

[23]Ibid., 401.

danger of sedition and civil war as the result of factional competition.

Such great parties and the conflicts that they produce, however, are unlikely within the system that the Constitution establishes. In addition to the protections afforded by the multiplication of interests and therefore factions in the extended republic that Madison details in *Federalist* No. 10, a number of other structural restraints are imposed upon such parties by the Constitution itself. Hamilton in particular points to the division of powers, the abandonment of the principle of unanimity, the large districts of Senators, the uniformity in the time of election, a unified executive, the reeligibility of the chief magistrate, and the veto power as curbing the power of factions.[24]

Under such constraints, parties may be a nuisance but they are not mortally dangerous. They are in fact the necessary consequence of peace and freedom and no attempt should be made to eliminate them. Madison in fact argues in *Federalist* No. 50 that the elimination of parties should not even be desired since this could only occur if the nation faced a danger to its very existence or succumbed to despotism.[25] Oddly, as Madison points out in *Federalist* No. 37 and No. 49, it was precisely such danger and alarm that was responsible for the absence of factionalism in the Constitutional Convention itself.[26] He recognizes, however, that this moment is transient and that ordinary politics under the new Constitution will involve party division and conflict.

Hamilton at one point in *Federalist* No. 26 even seems to suggest that the existence of party opposition may be of signal benefit to the new system:

As the spirit of party in different degrees must be expected to infect all political bodies, there will be no doubt, persons in the national legislature willing enough to arraign the measures and criminate the view of the majority. The provision for the support of a military force will always be a favorable topic for declamation. As often as the question comes forward, the public attention will be roused and attracted to the subject by the party in opposition; and if the majority should be really disposed to exceed the proper limits, the community will be warned of the danger.[27]

---

[24]Ibid., 71, 117, 148, 175, 375, 426, 431, 443.
[25]Ibid., 320.
[26]Ibid., 231, 315.
[27]Ibid., 171–72.

He clearly recognizes here that there will be "parties in the national legislature itself" and tries to show that they will in some instances serve a beneficial purpose.[28] While this is an isolated claim in *The Federalist Papers*, it is a revealing one, especially in a series of papers otherwise so hostile to party. If the parties under the Constitutional system are beneficial on some occasions, these are at best exceptions, since even such relatively pacific parties corrupt the public's capacity for rational deliberation and justice. Madison in particular stresses this danger and clearly believes it will continue to be a problem under the new Constitution. In *Federalist* No. 10 he explains that such a distortion of rational deliberation is inevitable because of the connection between man's reason and his self-love. Because of this connection man's opinions and his passions have a reciprocal influence on each other, the former being the objects to which the latter attach themselves.[29] Even those "men who possess the most attractive merit and the most diffusive and established characters," and who, Madison argues, will most likely be elected under this new system, will not be entirely free from this malign influence of interests and passions although they will not be as dominated by it as others.[30] There thus can be no simply rational and good legislative body. Hamilton comes to a similar conclusion in *Federalist* No. 15: "A spirit of faction, which is apt to mingle its poison in the deliberations of all bodies of men, will often hurry the persons of whom they are composed into improprieties and excesses for which they would blush in a private capacity."[31] He argues in *Federalist* No. 73 that the presidential veto is a necessity because the continuation of party spirit in the legislature is inevitable and "a spirit of faction may sometimes pervert its deliberations."[32]

Hamilton, like Madison, understands the practical consequences of the corruption of rational deliberation. He argues in *Federalist* No. 76 that in every appointment of men left to legislative bodies, parties clash and one wins or some compromise between the parties is attained. He concludes that "it will rarely happen that the advancement of the public service will be the primary object either of party victories or party negotiations."[33]

[28]Ibid.
[29]Ibid., 78.
[30]Ibid., 83.
[31]Ibid., 111.
[32]Ibid., 443.
[33]Ibid., 456.

Thus, he argues in *Federalist* No. 77 that in such situations, "the desire for mutual gratification will beget a scandalous bartering of votes and bargaining for places."[34] Members of the different parties, if given a chance, will reach an agreement to fill the positions in public service with their friends and relatives. Such scandalous party bargaining, Hamilton argues, is what generally occurs in New York. The proposed Constitution, by contrast, will help to ameliorate this problem by giving the President the appointment power and requiring that his appointments be confirmed by the Senate. Hamilton does not assert that this organization of powers will eliminate parties under the new Constitution. Indeed, he is convinced that they will continue to be an important force. He believes rather that the force of interest and passion that manifests itself in parties will be blunted by the structures of power established by the new Constitution. As a result, rational deliberation will play a relatively more important role and justice consequently be more often attained.

Madison and Hamilton draw many of the arguments they present in *The Federalist* from arguments that were first presented in the Federal Convention. What is surprising is that the question of party *per se* seldom arose in the course of the Convention debates. The discussion of party there can be briefly summarized. In opposing remuneration for public officials, Franklin argues early in the Convention that it is the combination of honor and profit in the organization of offices that is the true source of the factions that perpetually divide the British nation and encumber its government.[35] Patterson and Govr. Morris suggest that parties are occasionally influential in the states and Gerry refuses to sign the Constitution because he is afraid that it will augment the party animosity in Massachusetts.[36] King suggests that granting the federal government the power to establish a bank will be the source of parties and Govr. Morris worries that party intrigue may unseat the President.[37] Beyond these few comments little is said about party or faction by anyone except Madison and Hamilton. Madison presents many of the arguments that later appear in *Federalist* No. 10 in an abbreviated form. In addition to the causes of faction listed in *Federalist* No. 10, he points to mere geographical differences and the allegiances that individuals have to particular leaders as potential sources of faction. Hamilton gives a somewhat more extensive

[34]Ibid., 462.
[35]*Records of the Federal Convention*, 1:82.
[36]Ibid., 1:276, 2:31, 647.
[37]Ibid., 2:104, 616.

account of what he sees as the danger of party and presents the English example as a model of how to remedy them:

In every community where industry is encouraged, there will be a division into the few & the many. Hence separate interests will arise There will be debtors & Creditors &c. Give all the power to the many, they will oppress the few. Give all power to the few they will oppress the many. Both therefore ought to have power, that they may defend agst. the other. To the want of this check we owe our paper money—installment laws &c To the proper adjustment of it the British owe the excellence of their Constitution.[38]

Hamilton's account here is generally Aristotelian and does not discuss the middle class solution at all. In part this is probably due to the fact that his argument here is part of the speech in which Hamilton presents his plan for a national government more or less modelled on England. For rhetorical purposes he thus needs to emphasize the depth of the vertical divisions between social groups and to paper over the horizontal character of many of the political differences. It is also clearly belied by what Hamilton says on many occasions elsewhere.

Hamilton's treatment of faction here, however, is typical on a deeper level of the implicit Aristotelian notion of society that many of the delegates to the Federal Convention seem to share and that shapes their perspective on future political activity in the United States. In particular they believe, as Hamilton's comments indicate, that the essential divisions in society are vertical and that the problem in forming a government is to balance the democratic and the aristocratic elements of society, to establish a mixed government. The governments in the states in their view have deviated too far towards democracy and a more aristocratic character must be given to the new federal government to balance the system. While their thinking is thus constrained in many ways by these Aristotelian categories, they also recognize on many occasions that they are not altogether appropriate to American society. In one of the most telling exchanges in the Federal Convention, Pinkney argues that the social conditions of the U.S. were significantly different than those of England. The United States is essentially a middle class society. In England there are three vertical classes whose interests are independent of one another. In the U.S. there are three classes, professional men, commercial men, and a landed interest, all at more or less the level of the Commons in

[38]Ibid., 1:288. See also ibid., 1:308–9.

England and all of whose interests are mutually dependent.[39] In reply Madison agrees that Pinkney's claim may not be entirely false but argues further that

we cannot however be regarded even at this time, as one homogeneous mass, in which every thing that affects a part will affect in the same manner the whole. In framing a system which we wish to last for ages, we shd. not lose sight of the changes which ages will produce. An increase in population will of necessity increase the proportion of those who will labour under all the hardships of life, & secretly sigh for a more equal distribution of its blessings. These may in time outnumber those who are placed above the feelings of indigence.[40]

The result will be a widespread leveling spirit of the sort that in his view had already appeared in the United States. While Madison may have believed that a relative equality of condition characterized contemporary American society, he was thus not sanguine that future developments would preserve it. Hence, he believed that the system should be arranged in such a way to make the sectoral interests of the middle class predominate over the vertical differences of the traditional classes. The Aristotelian analysis of society is thus matched by a kind of Aristotelian solution that confines political activity to the middle class. This solution, however, recognizes that political ambition and political competition will continue and tries to focus this competition in parties that are horizontally and not vertically divided.

In conclusion we can thus say that the Federalists were opponents of party and sought ways to limit party influence in the Federal government but they did not aim at the abolition of parties and did not even believe that it would be a good idea. It would be incorrect to assume, however, that they saw parties as the legitimate representatives of various particular interests. In part their inability or unwillingness to see parties in this light is the result of their notion of what a representative ought to be and do. The Federalists believed in "loose" representation. This notion of representation, which traces its lineage back to Hobbes and finds its foremost proponent in Burke, envisages a representative, guided by prudence and conscience, who tries to determine what constitutes the public good. While the representative is elected from a particular district and needs to make the needs and wishes of his constituents known to his fellows, he is in reality a representative of the people

[39]*Records of the Federal Convention,* 1:402–3.
[40]Ibid., 1:422–23.

as a whole and must ultimately concern himself with the permanent and aggregate good of the community. This representative thus should not be bound by his constituents, either directly by their instructions or indirectly by their interests and wishes. In this respect the Federalists were greatly at odds with the Anti-Federalists.

It would be a mistake to think that the Anti-Federalists were supporters of parties. While they seldom mention the topic, whenever they do it is almost invariably with the harshest criticism, often in a manner quite similar to that of Madison and Hamilton. Federal Farmer, for example, argues that "it is interested combinations and factions we are particularly to guard against in the federal government, and all the rational means that can be put into the hands of the people to prevent them, ought to be provided and furnished for them."[41] William Symmes argues similarly that

faction, Sir, is the vehicle of all transactions in publick bodies, and when gentlemen know this so well, I am rather surprized to hear them so sanguine in this respect [i.e., with respect to Congress's power to tax]. . . . we know that all governments have degenerated, and consequently have abused the powers reposed in them, and why we should imagine better of the proposed Congress than of myriads of publick bodies who have gone before them, I cannot at present conceive.[42]

Cato saw the Kingdom of Poland as a lamentable example, "divided into parties; which are equally impelled by interested motives, and wandering from the line of rectitude and patriotism."[43] Sydney points to the violent parties in colonial America.[44] Finally, Mercy Warren argues in the most extended Anti-Federalist discussion of parties that

both history and experience have proved, that when party feuds have thus divided a nation, urbanity and benevolence are laid aside; and, influenced by the most malignant and corrupt passions, they lose sight of the sacred obligations of virtue, until there appears little difference in the ferocious spirits of men in the most refined and civilized society, or among the rude and barbarous hordes of the wilderness. Though some symptoms of this degradation of human character have appeared in America, we hope the cloud is fast dissipating, and that no vicissitudes in human affairs, no intrigues of the interested, nor any mistakes of

[41] Herbert Storing, ed., *The Complete Anti-Federalist*, 6 vols. (Chicago: University of Chicago Press, 1981), 2.8.147.
[42] Ibid., 4.5.12.
[43] Ibid., 5.10.2.
[44] Ibid., 6.9.18.

upright men will ever damp the prospect of the establishment and continuance of a republican system, which appears to be best adapted to
the genius of Americans. . . .

Yet there is still a division of parties, and a variety of sentiment,
relative to a subject that has heated the imaginations, and divided the
opinions of mankind, from the rise of the Roman republic to the destruction of her splendid empire; and from that day to the present,
when the divisions of the literati of every age, have called the attention
of genius and ability to speculate and to dissent in their ideas of the best
modes and forms of government.[45]

Mercy Warren, like Madison and Hamilton, saw the disquieting
manifestations of factionalism in the American republics of the
Confederation period but, in contradistinction to the two Federalists, she argues that such factionalism is transient, the result of
the unsettled constitutional questions of the structure and authority of government. Presumably, when stable government has been
reestablished, man will become civilized and therefore virtuous
again. In contrast to Madison she thus equates civilization with virtue and an absence of party spirit, whereas Madison saw civilization as the source of a new kind of (middle class) party spirit.

Despite the superficial resemblance of the Anti-Federalist critique of party to that of Madison and Hamilton, there are real differences between the two views. The principal difference is implicit
in Mercy Warren's analysis of party. When the Anti-Federalists
speak of parties they are generally speaking in an Aristotelian
fashion of class based parties and not of the middle class parties
that Madison and Hamilton, for example, foresaw. They consequently view parties as a reflection of the vertical divisions of society into classes. Their great fear is thus not the advent of
factionalism but the establishment of aristocracy or oligarchy at
odds with the republican genius of the American people. The parties that they dreaded were thus not factions representing a mercantile or money or landed interest but aristocratic parties that
included the elite members of all of these groups. Moreover, because the Anti-Federalists believed that these were great parties in
the Aristotelian sense and represented the unchanging and necessarily antagonistic interests of different parts of the community instead of the shifting interests of different groups within the middle
class, they were much less sanguine that the interests the parties
represented could be reconciled in the manner Madison and
Hamilton suggested. Indeed, as Wilson Cary McWilliams has

[45]Ibid., 6.14.11–13.

pointed out, the Anti-Federalists believed that in practice "a large republic with a fragmented and dispersed citizenry gave decisive advantages to organized elites—specifically government officials, the wealthy, and men of commerce."[46] In short the Anti-Federalists believed that the extended republic which Madison saw as eliminating the power of great parties and limiting the power of the parties of the middle class in fact served only to secure the power of one great party, the party or junto of a wealthy elite.

In contrast to the Federalists, they were convinced that more "independent" representatives would be captured by such parties. Therefore, the development of such an aristocracy could be prevented only by a numerous and "close" representation of the people. A representative in their view should be responsive to the principles and interests of his constituents. Indeed, the people should be able to instruct their representatives how to vote and to recall them if they violate their instructions. The Anti-Federalists like the Federalists were generally convinced that men's passions and interests exercised a decisive influence on their reason. They were less convinced, however, that the elite, those "men who possess the most attractive merit and the most diffusive and established characters," to use Madison's terminology, could or would rise above partisanship in the way Madison predicted. They agreed with Madison that the new system was likely to be filled with such characters but they were convinced that this would only secure the interests of the wealthy and better educated, not "the aggregate and permanent interest of the community." In this respect they saw vertical partisanship as much more difficult to eradicate. In part this is certainly because they did not think in terms of middle class interest groups that had mutual interests that could be secured by cooperation but of antagonistic parties involved in a zero sum game. The Federalist argument that the extended republic would solve the problems of parties and secure a generally just result thus seemed to them to be merely a rhetorical gambit of a class and a party that sought only its own advantage.

The suspicion that the issue of the Constitution evoked was carried over into the first Congress and played a crucial role in the formation of the first parties. Madison and Hamilton along with many of the other Federalists and Anti-Federalists who had been active in the debate over the Constitution were responsible for organizing the first competitive national parties in the early years of the American republic. These parties reflected real differences

[46]"The Anti-Federalists, Representation, and Party," *Northwestern Law Review* 84:12 (1989):30.

among Americans, including the divisive and often reinforcing distinctions between the New England and the southern states, nationalists and advocates of the states, the allies of England and the allies of France, the champions of order and the proponents of popular participation, and supporters of manufacturing and advocates of agriculture. While these differences were important and politically divisive, they do not in themselves explain the formation of political parties. Without such salient differences it is unlikely that parties would have come into being, but the institutionalization of these differences in antagonistic political parties cannot be explained by these differences alone. The Constitution itself made available alternative mechanisms for dealing with these problems and the strong anti-party sentiment and rhetoric among both Federalists and Anti-Federalists seemed on the surface at least to delegitimize any efforts to found parties.

Both the Federalists and Anti-Federalists, however, recognized that some parties were legitimate. They agreed that the party of the Revolution had been legitimate. They disagreed, however, about the legitimacy of middle class parties. The Federalists believed that such parties would be an inevitable if unfortunate aspect of the new system. The Anti-Federalists were convinced that such parties would lead to the corruption of the republican spirit and the degeneration of the system into an aristocracy or monarchy. The origin of the first parties during the 1790s is in part a result of the failure of these opposing groups to understand the different views of party that each held. As a result, each group understood its own party organization to be compatible with and indeed essential to the preservation of republican government, while at the same time viewing the opposition party as a threat to the continued existence of republicanism.

While political parties had long been widespread within the states, the first national parties arose only with the increasingly vocal demand for separation from England.[47] This revolutionary party, centered first around the Committees of Correspondence and then around the Continental Congress was, however, little more than a loose coalition of relatively like-minded men, brought into being and more or less unified for the specific purpose of securing independence. When this goal was achieved the *raison d'être* of the party disappeared and the party itself and the fragile na-

---

[47]On the pre-Constitutional state parties see Jackson Turner Main, *Political Parties Before the Constitution* (Chapel: University of North Carolina Press, 1973) and Stephen Patterson, *Political Parties in Revolutionary Massachusetts* (Madison: University of Wisconsin Press, 1973).

tional unity that it represented began to crumble. The question of the Constitution reawakened national questions and with these questions national parties or what we might more accurately call protoparties, the Federalists and the Anti-Federalists. These protoparties, however, were little more than diffuse groups of disparate men in various states who were connected principally by the issue of the Constitution. There were also profound differences within both groups over the meaning of the Constitution.[48] All of these factors notwithstanding, the struggle over the ratification of the Constitution was the first partisan national campaign.

This campaign was more or less a victory for the Federalists. The Constitution was ratified with a number of states recommending amendments which, it was generally believed, would be accepted by the first Congress. The contest did not end with the ratification of the Constitution. Everyone recognized that the plan would only be given concrete form by the legislation establishing the whole system of administrative offices and powers in the first Congresses. The first elections for the seats in the national legislature were thus hotly contested, and every legislative question, however trivial, that arose in the course of the first years of the new republic was treated with great seriousness, for everyone recognized that each decision set a precedent for all the decisions to come. Members of the first Congresses thus saw themselves dealing not with ordinary legislative questions but with questions of supreme constitutional importance. Under such circumstances it is thus not surprising that suspicion was widespread. This situation was exacerbated by the outbreak of the French Revolution and the war between Britain and France which further reinforced existing political cleavages.

As we have seen, both the Federalists and the Anti-Federalists were exceedingly suspicious of parties. The Federalists, however, distinguished the truly dangerous parties from the merely troublesome parties of the middle class. The Anti-Federalists by and large conceived of all parties in Aristotelian fashion as great parties that sought a constitutional change. To the Anti-Federalists such parties were unacceptable. Both groups were convinced that such parties were the likely consequence of free government. Both were also convinced that a great party in support of republican institutions was legitimate. Given the highly charged circumstances of the first Congresses, it is thus not surprising that republicans on

---

[48]The great diversity of both of these groups is brought out in Michael Allen Gillespie and Michael Lienesch, eds., *Ratifying the Constitution* (Lawrence: University Press of Kansas, 1989).

both sides should come to see their opponents as great parties striving to overthrow the republican order and themselves as its defender. In this sense their misunderstanding of one another played an integral role in the formation of the first national political parties.

Three questions dominated the first Congress, the formulation of a Bill of Rights, the place of the Capital, and the establishment of a government administration to manage the political and economic affairs of the new nation. While the first two occupied a great deal of the representatives' time, it was the last that was substantively the most important. The principal defect of the Articles of Confederation had been the inability of the Continental Congress to meet its financial obligations and regulate commerce between the states and between the states and foreign countries. This had led first to the Annapolis Convention and then to the Constitutional Convention in Philadelphia. The desire to have a government capable of achieving these goals also was the principal cause in securing the ratification of the Constitution.

As Secretary of the Treasury in Washington's administration, Hamilton developed a plan for meeting the federal government's financial obligations and regulating commerce. This plan had several components. The first and perhaps foremost of these was Hamilton's highly contentious plan for the assumption of state debts that included the payment of all debts at face value, despite the fact that much of this debt had been purchased by speculators at deeply discounted rates. The goal of this plan was to win the loyalty of the financial class to the new government, an indispensable condition in Hamilton's view for the security of the Constitutional system.[49] His additional plans for a national bank and the encouragement of manufactures further laid out the foundations he believed necessary for the development of a national middle class which in his view was the *sine qua non* of republican government. He himself did not perceive these actions as factional despite their inegalitarian consequences. Rather he believed they were in the permanent and aggregate interest of the community and viewed opposition to them as essentially selfish and sectional. Moreover, to the extent these institutions might be factional, they were not subversive of the constitutional order but only

[49]In his first Report on Public Credit Hamilton argues that "If all the public creditors receive their dues from one source, their interests will be the same. And having the same interests, they will unite in support of the fiscal arrangements of government." Harold C. Syrett et al, eds., *The Papers of Alexander Hamilton*, 28 vols. (New York: Columbia University Press, 1960–1979), 6:80–81.

an attempt to secure the interests of the middle class and middle class parties within this order. In this respect Hamilton clearly saw the situation of the United States as analogous to that of England after 1688 and consciously attempted to manage American problems and form a strong national union using similar financial tools.[50]

Jefferson and his supporters including Madison, however, saw Hamilton's actions as part of a concerted plan to overthrow the republic and to establish monarchy in its stead. Despite his explicit antiparty sentiment, Jefferson, for example, helped to organize the Republican party because of the threat to republicanism that he perceived in Hamilton's plans. He sincerely believed that, "the contests of that day were contests of principle, between the advocates of republican, and those of kingly government."[51] Hamilton, in Jefferson's view, had long been a supporter of monarchy, from his plan in the Constitutional Convention for a more monarchical government to his plans for debt assumption and a national bank which in Jefferson's view aimed at establishing not merely a monarchy but a monarchy like that of England based upon corruption.[52]

---

[50]On this point see his letter to Duane and his letter to an unknown recipient. *Papers of Alexander Hamilton*, 2:414 and 2:244–45, 248. For a comprehensive account of Hamilton's pro-development stance see Cathy D. Matson and Peter S. Onuf, *A Union of Interests: Political and Economic Thought in Revolutionary America* (Lawrence: University Press of Kansas, 1990).

[51]Thomas Jefferson, *The Life and Selected Writings of Jefferson*, ed. Adrienne Koch and William Peden (New York: Random House, 1944), 117.

[52]Ibid., 120–26. Jefferson apparently came to this conclusion at least in part as a result of several of Hamilton's remarks at a dinner Jefferson hosted. Jefferson recounts how after dinner the discussion turned to the English constitution,

Mr. [John] Adams observed,"purge that constitution of its corruption, and give to its popular branch equality of representation, and it would be the most perfect constitution ever devised by the wit of man." Hamilton paused and said, "purge it of its corruption, and give to its popular branch equality of representation, and it would become an *impracticable* government: as it stands at present, with all its supposed defects, it is the most perfect government which ever existed." And this was assuredly the exact line which separated the political creeds of these two gentlemen. The one was for two hereditary branches and an honest elective one; the other, for an hereditary King, with a House of Lords and Commons corrupted to his will, and standing between him and the people.

Ibid., 126–27. See also 608.

This opinion was reinforced in Jefferson's imagination by Hamilton's subsequent remark the same evening that Julius Caesar and not Bacon, Newton, or Locke (Jefferson's heroes) was the greatest man who ever lived. Ibid., 609. On the basis of these remarks Jefferson came to see Hamilton's plans in a new light as an

The political struggle between Jefferson's Republicans and Hamilton's Federalists that ensued was consequently interpreted in Jefferson's mind as a struggle between two great parties, the Federalists favoring monarchy and his party the preservation of the republic. He wrote to John Melish on 13 January 1813 that

> the principle of difference between the two great political parties here . . . [is not], "whether the controlling power shall be vested in this or that set of men." That each party endeavors to get into the administration of the government, and exclude the other from power, is true, and may be stated as a motive of action: but this is only secondary; the primary motive being a real and radical difference of political principle. I sincerely wish our differences were but personally who should govern, and that the principles of our constitution were those of both parties. Unfortunately, it is otherwise; and the question of preference between monarchy and republicanism, which has so long divided mankind elsewhere, threatens a permanent division here.[53]

Jefferson's interpretation of this struggle as a contest between two great parties was in part the result of the fact that he saw parties as vertical, class based parties and not as horizontal, middle class parties.[54] In contrast to Hamilton he saw events not through the lens of English history but through that of the *ancien regime* in France. The struggle in America from the 1760s until the present, Jefferson claimed, was nothing other than this age old class struggle. While the Federalists favored monarchy,

---

effort to transform the government into a monarchy. He reached this conclusion despite the fact that he generally admired Hamilton's character. Jefferson believed that, "Hamilton was, indeed, a singular character. Of acute understanding, disinterested, honest, and honorable in all private transactions, amiable in society, and duly valuing virtue in private life, yet so bewitched and perverted by the British example, as to be under thorough conviction that corruption was essential to the government of a nation." Ibid., 127. Hamilton's later support of Jefferson over Burr belies this conclusion.

[53]Ibid., 621–22.

[54]He wrote to John Adams on 27 June 1813: "Men have differed in opinion, and been divided into parties by these opinions, from the first origin of societies, and in all governments where they have been permitted freely to think and to speak. The same political parties which now agitate the United States, have existed through all time. Whether the power of the people or that of the aristoi should prevail, were questions which kept the States of Greece and Rome in eternal convulsions, as they now schismatize every people whose minds and mouths are not shut up by the gag of a despot. And in fact, the terms of whig and tory belong to natural as well as to civil history. They denote the temper and constitution of mind of different individuals." Ibid., 627.

the party called republican is steadily for the support of the present constitution. They obtained at its commencement, all the amendments to it they desired. These reconciled them to it perfectly, and if they have any ulterior view, it is only, perhaps, to popularize it further, by shortening the Senatorial term, and devising a process for the responsibility of judges, more practicable than that of impeachment.[55]

Hamilton was first surprised and puzzled by the opposition that his plan met, especially from his former ally Madison. In contrast to both Madison and Jefferson, however, he had never been attracted to the civic republicanism of the time and placed much less emphasis than any of his contemporaries on the necessity of virtue for republican government. Indeed, he saw self-interest and economic diversity as a much surer foundation for political stability, and his economic proposals were intended to foster such a self-interested, diverse, middle class society. He thus saw the resistance to this plan as the result of sectional selfishness and a desire for ambitious individuals to use factional fighting to gain personal position and power.[56] While decrying the rising party spirit of his opponents, he could still ask in the period between 1792–1795 how it is possible to "distinguish the virtuous Patriot, who is endeavouring to inflict punishment upon delinquency and disgrace upon demerit from the factious Partisan who is labouring to undermine the faithful friend of his Country and to destroy the Rival he envies & the Competitor he fears?"[57] Despite the vehement party conflict of the 1790s, in 1800 he supported Jefferson, with all of his faults, over Burr, whom Hamilton was convinced would seek to establish precisely the kind of corrupt regime that the Republicans had long believed Hamilton himself to desire. By 1801, however, he had come to believe that the opposition party was irremediably Jacobin, dedicated to the overthrow of the Constitutional system. He argued in "An Address to the Electors of the State of New York on 21 March 1801 that

the pernicious spirit which has actuated many of the leaders of the party denominated antifederal, from the moment when our national constitution was first proposed . . . seems now to have laid aside all reserve; . . .

[55]Ibid., 623.

[56]Forrest McDonald argues that Hamilton wanted to transform what he believed to be a indolent, hierarchical society in which landholding elites held sway into a commercial society in which position was determined by hard work and ability. *Alexander Hamilton: A Biography* (New York: Norton, 1979), 122, 216, 232.

[57]"The Defence" No. 1. (1792–1795), *Selected Writings and Speeches of Alexander Hamilton*, ed. Morton Frisch (Washington: AEI, 1985), 390–91.

[This] will serve to shew, that moderate men, who have seen in our political struggles, nothing more than a competition for power and place, have been deceived; that in reality the foundations of society, the essential interests of our nation, the dearest concerns of individuals are staked upon the eventful contest.

[A]s a party, and with few exceptions, they were violent opposers of the adoption of the constitution itself; predicted from it every possible evil, and painted it in the blackest colours, as a monster of political deformity.

It is because the amendments subsequently made, meeting scarcely any of the important objections which were urged, leaving the structure of the government, and the mass and distribution of its powers where they were, are too insignificant to be with any sensible man a reason for being reconciled to the system if he thought it originally bad. . . .

[T]hey have openly avowed their attachment to the excessive principles of the French revolution. . . .

In regard to these sects, which compose the pith and essence of the antifederal party, we believe it to be true, that the contest between the tyranny of jacobinism, which confounds and levels every thing, and the mild reign of rational liberty. . . .

'Tis against these sects that all good men should form an indissoluble league.[58]

This quotation makes clear in an exceptionally cogent form the Federalist view of the Republicans. They were not merely a group of men concerned with their own aggrandizement; they were a great party whose consistent aim for over a decade had been the overthrow of rational republican government and the establishment in its place of a radically egalitarian Jacobinism. The Republican opposition to the Federalists is thus in Hamilton's view thoroughly disingenuous, mere camouflage for their real, revolutionary notions.

Both the Federalists and the Republicans thus saw themselves as great parties organized in defense of the Constitutional order and saw their opponents as motivated by a desire to overthrow this order. Hamilton, the Republicans proclaimed, was attempting to administer the government into a monarchy or aristocracy. Jefferson, the Federalists countered, aimed to replace the Constitutional republic with a Jacobin dictatorship. In fact Hamilton was trying to create the basis for a stable middle class republic with middle class rather than great parties using financial tools that the Republicans themselves after 1808 were increasingly driven to employ. The Republicans, however, misunderstood Hamilton's goals

[58]Ibid., 465–78.

in part because (Madison excepted) they did not have a comprehensive grasp of modern political economy and in part because they saw parties in an Aristotelian manner as vertical class based parties. Their very civic republicanism in this sense misled them. By contrast Hamilton and the Federalists were at first perplexed by the opposition to their plans in part because they did not have any real understanding of the depth of their opponents commitment to the civic republican ideals and in part because they did not see their plans as inimical to the republican order.

The organization of the first parties by the American Founders was thus not at odds with their principled antiparty stance during the period of the formation and ratification of the Constitution. The principles that they espoused were not merely rhetorical positions defended for simply expeditious reasons. They were sincerely believed and sincerely argued. Moreover, the parties they eventually formed were not at odds with the principles and were organized only because they saw these principles threatened in fundamental ways. Both the Federalists and the Republicans were in this sense striving to defend the republican form of government that they believed the Constitution had more or less adequately established.

The parties that they established were thus not factions: they did not seek to undermine the rights of their fellow citizens and did not aim at a goal that was adverse to the permanent and aggregate interest of the community. The real interests that lay behind the parties were middle class interests and particularly the conflict between the commercial and agricultural sectors of society. If both sides had been able to recognize this fact, the fervor of party competition would have been much muted. The vehemence of the first parties arose out of the fact that each saw itself defending the republican order against its worst enemies. If they had not thought of themselves in such a way, however, they could not have formed as parties. They were unable to think of themselves as merely middle class parties, however, not because the conceptual tools for such a conclusion were lacking. Rather they were unable to recognize themselves for what they were because to do so would have required that they recognize that the days of the Revolution were behind them and that they were now concerned not with the great questions of those days but with the mundane questions of everyday life. While they all recognized that such a time would come, they could not face the fact that it was already upon them.

LINCOLN AND THE
REPUBLICAN REALIGNMENT

Glen Thurow

IN EXAMINING THE BEHAVIOR AND FOUNDATION OF AMERICAN POLIT-
ical parties, political scientists have developed the theory of "critical realignment." This theory holds that the history of American
parties can be understood as a series of periodic realignments of
voter loyalties. These realignments take place in "critical elections"
or are revealed in such elections. Sometimes they take the form of
voters deserting a party or parties to form a new party; sometimes
they take the form of new alignments of voters between existing
parties. Between such elections, in non-critical elections, voters
are consolidated in their voting habits and both parties have to
adapt to the views endorsed by the voters in the last critical election if they are to have a chance of electoral success. Historians
of parties have argued that such realignments take place every
28–36 years.

This theory has suffered recently because the last realigning
election was that of 1932. The New Deal coalition then formed
dominated American politics through the 1960s. Beginning with
the election of 1968 this coalition progressively fell apart. Both
Democratic and Republican parties took a new shape. In spite of
Republican triumphs on the Presidential level in all elections but
one since 1968 there has been no decisive realignment of the parties that would give either political party a dominant position.
Rather, there seems to be a stand-off in which the Democrats dominate the Congress and the Republicans the Presidency. The
causes and significance of this lack of a critical election have been
the subject of considerable speculation among political scientists.
Theories propounded range from the view that the realignment is
only slower than in previous realignments, to the contention that
realignments are impossible under the conditions of modern
welfare-state politics.

Perhaps one can begin to understand better the failure of our contemporary parties to be able to effect a realignment by looking at the party responsible for the most decisive realignment in American history, the Republican Party of the 1850s. It has been said that the Civil War is the most revealing event in American history. The extremity of that conflict revealed the tensions within American politics and forced (and still forces) Americans to reflect on the fundamental principles of their political order. It might equally be said that the formation and rapid rise to power of the Republican Party as a prelude to that war reveal the character and potential of American political parties.

The Republican Party was born and rose rapidly to electoral triumph in the 1850s. Formed in opposition to the Kansas-Nebraska Act of 1854, by 1860 it had destroyed an old party (the Whig), captured the Presidency and both houses of Congress, helped to split its rival, the Democratic Party, and left the country sectionally divided, a situation it remedied only by leading the nation in a Civil War which ended the reign of the institution of slavery it had been born to fight. No other realignment has had such great immediate effects or so long-lasting an impact upon American politics.

What enabled the Republican Party to accomplish so much? There are, of course, many causes that contributed to its success. But there is also one simple answer to the question posed: the party became led by—even dominated by—Abraham Lincoln. In his hands the party, for all its gradations of opinion, became a powerful instrument for bringing about precisely those changes for which he strove. Lincoln was able to accomplish this not by a blind act of will, but by understanding thoroughly the character of party in the context of American politics and by acting on this understanding at the critical times.

I do not propose in this essay to give a comprehensive account of Lincoln's leadership of the Republican Party. Rather, I wish to show the kind of party he worked to create and how it related to his statesmanship more generally. In order to do this I will first set out why political parties are a problematic form of political organization, a form the American Founders sought to prevent or at least to keep weak. Then I will attempt to show how the problem posed by parties is made more pointed by the particular character of the United States. Having sketched the background, I will then turn to the formation of the Republican Party and Lincoln's role in it. I will show the kind of unity he sought to create in the party and the diversity it allowed, the goals he sought for it, and the room it left for statesmanship.

THE PROBLEM OF POLITICAL PARTIES

Although contemporary Americans may object to particular political parties (such as Communist or Nazi parties), in general they consider parties to be a good, even essential, element of democratic government. It is well known among students of the American founding, however, that the authors of the Constitution did not share this sanguine view of parties. The most famous paper of *The Federalist*, No. 10, makes no secret of its belief that one of the great accomplishments of the Founders was the discovery of a republican way to control the mischief of faction or party. (The non-republican way was either to suppress parties altogether by denying people liberty, or to attempt to give everyone the "same opinions, passions, and interests" so that they would not divide into parties.) This view was shared by all the Founders. So important did George Washington consider it to control parties that when the Framers' discovery did not prevent the rise of party conflict in the 1790s, he rose in his Farewell Address, as if from his deathbed, to warn his countrymen of the evils of party:

Let me now take a more comprehensive view and warn you in the most solemn manner against the baneful effects of the spirit of party generally.

This spirit, unfortunately, is inseparable from our nature, having its root in the strongest passions of the human mind. It exists under different shapes in all governments, more or less stifled, controlled, or repressed; but, in those of the popular form, it is seen in its greatest rankness and is truly their worst enemy.[1]

The basis of this anti-party view of the wisest generation of men to have led the United States is not difficult to state.[2] According to this view, parties undermine the unity of a country, bedevil its administration, and thwart the possibility of true statesmanship.

To have parties, as the name suggests, is to divide a country into parts threatening to undermine its unity. Can one have a whole made of diverse parts? The answer depends upon the character of the parts and the kind of whole one seeks to make.

[1] George Washington, "Farewell Address", in *The People Shall Judge: Readings in the Formation of American Policy* (Chicago: University of Chicago Press, 1949), 491–492.

[2] It is not difficult because it has been clearly laid out by Harvey C. Mansfield, Jr. I owe the following understanding of the general problem of parties to him. See his *Statesmanship and Party Government* (Chicago, University of Chicago Press, 1965).

Political parties differ from each other in presenting disputing claims about who or what should rule. Members of today's Republican Party believe that a certain sort of person with certain views should hold office, while Democrats believe a different sort with different views should lead. What is the character of these differences?

The disputes between parties may be over relatively large matters or over relatively small matters. The traditional view holds that either kind of dispute is dangerous to good politics. If men split about large matters, such as whether Catholics or Protestants should rule, the result is likely to be strife and civil war. If they split about small matters, such as whether twiddle-dee or twiddle-dum should be in office, then politics becomes petty and enervating. There is also the danger that petty disputes may turn into momentous disputes, leading again to war and strife. (Evidence that this fear is not groundless is to be found in the tremendous significance given to whether young men wore their hair long and on their faces, or short and only on top of their heads during the Vietnam War.)

Because the unity of a country is itself based upon an agreement about who and what should rule, parties divided by important differences of principle create a potentially revolutionary situation. At the very least, all but one of the disputing parties must be potentially revolutionary because they must disagree either wittingly or unwittingly with the agreement upon which the country is based. Hence, according to the traditional view, political parties of principle undermine the necessary unity of a country. Parties divided by petty matters might be tolerated, but the only reason to tolerate them is that there may be no good way to get rid of them. Both kinds provide fertile soil for the growth of leaders willing to exploit these passions and divisions.

The second major charge against political parties is that they undermine the prudence necessary for wise political leadership. To be politically prudent means to do the right thing at the right time for the good of one's country. If parties are simply collections of men seeking their own advantage rather than the country's, then they constitute organized opposition to prudent action for the common good. If, on the other hand, they represent principles, not narrow self-interest, they are equally if not more dangerous to good statesmanship. Even if their principles do not conflict with the principles of the country, they are likely to undermine the flexibility needed for wise leadership. Organized parties create bodies of men wedded by both belief and interest to particular policies. Even if the stand of the party is at one time for the common good, the circumstances that make policies good can rapidly change, while it is a difficult and slow business to change the views of large numbers of people organized into a party.

This critique leaves us with two questions: 1) Under what conditions, if any, is it possible to have decent political parties that do not threaten the unity of a country? and 2) Is it possible to reconcile the flexibility required by statesmanship with the brute sluggishness of political parties directed towards fixed policies?

American Unity

The way in which parties might threaten the unity of a particular country depends in large part upon the kind of unity a particular country has. Since statesmanship consists in advancing the union or the common good, it too cannot be understood without understanding the basis of unity in a particular country. The basis of national unity was, of course, the question of the Civil War, and was one to which Lincoln devoted considerable thought.

Lincoln understood the American union to essentially consist in a commitment to the principle of the Declaration of Independence that all men are created equal. He did not think the basis of union was to be found simply in a common history, a common ethnic stock, or even common traditions in general.

Perhaps Lincoln's clearest exposition of the nature of the American union is to be found in a speech delivered in Chicago on July 10, 1858. In this speech, Lincoln reflected on what tied Americans together. Explaining why we celebrate the Fourth of July, he noted that we can look back to

a race of men living in that day whom we claim as our fathers and grandfathers; they were iron men, they fought for the principle that they were contending for; and we understand that by what they then did it has followed that the degree of prosperity that we now enjoy has come to us. We hold this annual celebration to remind ourselves of all the good done in this process of time, of how it was done and who did it, and how we are historically connected with it; and we go from these meetings in better humor with ourselves—we feel more attached the one to the other, and more firmly bound to the country we inhabit.[3]

But Lincoln goes on to note that many citizens cannot literally look back to those men as their fathers and grandfathers. They, or their

[3]Abraham Lincoln, *Collected Works*, ed. Roy P. Basler, 9 vols (New Brunswick, New Jersey: Rutgers University Press, 1953), vol. 2, 499.

ancestors, came from Europe after the Revolution and have no
common ties of blood to that earlier race:

[B]ut when they look through that old Declaration of Independence
they find that those old men say that "We hold these truths to be self-
evident, that all men are created equal," and they feel that that moral
sentiment taught in that day evidences their relation to those men, that
it is the father of all moral principle in them, and they have a right to
claim it as though they were blood of the blood, and flesh of the flesh
of the men who wrote the Declaration, and so they are. That is the elec-
tric cord in that Declaration that links the hearts of patriotic and
liberty-loving men together, that will link those patriotic hearts as long
as the love of freedom exists in the minds of men throughout the
world.[4]

Lincoln argues that the Union can assimilate newcomers because it
is based on a principle that is the "father of morality" in men. We
do not have a union because of a common history, but we have a
common history because the Union is the triumph of moral principle within ourselves.

Lincoln always made clear that in working for the preservation
of the Union, he was not so much working for the mere adherence
of one state to another as he was working for the principle upon
which the Union was based. He always maintained that the "Union
must be preserved in the purity of its principles as well as in the
integrity of its territorial parts."[5] If the territorial union could be
saved only by giving up the principles of the Declaration, Lincoln
once said, "I would rather be assassinated on this spot than to surrender it."[6]

But it is not sufficient to recognize that American unity is to be
found in adherence to the abstract principle of the Declaration, a
principle natural to all men in the sense that it lies at the foundation of their morality. Although the principle is natural in this
sense, men do not automatically adhere to it. It is perfectly possible for them to believe something else. The greatest threat, as
Lincoln saw it, in the political events leading up to the Civil War
was the threatened erosion of the principle of equality. As he once
explained:

But, soberly, it is now no child's play to save the principles of Jefferson from total overthrow in this nation.

[4]Ibid., vol 2, 499–500.
[5]Ibid., vol. 2, 341.
[6]Ibid., vol. 4, 240.

One would start with great confidence that he could convince any sane child that the simpler propositions of Euclid are true; but, nevertheless, he would fail, utterly, with one who should deny the definitions and axioms. The principles of Jefferson are the definitions and axioms of free society. And yet they are denied and evaded, with no small show of success.[7]

For this reason, the maintenance of the principle of equality in men's minds and hearts was the chief task of American statesmanship. As Lincoln put it, "He who molds public sentiment goes deeper than he who enacts statutes and pronounces decisions. He makes statutes or decisions possible or impossible to execute."[8] To be effective, the principle of equality requires the weight that public opinion, the ruling opinion of a democracy, can give to it:

Our government rests in public opinion. Whoever can change public opinion, can change the government, practically just as much. Public opinion, on any subject always has a "*central idea*," from which all its minor thoughts radiate. That "central idea" in our political public opinion, at the beginning was, and until recently has continued to be, "the equality of men."[9]

In Lincoln's analysis, the unity of the country is based upon two things: the truth of human equality, and the adherence of public opinion to this truth. The political effectiveness of the truth of human equality depends upon the maintenance of a nation committed to it because people hold the universal truth of human equality not as an unshakable rational truth but as a belief fostered by the dominant opinion of a particular nation.

It is the highest task of statesmanship as understood by Lincoln to maintain the public opinion that supports the principle of human equality. This requires that a statesman understand both the centrality of the principle of equality and its dependence upon public opinion.

The general difficulties posed by political parties are enhanced by the particular character of the United States. Its foundation upon an abstract truth fosters, even requires, a politics looking to abstract truths. Parties formed around abstract principle are the most dangerous kind of party, as the traditional view maintains. At the same time its character seems to require some

[7]Ibid., vol. 3, 375.
[8]Ibid., vol. 3, p. 27.
[9]Ibid., vol. 2, 385.

method for molding public opinion in support of its founding principle, a function which might provide a justification for party.

THE PRINCIPLE OF EQUALITY AND THE REPUBLICAN PARTY

The history of the 1850s might seem to vindicate the Founders' fears and the traditional charge against political parties. Did not the formation of the Republican Party divide the country, and was it not largely responsible for bringing on the Civil War? Was it not, as its opponents charged, a sectional party? In the election of 1860, Lincoln's name did not even appear on the ballot in most of the Southern states; his strength was entirely concentrated in the North. The reason for that was that the Republican Party threatened the interests and the rights of the South.

In the eyes of its critics the Republican Party seemed to be the perfect representation of faction, the danger most feared by Publius. Fitting precisely the definition of *Federalist* No. 10, it was a group of people united by a common interest and passion adverse to the rights of the South and the common good of the country. Furthermore, it was the most dangerous kind of faction—a territorial faction—and it led inexorably to the evils the Founders predicted. It led both to the triumph of someone willing to exploit those passions and to civil war. As we have seen, the traditional view argued that parties that disputed about minor matters might be tolerated, but the Republican Party was a party of high principle. No one strove harder to form the party around high principle than did Abraham Lincoln. He, and others, invested the principle of human equality with a passion as great as that embodied in the religious parties of Europe, with the same consequence of civil strife.[10]

In order to understand the character of this party as Lincoln wished it to be, it is necessary to look more closely at the Republican Party and Lincoln's relationship to it. The Republican Party was formed in response to the introduction by Stephen Douglas of the Kansas-Nebraska Bill in 1854. The party was not the creation of one or a few men, but grew out of groups in various states who had coalesced in opposition to the bill. Lincoln was not the first to join the Republican Party; indeed, he refused to join the Party

[10]For a discussion of the way in which Lincoln impassioned the principle of equality, see my "Abraham Lincoln and American Political Religion," in Gabor Boritt, ed., *The Historian's Lincoln: Pseudohistory, Psychohistory, and History* (Urbana and Chicago: University of Illinois Press, 1988), 125–143. See also my book of the same title (Albany: State University of New York press, 1976).

when it initially developed in Illinois, preferring to remain a Whig. However, he very quickly gave up on the Whig Party and joined the Republicans. Lincoln may be considered to be one of the founders of the Republican Party, not because he was among the first to join its ranks, but because he helped to shape its character both in the pivotal state of Illinois and nationally, laying the groundwork for both his own and his party's triumph in 1860.

By opening the Nebraska territory to slavery, the Kansas-Nebraska Act raised the possibility that slavery might be extended into territory in which slavery had been prohibited by the Missouri Compromise of 1820. But the Act was not a mere tacit violation of this compromise; it explicitly overturned the Missouri Compromise in the name of a universal principle, the principle of "popular sovereignty." This doctrine, developed and championed by Stephen Douglas, held that the extension of slavery was a matter to be decided by the people of the territory or state concerned, not by the national government. It was a proper principle of self-government that the people of the states and territories be free to have slavery or not, in accordance with their own wishes.

Lincoln's problem, as Harry V. Jaffa shows so well, was that he faced a formidable opponent.[11] Stephen Douglas sought a comprehensive settlement of the slavery issue by setting the issue on new ground, on ground that denied the equality of men enunciated in the Declaration. Lincoln understood his fundamental task to be to resist not merely the particular measures that Douglas supported, but to counter the new ground, the ground of "popular sovereignty" on which Douglas sought to set the slavery issue altogether. It was this point that Lincoln returned to again and again in his debates with Douglas. The alternative to popular sovereignty was the Declaration of Independence. Lincoln sought to show that although "popular sovereignty" sounded democratic, it stood in opposition to the fundamental principle that "all men are created equal."

Lincoln thus insisted upon making the Republican Party a party of principle. Because what was at stake was the "central idea" of public opinion, it was not sufficient for the party to stand right on particular issues. More importantly, it needed to stand right on the fundamental issue—the principle at stake. The only possible justification for such a party, which so threatened to divide the country, was that Lincoln was right that there was a threat to subvert the fundamental character of the country.

[11]Harry V. Jaffa, *Crisis of the House Divided* (Garden City, New York: Doubleday, 1959).

Again, it is this claim that justifies Lincoln's unwillingness to ally with others when he thought that alliance might undermine the central principle of the party. This aspect of Lincoln's statesmanship can be seen in his response to those who would have allied with Senator Douglas in the Lecompton Constitution affair. In 1858, the Buchanan administration pushed the acceptance of Kansas as a state under a constitution which had been made by a convention elected by a small part of the electorate because the anti-slavery forces had boycotted the polls. This Lecompton Constitution protected the existing slavery in Kansas. The convention decided that voters were not to be allowed to vote on the whole constitution, but only on the question of whether they preferred the constitution with slavery or with a provision prohibiting new slaves from being brought into the state. Douglas opposed the Lecompton Constitution as violating popular sovereignty. Many Republicans thought of making an alliance with him, since they, too, opposed the Lecompton Constitution.[12]

From the beginning of the affair, Lincoln was aware of the danger that Republicans might side with Douglas against Buchanan. He wrote to Lyman Trumbull in November of 1857, "What think you of the probable 'rumpus' among the democracy over the Kansas constitution? I think the Republicans should stand clear of it. In their view both the President and Douglas are wrong; and they should not espouse the cause of either, because they may consider the other a little the farther wrong of the two."[13] Although Lincoln was willing to attract whomever he could to his cause, he saw the danger that the alliance would mean the endorsement of the lesser evil, which in this case was the doctrine of popular sovereignty.

Later, in explaining that the Republicans could reasonably vote with Judge Douglas against Buchanan, Lincoln nevertheless insisted on the clear difference of principle between Douglas and the Republicans: "*they* insisting that Congress *shall,* and *he* insisting that congress *shall not,* keep slavery out of the Territories *before &* *up to the time* they form State constitutions."[14] Lincoln said that the difference was "that he [Douglas] cares not whether slavery is voted down or up," but Republicans "think slavery is wrong; and that, like every other wrong which some men will commit if left

[12]For an account of the divisions within the Republican Party over alliance with Douglas, see Allan Nevins, *The Emergence of Lincoln* (New York, London: Charles Scribner's Sons, 1950), esp. 367–370.
[13]Lincoln, vol. 2, 427.
[14]Ibid., vol. 2, 446.

alone, it ought to be prohibited by law. They consider it not only morally wrong, but a 'deadly poison' in a government like ours, professedly based on the equality of men."[15]

This line of argument culminated in the House Divided Speech. This speech was attacked because it was designed to destroy the apparently moderate middle by arguing that there were only two alternatives—pro-slavery or anti-slavery—and that a conspiracy was bringing about the victory of the pro-slavery opinion. Lincoln's justification was that the middle ground was that occupied by Senator Douglas, and his view undermined the fundamental principle of equality. Stand firm, was Lincoln's advice:

> Of *strange, discordant,* and even, *hostile* elements, we gathered from the four winds, and *formed* and fought the battle through, under the constant hot fire of a disciplined proud and pampered enemy.
>
> Did we brave all *then,* to *falter* now?—now—when that same enemy is *wavering,* dissevered and belligerent?
>
> The result is not doubtful. We shall not fail—if we stand firm, we shall not fail.[16]

Lincoln was instrumental in keeping the Illinois, and thereby the national, Republican Party committed to the principle of human equality in spite of the temptations to compromise. This was the very purpose of the party. Lincoln also saw that the temptation to compromise in order to increase the reach of the party was misguided. The Republican Party was not held together, nor could it be held together, by mere horse trading. In notes he made in preparation for speeches in 1859, he wrote:

For the sake of their principles in forming their party, they broke and sacrificed, the strongest mere party ties and advantages which can exist. Republicans believe that slavery is wrong, and they insist, and will continue to insist upon a national policy which recognizes it, and deals with it, *as a wrong.* There can be no letting down about this. Simultaneously with such letting down, the republican organization itself would go to pieces, and half its elements go in a different direction, leaving an easy victory to the common ene[my.] No ingenuity of political trading could possibly hold it together.[17]

This insistence upon maintaining the principle of the party did not mean that Lincoln was unwilling to compromise where it was not at stake; he was merely unwilling to compromise on the

[15]Ibid., vol. 2, 449.
[16]Ibid., vol. 2, 468.
[17]Ibid., vol. 3, 432–433.

central principle at stake. Lincoln was perfectly willing to unite with people with whom he disagreed, even profoundly, on many other issues. Lincoln knew well, and approved the fact, that the Republican Party was composed of *"strange, discordant,* and even, *hostile* elements."

THE REPUBLICANS AND THE KNOW-NOTHINGS

The way in which Lincoln responded to the American or Know-Nothing Party, a party dedicated to anti-immigrant and anti-Catholic sentiment, perhaps best reveals the lengths to which Lincoln was willing to go to attract people to the party in spite of profound differences of opinion.

From early on, Lincoln's policy with regard to the Know-Nothing Party was to maintain a public silence in spite of disagreement with its goals. That disagreement is apparent from the start, as is his silence. The first time the party is mentioned in the extant speeches of Lincoln, Lincoln indicates that he doubted such an organization existed, but if it did and "had for its object interference with the rights of foreigners," then he was against it.[18] In a letter to his friend Joshua Speed written in August of 1855, Lincoln privately made clear his views:

I am not a Know-Nothing. That is certain. How could I be? How can any one who abhors the oppression of negroes, be in favor of degrading classes of white people? Our progress in degeneracy appears to me to be pretty rapid. . . . When the Know-Nothings get control, [the Declaration of Independence] will read "all men are created equal, except negroes, *and foreigners, and catholics."* When it comes to this I should prefer emigrating to some country where they make no pretense of loving liberty—to Russia, for instance, where despotism can be taken pure, and without the base alloy of hypocrisy.[19]

This passage makes clear that Lincoln not only abhorred the views of the Know-Nothings, but that he thought that the principle involved was exactly the same as that involved in the issue of slavery. Yet despite his abhorrence and his belief that a vital issue of principle was at stake, he did little publicly to try to stop them. This was because he believed that the party would not last in any event and that to denounce it would make it difficult to win its adherents for the Republicans. "They were," he wrote, "an ephemeral

[18]Ibid., vol. 2, 234.
[19]Ibid., vol. 2, 323.

party, and would soon pass away."[20] Writing in August of 1855, he noted that opposition to the Nebraska principles could not succeed without elements from the Know-Nothing party, and fretted that it "has not yet entirely tumbled to pieces." But he expressed his fear that "an open push by us now, may offend them, and tend to prevent our ever getting them."[21]

Lincoln sought to get the Know-Nothings under the Republican banner. His willingness to woo them had nothing to do with liking their principles. Lincoln looked to the grounds on which common cause with others could take place, not on a person's intrinsic merits or overall position. As he put it, "I have no objection to 'fuse' with any body provided I can fuse on ground which I think is right."[22] This view extended not only to getting the pro-Know-Nothing vote, but the anti-Know-Nothing vote as well.

Writing to a prominent German-American leader in Springfield in 1858, Lincoln noted that there were reports that half the Know-Nothings in the county were going for Douglas, a disastrous result if true. However, Lincoln thought that if it were true, it might be turned to account by getting the German vote. Lincoln wrote, "It appears to me this fact of itself, would make it, at least no harder for us to get accessions from the Germans. . . . Every edge must be made to cut. Can not you, Canisius, and some other influential Germans set a plan on foot that shall gain us accession from the Germans, and see that, at the election, none are cheated in their ballots?"

But while Canisius would be getting the anti-Know-Nothing vote, Abe would be getting the pro-Know-Nothing vote: "Others of us must find the way to save as many Americans as possible. Still others must do other things. Nothing must be left undone."[23] One takes one's allies wherever one can find them, and in pursuing the main issue, one does not let side issues detract from the central objective.

During the election of 1858, Lincoln's previous public silence had been so complete that it was possible to start a rumor that Lincoln had in fact been connected with the Know-Nothings. Lincoln publicly denied the charge, but even as late as 1860 the charge resurfaced.[24] Lincoln refuted the particular charges in detail in a confidential letter, but ended the letter by noting:

[20]Ibid., vol. 2, 373.
[21]Ibid., vol. 2, 316.
[22]Ibid., vol, 2, 316.
[23]Ibid., vol., 2, 524.
[24]Ibid., vol, 3, p. 329, 333.

And now, a word of caution. Our adversaries think they can gain a point, if they could force me to openly deny this charge, by which some degree of offence would be given to the Americans. For this reason, it must not publicly appear that I am paying any attention to the charge.[25]

In Lincoln's dealing with the Know-Nothing issue, we can see his skill in keeping his own attention focused on the central issue, that of extension of slavery into the territories, in spite of his deep conviction that the principles of Know-Nothingism were abhorrent and contrary to the great principle he was trying to defend. This was because of his sound political judgment that it was over the issue of the extension of slavery, not the issue of immigration, that the principle of human equality was going to be won or lost. By keeping the Republican Party focused on the vital issue of slavery extension, the lesser issues would fade and their adherents could be won to the Republican side. They could be won not by concessions to their principles, but by being persuaded that there were bigger fish in the sea.

Lincoln even went further than this in the direction of being willing to absorb men into the party. To return to the issue of Douglas, Lincoln believed, as we have seen, that the principles of the Republican Party were rooted in men's nature and hence those principles would survive even an alliance with Douglas. But, he warns,

in the meantime all the labor that has been done to build up the present Republican party would be entirely lost, and perhaps twenty years of time, before we would again have formed around that principle as solid, extensive, and formidable an organization as we have, standing shoulder to shoulder tonight in harmony and strength around the Republican banner.[26]

Lincoln goes on to say that the party in various places had supported people with the views of Douglas, and that was likely wise. Lincoln notes that these other men "were comparatively small men, and the Republican party could take hold of them, use them, elect them, absorb them, expel them, or do whatever it pleased with them, and the Republican organization be in no wise shaken." But Senator Douglas was another matter:

[25]Ibid., vol. 4, 86.
[26]Ibid., vol. 3, 367.

Let the Republican party of Illinois dally with Judge Douglas; let them fall in behind him and make him their candidate, and they do not absorb him; he absorbs them. They would come out at the end all Douglas men, all claimed by him as having indorsed every one of his doctrines upon the great subject with which the whole nation is engaged at this hour.[27]

Lincoln was willing to make common cause even with men of Douglas' persuasion as long as they were not sufficiently numerous or weighty to tilt the party away from its central principle. One can almost say that there is an infinite flexibility in Lincoln's political maneuvering, except that it was all directed to the goal of developing a triumphant party unwilling to make any compromise on the most important issue, whether slavery was a good or a bad idea.

LINCOLN'S STATESMANSHIP AND PARTY

The traditional argument against parties, as we have said, contends that they limit statesmanship as well as threaten the unity of a country. Lincoln thought about this problem too. He considered it inevitable that, in a free country, anyone who wished to have political influence would have to join a political party. In his eulogy of Henry Clay he notes:

A free people, in times of peace and quiet—when pressed by no common danger—naturally divide into parties. At such times, the man who is of neither party, is not—cannot be, of any consequence. Mr. Clay, therefore, was of a party.[28]

As implied in this quotation and made clear in the remainder of the Eulogy, Lincoln also thought it was possible for statesmen to rise above party, as Clay had in playing a leading role in bringing about the compromises of 1820 and 1850. But the necessity of joining a party did mean that a statesman who won election on a party platform was bound to follow that platform once in office. To fail to do so would be to violate the very principles of representative democracy. After his election and before assuming office, he resisted urging to back down from party positions in order to prevent civil war, saying:

I thought such refusal was demanded by the view that if, when a chief Magistrate is constitutionally elected, he cannot be inaugurated until

[27]Ibid.
[28]Ibid., vol. 2, 126.

he betrays those who elected him, by breaking his pledges, and surren-
dering to those who tried and failed to defeat him at the polls, this government and all popular government is already at an end. Demands for
such surrender, once recognized, are without limit, as to nature, extent
and repetition. They break the only bond of faith between public and
public servant; and they distinctly set the minority over the majority.[29]

Not only should those elected by a party follow its platform,
but Lincoln followed the traditional critique of party in believ-
ing that parties could not easily change their principles: "[N]o
party can command respect which sustains this year, what it opposed last."[30]

If it was a requirement for making parties consistent with representative democracy that those they elect follow their platforms,
Lincoln also recognized that this principle could be inconsistent
with constitutional government. The following was reported of a
speech given in support of General Taylor for President in 1848:

Mr. Lincoln proceeded to examine the absurdity of an attempt to
make a platform or creed for a national party, to *all* parts of which *all*
must consent and agree, when it was clearly the intention and the true
philosophy of our government, that in Congress all opinions and principles should be represented, and that when the wisdom of all had been
compared and united, the will of the majority should be carried out.[31]

Rigid party platforms undermined the deliberative character
of Congress; they also made it difficult to gather the diverse elements together needed to form a majority. Lincoln's mitigation of
these difficulties was to argue that a party ought to be built
around a central principle which needed to be established or reinforced, and that other matters be muted. Thus, as we have already seen, the Republican Party ought to be built around the
central principle of opposition to the extension of slavery and
other issues ought to be laid to the side. This would both leave
room for flexibility and deliberation in government and allow men
of diverse opinions to join the party even while the party remained
principled. Speaking in 1859 Lincoln noted:

---

[29]Ibid., vol. 4, 201. See also the preliminary draft for Lincoln's First Inaugural
Address. Lincoln, vol. 4, 250. For a detailed account of Lincoln and the Republican
Party between his election and the fall of Fort Sumter, see David M. Potter, *Lincoln
and His Party in the Secession Crisis* (New Haven & London: Yale University Press,
1942).
[30]Ibid., vol. 3, 394.
[31]Ibid., vol. 2, 2–3.

I am afraid of the result upon organized action where great results are in view, if any of us allow ourselves to seek out minor or separate points on which there may be difference of views as to policy and right, and let them keep us from uniting in action upon a great principle in a cause on which we all agree, or are deluded into the belief that all can be brought to consider alike and agree upon every minor point before we unite and press forward in organization, asking the cooperation of all good men in that resistance to the extension of slavery upon which we all agree.[32]

Principled parties are justified because public opinion needs to be principled. It is in shaping public opinion that parties, like statesmen, perform their most important function. Such parties must be based upon the core principles of the republic, and leave secondary matters to the deliberation and discretion of statesmen. Otherwise, it is neither possible to form a majority nor to govern the country well once elected.

CONCLUSION

What are the characteristics that enabled the Republican Party to bring about a decisive change in the direction of the American polity? Under Lincoln it was able to penetrate to how the issue of the times related to the fundamental principles of the country and of human nature. Upon this bedrock was built an edifice capable of gathering a majority to its banner. This required that all other issues be subordinated to the central issue of the extension of slavery. A coalition was built, not by giving something to everybody, but by leaving people free to disagree on secondary issues (even issues of great importance) while making the central issue so compelling that men saw why other issues needed to be subordinated to it. The party could be a motley collection of people, but it could not itself be motley. The party transformed groups of people seeking a variety of ends into one whole seeking the end of slavery extension and the preservation of the principle of human equality.

There may be many reasons why we have not seen a realigning election with the end of the New Deal coalition. But the Republican Party of the 1850s shows us what a party both worthy and capable of leading a realignment would look like.

---

[32]Ibid., vol. 3, 366. For a good summary of the opinions about Lincoln's party activity after his election as President, a topic I do not deal with in this essay, see Don E. Fehrenbacher, *The Leadership of Abraham Lincoln* (New York, London, Sydney, Toronto: John Wiley & Sons, 1970), 69–110.

Representation, Deliberation, and Presidential Nominations: Improving the Performance of American Political Parties

William A. Galston

While the Framers of the U.S. Constitution did not explicitly contemplate the formation of political parties—indeed, attempted as best as they could to obstruct such a development—it became evident soon after 1787 that parties would be both politically unavoidable and structurally indispensable to the operation of the constitutional order. The terms of political evaluation have shifted correspondingly: our political health is no longer defined by the *absence* of party competition, but rather by the *nature* of that competition, and that competition is understood in relation to the constitutional functions that our political parties are now expected to play.

To explore some of the issues raised by the evolving role of American political parties, this chapter is divided into three sections. The first explores, in summary form, the constitutional functions that our parties have assumed. The next section probes, in somewhat greater detail, one of these functions—nominating candidates for the presidency—and suggests that in recent times this task has been performed with decreasing adequacy. The final section explores some reforms that might render the presidential nominating process both more representative and more deliberative.

During the course of our political history, political parties have come to serve the Constitution in a number of different ways.

1. **Parties help organize and channel the conflicts inherent in a free society.** There are three different kinds of political conflict:

over *interests,* when different individuals and groups agree as to the nature of the good to be pursued and struggle to gain the largest possible share for themselves;

over *principles,* when disagreement arises as to the basic manner in which the public interest is to be defined and pursued within the basic structure of a given political order;

over *regimes,* when disagreement arises over principles and institutions that define the nature of the political order itself.

During periods in which the primary conflict is over interests, parties provide the arena within which the multiplicity of interests in a diverse society can be welded together into a governing majority. (This was the function of urban party "machines" in their heyday, and of the national parties in several periods, notably between the end of the Civil War and the rise of the Populist movement.)

During periods in which the primary conflict is over principles, political parties serve as a vehicle through which the conflict can be organized and expressed. It is in these periods that parties most closely conform to Burke's famous definition: "Party is a body of men united for promoting by their joint endeavors the national interest upon some particular principle in which they are all agreed."[1] In 1984, for example, the two parties stood for—and set forth in publicly comprehensible terms—conflicting principles concerning the conduct of economic, social, and foreign policy. In voting for President Reagan over his challenger, voters chose, *inter alia,* strict limits on government intervention in the economy, staunch opposition to abortion on demand, and a foreign policy squarely focused on the struggle between the United States and the Soviet Union.

During periods in which the primary conflict is over the regime itself, political parties offer what is frequently the last best hope of resolving the conflict through means short of force. There have arguably been three regime-threatening conflicts in American history: over the possibility of legitimate opposition, in 1794–1801; over slavery; and over government's power to manage the economy and society, in 1934–1937. In two of these cases, the van-

[1] For a discussion of Burke's views, see Richard Hofstadter, *The Idea of a Party System* (Berkeley: University of California Press, 1969), 29–35.

quished parties acquiesced in the people's verdict. In the third, political parties were the last of the bonds of union to be severed.

2. **In a system of divided powers, political parties help make effective governance possible by providing some basis for organized cooperation between the executive and legislative branches.** Political parties, that is, provide a better than random chance of selecting legislators whose stance towards the President's proposals will conform to the wishes of the electorate. Parties provide as well a way for presidents to organize legislative support for their program.

3. **Through their jealous mutual opposition, parties help preserve free government and public liberty.** The Founders anticipated that the struggle between the legislative and executive branches, and between the two legislative houses, would suffice to defend government and the people against overreaching lust for power. But at critical junctures in our history, the struggle between the parties has proved to be an important auxiliary precaution. In the Watergate period, for example, many abuses of power came to light only because the Congress—hence the investigation—was dominated by legislators of the party opposed to the incumbent president. More recently, during the Iran-contra affair, abuses of legal and even constitutional significance came to light in part because of partisan strife.

4. **Through their zealous competition for public support, parties help promote the public good.** The public benefits of party competition may be understood on the analogy of free market economic competition. Just as firms vie for consumer support by devising products that more efficiently satisfy consumer demand, so political parties contend for voter support by devising programs that minister more effectively to public problems. Alternatively, the benefits of party competition may be understood on the analogy of the adversary legal system. Just as facts and perspectives pertinent to sound verdicts are more likely to emerge from the clash between prosecution and defense than from any other system yet devised, so too are sound political judgments likely to emerge from a competitive political process in which each side has great incentives to discredit the other. Of course, just as markets and juries are subject to distortions, so too is party competition. Consumers may be frivolous and insatiable, jurors ignorant and biased, voters unrealistic and shortsighted. The point is not that wise policies and sound judgments automatically result, but rather that party competition seems more conducive to such outcomes than does any other system yet tested in the crucible of experience.

5. **Political parties help link a numerous and geographically dispersed electorate to the electoral process.** In a Madisonian extended republic, parties stand in the same relation to elections as do representatives to governance: they mediate between large numbers of citizens, who cannot possibly convene in person to conduct their affairs, and the decisions that must be made. Parties provide, not only the arena for agenda-setting choices, but also the political shorthand that helps citizens make choices without necessarily possessing detailed first-hand knowledge of either individual candidates or particular policies. The average congressional district now contains half a million citizens. Most of them will not, and cannot, directly know the characters and opinions of their district's congressional candidates. Party affiliation thus provides essential information about the candidates' likely predilections, and party nominating processes give citizens some confidence that candidates' personal fitness for office has undergone at least a modicum of scrutiny.

6. **Political parties play the leading role in selecting nominees for public office.** In most states, the candidate selections of recognized major parties are automatically placed on the general election ballot while other potential candidates must run the gauntlet of a demanding petition process. From a very large pool of potential office-holders, out parties reduce general elections to a choice among just two persons. If the meaningfulness of an act of choosing is dependent upon the character of the alternatives between which we can choose, then American political parties in effect define the significance of most citizens' political choices.

I turn now to what is arguably the single most important function of political parties—the selection of presidential nominees. The proposition for which I wish to argue is that changes in the past generation have rendered our parties significantly less able to execute this function and that this decline has potentially serious consequences for our polity. But before reaching the sorry facts of recent history, I must begin with some theoretical reflections.

My first contention is this: in republics, defined by Madison as governments in which all powers are derived directly or indirectly from the people, the most critical political challenge is to conjoin wisdom and virtue to consent. Some interpreters of *The Federalist* believe that its authors understood the Constitution to substitute institutional restraints (checks and balances, ambition counteracting ambition, and so forth) for the traditional political necessities of prudence and moderation. I believe that this is at best a one-sided interpretation of the Framers' intent—and of the actual operation of our political institutions. The pages of *The Federalist* are replete with references to the qualities of mind and character legislators, judges, presidents (and for that matter, citizens) must have if our republic is to be well-ordered. This is not to deny that the Founders saw fit to make use of "auxiliary precautions." But it is to say that these institutional restraints were not viewed as in themselves sufficient to ensure either wise policies or individual liberties. Thomas Jefferson summed up this understanding when he wrote to John Adams that "there is a natural aristocracy among men. The grounds of this are virtue and talents. . . . May we not even say, that that form of government is the best, which provides the most effectively for a pure selection of these natural *aristoi* into the offices of government?"[2]

This brings me to my second point: the Founders saw the presidency as requiring unusual "virtues and talents," and they took pains to devise an institution that they regarded as the most likely to discern these special qualities and to employ them as the primary basis of presidential selection. This was of course the original conception of the Electoral College: "a small number of people, selected by their fellow-citizens from the general mass, [who] will be most likely to possess the information and discernment requisite to so complicated an investigation." Free from the pressures of other federal offices and from the temptations of "cabal, intrigue, and corruption," the electors' "transient existence" and "detached situation" would minimize the danger of "sinister bias." Instead, electors would deliberate in a disinterested manner. Concluded Publius:

This process of election affords a moral certainty that the office of President will seldom fall to the lot of any man who is not in an eminent degree endowed with the requisite qualifications. Talents for low intrigue, and the little arts of popularity, may alone suffice to elevate a man to the first honors in a single State; but it will require other talents, and a different kind of merit, to establish him in the esteem and confidence of the whole Union . . . It will not be too strong to say that there will be a constant probability of seeing the station filled by characters pre-eminent for ability and virtue.[3]

It is of course perfectly true that the Electoral College is the constitutional institution whose operations most quickly and

[2]Thomas Jefferson, letter to John Adams, October 28, 1813.
[3]Clinton Rossiter, ed., *The Federalist Papers* (New York: New American Library, 1961), No. 68, 412–414.

decisively diverged from the Framers' intent—indeed, one of only two institutions subjected to constitutional amendment prior to the Civil War. But notwithstanding this change, two key arguments underlying the Electoral College were long left unchallenged: that the selection of the president was not a mechanical majoritarian act but rather a deliberative process requiring special information and discernment; and that this deliberation was therefore to be carried out by individuals ultimately responsible to the people yet distinct from them. The Twelfth Amendment restructured the Electoral College in response to the emergence of organized party competition. But this did not altogether remove the element of deliberation from presidential selection. Rather, the venue of that deliberation was shifted from the ultimate presidential choice to the selection of party nominees, first in congressional caucuses, and later in party conventions. For more than a century, until only a generation ago, conventions were deliberative bodies in the sense that they were free to examine the merits of individual candidates, always of course in conjunction with the perceived requirements of electoral victory.

We have now arrived at the third step in my argument: today, for the first time in American history, we have a system of presidential selection in which the element of deliberation is almost completely absent. Presidential nominating conventions are mere rubber-stamps for decisions made in primaries and caucuses. And the influence of elected officials—national, state, and local—has been largely displaced by two other forces: the media of mass persuasion, principally television; and party activists organized into small groups, each of which seeks to impose its own narrow litmus-test issues on candidates seeking their party's nomination. It is my contention that this new non-deliberative process is systematically less likely to produce good presidents than was the process it displaced. To see why, it is necessary to advert to some special characteristics of the presidency and of political judgment.

In parliamentary systems, the head of *state* is typically distinguished from the head of *government*—in Great Britain, the Queen versus the Prime Minister, in France and West Germany, the President versus the Prime Minister, and so forth. In the United States, on the other hand, the functions of head of state and head of government are combined in one office. An effective president must have the virtues and talents required to discharge both these functions. Therein lies the problem. The contemporary system of presidential selection bears some relation to the choice of head of state. Television at least reveals the presence (or absence) of the character and demeanor needed to represent the nation as a whole. But neither television nor vetting by interest groups provides much evidence bearing on an individuals' fitness to serve as head of government—that is, to carry out the kinds of executive duties discharged by parliamentary prime ministers. The current system of presidential selection is thus biased in favor of the ability to inspire emotion, to capture a mood, to incarnate virtues, and against the competencies required for the effective management of the government.

This difficulty is reinforced by another. Relative to every political office, there are two different forms of political judgment—retrospective and prospective. Retrospective judgments deal with an individual's performance in office. Because many aspects of performance are matters of direct citizen perception and experience, the judgment of performance falls within the purview and competence of the citizenry as a whole. Citizens can properly decide for themselves whether the president has reduced inflation, restored national pride, and so forth. Prospective judgments, on the other hand, deal with an individual's fitness for an office he has not yet held. Some of these judgments as well are in the broad public purview: gross misconduct can be seen and judged by all. But many prospective judgments rest on information known only to a relatively few people, and inferences from this information that only individuals with direct political experience can make. Was X a good governor or senator? Are there important gaps in his knowledge? Can he manage effectively? These are judgments that call not just for public review, but also for peer review. When elected public officials played a dominant role in presidential nominations, there was at least an institutionalized forum for rendering such judgments. But now, because that forum has virtually disappeared, questions of competence cannot be systematically addressed.

The decline of peer review in presidential selection has expanded the influence, not only of the media, but also of narrow-agenda organized groups. These groups have a number of unfortunate characteristics. They are by and large composed of true believers uninterested in compromise. They care far more about a candidate's pure fealty to their litmus-test issues than about his prospects of victory in the general election. And they tend to be dominated by the most extreme elements of each party. These group characteristics produce systematic consequences. Most Americans, for example, are deeply troubled by abortion, wish to limit it in various ways, but are willing to countenance it in a fairly wide range of circumstances. Not our presidential candidates. No Democrat can receive his party's nomination without endorsing

Roe v. *Wade.* No Republican can be nominated without condemning it. Similar party litmus-tests are now to be found for nearly every issue.

The consequences are not confined to single issues. Because key groups are dominated by the most extreme elements within each party, it becomes increasingly difficult for more moderate candidates to receive their party's presidential nomination. This structural fact has two important political consequences, both much in evidence in our recent political history: many moderate candidates choose not to vie for the presidency, and those moderates who do run seek to disguise their true colors and to adopt positions congenial to the extremes.

Three related but distinct causes underlie the past quarter-century's transformation of the American party system. The first was a kind of populist revolt against party elites: among Republicans, against the "Eastern establishment"; among Democrats, against big-city bosses and labor leaders. The second was a growing tendency to measure political institutions against their conformity to abstract democratic procedures rather than against their propensity to engender good results. The third, and perhaps most fundamental, was a swelling preference for political processes that responded to the people directly rather than indirectly—a preference, that is, for "direct democracy" at the expense of meditation and representation. In the conduct of our political parties, the classic Madisonian arguments for representative choice—information, deliberation, and expression of the people's reason and common sense rather than its passion of the moment—have been set aside. In their place, we find the norms and institutions of unmediated responsiveness—parties, that is, in which choices are dominated by pollsters, reporters, and activists.

As I have suggested, direct democracy in the selection of presidential nominees is actually less representative than was the system it replaced. The elected officials who once dominated presidential nomination processes were compelled by the logic of self-interest to pay some attention to the preferences of citizens who were not party activists, who might not have the time or inclination to participate in primaries or caucuses, who might not even be affiliated with a party, but whose support in the general election would be critical. Today, virtually no one reflects the views, or defends the interests, of these citizens. Thus, although many more people now participate in presidential nominations than was the case a generation ago, the nominating process is less rather than more representative of party rank-and-file, and of the electorate as a whole, than it was in 1960. Direct democracy in presidential nominations is not the rule of the people; it is an oligarchy of zealots.[4]

What then is to be done? The distinctive position of American political parties—outside the written constitution yet decisive for the operation of our constitutional institutions—creates a peculiar difficulty for would-be party reformers. For the most part, reforms cannot come from the outside, through congressional legislation or constitutional amendment. They must rather come from within. But this means, in effect, asking those who have increased their power under the current system to voluntarily relinquish a portion of that power. History offers an eloquent testimony to the improbability of such events. I therefore offer a few closing thoughts with no great expectation of efficacy.

As I have suggested throughout this discussion, our political parties must be made both more *representative* and more *deliberative* if they are to perform their constitutional role more adequately.

Representation could be enhanced by a simple expedient: each party could set aside no fewer than half the delegate seats for elected public officials—national, state, and local—at its presidential nominating conventions. To the extent that, as I have argued, elected officials have both the information and the incentive to respond to broad coalitions rather than narrow factions, this provision could have a dramatic effect on both party platforms and party nominations.

Deliberation could be enhanced by a second expedient: each party could abolish both formal requirements and informal understandings that "bind" delegates to particular candidates. To be sure, many delegates would continue to be selected through primaries and caucuses under the presumption that they would cast at least their first ballot for the candidate on behalf of whom they campaigned. Nevertheless, they would be legally and morally free at the convention to reexamine commitments made months ago in light of new information and new alternatives.

A third avenue of reform has recently been offered by the political scientist James Fishkin. Under this proposal, a random sample of citizens, large enough to be statistically valid, would be

[4]For parallel reflections, see Nelson Polsby, *Consequences of Party Reform* (New York: Oxford University Press, 1983); and James Ceaser, "Political Change and Party Reform," in Robert Goldwin, ed., *Political Parties in the Eighties* (Washington, D.C.: American Enterprise Institute, 1980), 97–115.

chosen, equipped with impartial information about the candidates contesting for their party's presidential nomination, and assembled at a single location early in the nominating process. The candidates would appear before these informed citizens to make presentations and to be interrogated in detail concerning their agendas for the country, after which the citizens would debate the relative merits of the candidates and indicate their preferences. The proceedings of this citizens' caucus would be broadcast nationwide and, if successful, could function in effect as the first presidential primary.

The appeal of this proposal is obvious. In an age that worships directness and mistrusts centers of power and expertise, substantial responsibility would be invested in average citizens with whom Americans around the country could identify. They would be (in John Adams's phrase) a "miniature of the people." But they would be an improved version of ourselves, with access to (and incentives to use) a wide range of relevant information, and with organized opportunities to question political candidates directly and to discuss in depth what they have heard. These citizens would, then, play leading roles in a process that is simultaneously direct, representative, and deliberative.

These three reforms would not cure all the vices of the current system, but they would ameliorate many of them. Beyond the obvious gains, let me cite two important collateral advantages. To the extent that elected officials are more intimately involved in the presidential nominating process, the two party nominees are more likely to possess the qualities needed to manage an administration effectively in both foreign and domestic policy. And to the extent that the system becomes more truly representative and deliberative, the power of the media would be diminished, and with it, all the ills to which a media-driven presidential nominating process is now subjected. Our politics would be less dominated by crazes, fads, stereotypes, and expectations, less affected by accidents and by marginally relevant personal facts, less responsive to fervor and factional mobilization, and more inclined to reward the soberer virtues of competence, experience, seriousness, and coalition-building.

For nearly three decades, our political system has been swept by the forces of party change. During this same period, public participation in politics has declined while public mistrust of government and politicians has soared. As E.J. Dionne has recently argued, the American people now sees both our major political parties trapped in a stylized, repetitive, polarized debate that is substantially, and increasingly, irrelevant to the real problems facing the country.[5] While this distressing situation is the outcome of many diverse forces, I believe that the changes in our party system must bear a substantial share of the responsibility. As unpromising as the prospect may appear, citizens interested in a more representative and deliberative politics more responsive to our real national challenges must give serious attention to the reform of our defective party structure.

[5]E.J. Dionne, Jr., *Why Americans Hate Politics* (New York: Simon and Schuster, 1991).

POLITICAL PARTIES ACROSS THE SEPARATION OF POWERS

Michael J. Malbin

PEOPLE WHO WORRY—NOT COLD-HEARTED ANALYSTS, BUT PEOPLE who really worry—about the future of political parties, generally believe there is a connection between the health of the party system and the health of the country. One of the clearest statements of this point of view comes in the popular textbook for introductory American government courses written by James MacGregor Burns, J.W. Peltason and Thomas E. Cronin:

> Our Constitution divides government by setting the legislative, executive, and judicial branches at odds with one another. . . . The purpose, you will recall, was to limit the government's power and influence. . . .
>
> But there was a flip side to this idea. Americans then also wanted efficient, orderly, and effective government—just as we do today. They wanted teamwork in government: a group of officials who would work together and collectively be held responsible for what they did or failed to do. So Americans in effect invented what could be called a "second constitution"—government by political parties.[1]

Burns, Peltason and Cronin thus seem to be arguing that strong political parties help fulfill the intentions the people had for their government when the Constitution was written.[2] The parties work across the branches of government, helping to bring some coordination to institutions that formally were separated.

---

[1] James MacGregor Burns, J.W. Peltason and Thomas E. Cronin, *Government By The People*, 14th ed., (Englewood Cliffs, N.J., 1990), p.230.

[2] Let us leave aside for the moment the textbook's statement that the separation of powers was intended to make the government weaker. I disagree strongly, but the issue is a sideshow for this chapter. The authors' main point about the parties would not have changed if they had acknowledged that the creation of an independent Presidency was meant to help empower the government.

75

Federalist No. 51 speaks of the intention to give public officials a personal stake in preserving their own office's independence. Such a stake would have the effect of reinforcing and preserving separation. Political parties—as seen by Burns, Peltason and Cronin—give these same public officials a stake that runs in the opposite direction. The parties' role in elections is said to give officials a self-interested reason for working together in government—to help them create a common record to bring before the voters as they seek reelection.

This chapter will question the assumptions expressed in this point of view. It is not at all clear that stronger political parties automatically would be good for the country in the future. Whether stronger parties would be likely, or possible, or helpful, will depend upon what precise aspect of the party is under review. It no longer makes sense—if it ever did—to assume that a party system that becomes stronger along some dimensions, automatically translates into a strengthened party system along all of the parties' main lines of activity. To the contrary, one of the most interesting developments of the past two decades is how parties have become both stronger and weaker at the same time, with some strikingly paradoxical effects.

There is a common belief to the effect that the strength of political parties in government is a direct function of the strength of political parties in the electorate. For example, one important study of party voting in the House of Representatives over the past century concluded that

declines in party coherence and conflict at the electoral level *lead to* declines in reliance on party as a vehicle for collective position-taking and action at the legislative level; these lead, in turn, to decreasing relevance and significance for party as a factor in electoral judgments.[3]

There can be no question, compared to a century ago, that the importance of political parties has declined both in the electorate and in the government. However, the developments of recent years should lead us to question the relationship between the two aspects of party strength.

If you think through the logic that might lead you to see party-strength-in-the-electorate as the *cause* of party-strength-in-government, the linkage would run something as follows: public

[3]David W. Brady, Joseph Cooper and Patricia A. Hurley, "The Decline of Party in the U.S. House of Representatives, 1887–1968," *Legislative Studies Quarterly,* 4:381–407 (1979), p.404.

officials follow party cues in government if it is in their self-interest to do so. Thus, when voters make party the basis of their electoral decisions, public officials have an incentive to give their party leaders the tools they need to help the party-in-government look strong, and united, to the electorate. In contrast, public officials will ignore their party leaders, and weaken the levers they are willing to put into their leaders' hands, when the voters ignore party at reelection time.

The problem with this argument is that it makes the connection between party-in-the-electorate and party-in-government a little too quickly, without pausing long enough to examine the intermediate step in the argument: the relationship between party strength, on the one hand, and the interests and goals of the legislators, on the other. Members of Congress are interested in policy as well as in reelection. Legislative party organizations sometimes can help the members secure their policy goals, and they can help shield members from electoral retribution, but they rarely do much positively to bring about a member's reelection. One striking result has been that members have chosen in recent years to strengthen their legislative parties at the same time as party in the electorate continues to weaken. Instead of mutually reinforcing each other, the two aspects of party almost seem to be on different tracks. If anything, the new style of party-in-government may help further weaken the role of party in the electorate.

PARTY IN THE ELECTORATE

The weakening importance of party-in-the-electorate is a familiar story. First, state and local political party organizations lost their ability to control who ran as the parties' candidates in the general election. Party leaders also lost their functions as caseworkers and stopped being the main sources of political information for voters. Voters identified more loosely with their party and ticket splitting increased. The results are well known.

Perhaps the most direct indication of the role of party-in-the-electorate are the surveys of Senate and House voters. The following table indicates party identifiers who voted for the candidate of their own party, identifiers who voted for the candidate of another party (defectors) and pure independents.

As these tables make clear, most voters still say they identify with, or lean toward, one or the other major party. Most of these identifiers and leaners also continue to vote for their own party's candidates. However, the percentage of defectors and pure independents has gone up from about 20 per cent of the Senate and

House vote in the late 1950s to something closer to 30 per cent in the 1980s. Moreover, the overwhelming thrust of these defections has been in favor of sitting incumbents.

One clear result of the weakening of party-in-the-electorate has been an increase in split-ticket results.

With this amount of ticket splitting at the district level, divided government has become normal at the national level. In the 22 years since 1969, Republicans have controlled the Presidency for 18 years, the Senate for six and the House not at all. Weaker party-in-the-electorate may not be synonymous with divided government, but it is surely a precondition. According to some of the

Table 1
Party-Line Voting in Congressional Elections, 1956–1988

Year	Senate elections			House elections		
	Party-line voters	Defec-tors	Pure independents	Party-line voters	Defec-tors	Pure independents
1956	79	12	9	82	9	9
1958	85	9	5	84	11	5
1960	77	15	8	80	12	8
1962	n.a.	n.a.	n.a.	83	12	6
1964	78	16	6	79	15	5
1966	n.a.	n.a.	n.a.	76	16	8
1968	74	19	7	74	19	7
1970	78	12	10	76	16	8
1972	69	22	9	75	17	8
1974	73	19	8	74	18	8
1976	70	19	11	72	19	9
1978	71	20	9	69	22	9
1980	71	21	8	69	23	8
1982	77	17	6	76	17	6
1984	72	19	8	70	23	7
1986	76	20	4	72	22	2
1988	72	20	7	74	20	7
1990	75	20	5	72	22	5

SOURCE: N. Orstein, T. Mann and M. Malbin, *Vital Statistics on Congress, 1991–92*, p. 67; taken from the Survey Research Center/Center for Political Studies, *National Election Studies*.

theses we presented earlier, that should go along with a weaker party in government. The irony is that divided control seems to be strengthening the role of party in government instead of weakening it.

PARTY-IN-GOVERNMENT

No one could sensibly argue that parties are as important in Congress now as they were at the end of the nineteenth century—or as they are in many state legislatures today. Nevertheless, the

Table 2
Ticket Splitting Between Presidential and House Candidates, 1900–1988

Year	Districts	Districts with split results	
		Number	Percentage
1900	295	10	3
1904	310	5	2
1908	314	21	7
1912	333	84	25
1916	333	35	11
1920	344	11	3
1924	356	42	12
1928	359	68	19
1932	355	50	14
1936	361	51	14
1940	362	53	15
1944	367	41	11
1948	422	90	21
1952	435	84	19
1956	435	130	30
1960	435	114	26
1964	435	145	33
1968	435	139	32
1972	435	192	44
1976	435	124	29
1980	435	143	33
1984	435	190	44
1988	435	148	34

SOURCE: N. Ornstein, T. Mann and M. Malbin, *Vital Statistics on Congress, 1991–92,* p. 64.

congressional parties clearly are more important in Congress today than two decades ago. A great deal has already been written about the specific steps that were taken by House Democrats during the reforms of the 1970s to weaken committee chairs and strengthen the legislative party.[4] In this section we shall focus on a few of the results.

The simplest indicators of the importance of party in Congress are the party unity scores compiled by *Congressional Quarterly*. These scores indicate for individual members, or groups of members, the percentage of votes cast with one's party on roll calls in which more than half of the Democrats disagreed with more than half of the Republicans.

This table shows significant increases in party voting during President Reagan's term of office. To some extent, as David Rohde argues in *Parties and Leaders*[5], the increase in unity on roll call votes merely reflects the fact that both parties have more homogeneous electorates across the nation than they did two decades ago. Thanks in large part to the importance of black voters to Democratic candidates in the post-Voting Rights Act South, that region's Democrats now behave more or less like their Northern compatriots in Congress. In addition, the Northeastern liberal wing of the Republican Party has all but disappeared, and has been replaced by a significant number of conservative Southerners and Westerners.

In other words, Rohde portrays changes in the electorate as being associated with less diversity, or increasing unity, within the two major legislative parties. Thus, he joins those authors who see electoral conditions as one root cause for the cohesion of party in government. However, he does *not* argue that the degree of party cohesion in the legislature rests upon the importance of party for voters. His idea that the parties have become more uniform nationally is perfectly consistent with our earlier tables showing that voters are more likely to split their tickets now than before.

Of course, party unity scores do not by themselves tell you a great deal. Under the terms of CQ's definition, unity scores are based solely on "party votes"—votes when more than half of one party opposes more than half of the other party. That leaves open the possibility for major misinterpretations. It is perfectly possible

---

[4]E.g., Burton Sheppard, *Rethinking Congressional Reform: The Reform Roots of the Special Interest Congress* (Cambridge, MA: Schenkman Books, *1985*); Leroy Rieselbach, *Congressional Reform* (Washington D.C.: CQ Press, *1986*).

[5]David Rohde, *Parties and Leaders in the Post Reform House* (Chicago, Ill.: University of Chicago Press, 1991).

Table 3
Party Unit Scores in Congress, 1954–1990

Year	All Dems.	South-ern Dem	Repub-licans	All Dems.	South-ern Dem	Repub-licans
1954	80	n.a.	84	77	n.a.	89
1955	84	68	78	82	78	82
1956	80	79	78	80	75	80
1957	79	71	75	79	81	81
1958	77	67	73	82	76	74
1959	85	77	85	76	63	80
1960	75	62	77	73	60	74
1961	n.a.	n.a.	n.a.	n.a.	n.a.	n.a.
1962	81	n.a.	80	80	n.a.	81
1963	85	n.a.	84	79	n.a.	79
1964	82	n.a.	81	73	n.a.	75
1965	80	55	81	75	55	78
1966	78	55	82	73	52	78
1967	77	53	82	75	59	73
1968	73	48	76	71	57	74
1969	71	47	71	74	53	72
1970	71	52	72	71	49	71
1971	72	48	76	74	56	75
1972	70	44	76	72	43	73
1973	75	55	74	79	52	74
1974	72	51	71	72	41	68
1975	75	53	78	76	48	71
1976	75	52	75	74	46	72
1977	74	55	77	72	48	75
1978	71	53	77	75	54	66
1979	75	60	79	76	62	73
1980	78	64	79	76	64	74
1981	75	57	80	77	64	85
1982	77	62	76	76	62	80
1983	82	67	80	76	70	79
1984	81	68	77	75	61	83
1985	86	76	80	79	68	81
1986	86	76	76	74	59	80
1987	88	78	79	85	80	78
1988	88	81	80	85	78	74
1989	86	77	76	75	69	79
1990	86	78	78	82	75	77

SOURCE: N. Ornstein, T. Mann and M. Malbin, *Vital Statistics on Congress, 1991–92*, p. 199–200, based on *Congressional Quarterly*.

for average party unity scores to increase in the same year as the number of party votes is dramatically reduced. To take an extreme example: it is perfectly conceivable (not likely, but conceivable) for a Congress to have no party votes at all, except for the votes to elect a Speaker, adopt the rules, and a few other procedural matters. If that were to happen, most members would probably have party unity scores of 100 percent, even though this hypothetical Congress had almost no partisan roll call votes. It would be absurd to treat such a Congress as if it were more partisan than one with a large number of party votes and average unity scores of "only" 80 percent. Therefore, it is important when looking at the party-in-Congress to look at the percentage of party unity votes as well as the party unity scores.

It is worth comparing this table with tables 1 and 2. It appears that the percentage of roll call votes that divided the parties in Congress dropped sharply in the mid-1960s (Table 4), at about the same time as the percentages of defectors among voters (Table 1) and split-ticket results (Table 2) were on the increase. That is no surprise. Much more surprising is what happened during the 1980s: the percentage of party votes in Congress increased dramatically, especially in the House, at a time when there was no change in the importance of party in the electorate.

One major reason for the increase in party voting does come, as Rohde argues, from the sea change among Southern Democrats. However, as we have argued, it would be a mistake to put all of the explanation's weight on the electorate. The percentage of party votes went up partly because the raw number of bipartisan votes went down in the 1980s after a surge in the 1970s. This happened because the majority party learned how to use the rules to keep potentially "damaging" amendments from a floor vote. This has been done largely by giving the Speaker of the House better control over the Rules Committee. With that has come a much greater use of restrictive special rules that permit the majority to structure debate—including which amendments will be offered and in what order—in a way that will favor the majority of the Democratic party's policy preferences. Before the 1980s, open rules were the norm. Since then, restrictive rules have become common.

The process of restricting House floor debate that was developed during the Speakership of Thomas P. O'Neill (1977–86), flourished under Speaker Jim Wright (1987–89). Interestingly, the behavior of the aggressive and partisan Wright has continued to be followed by his supposedly more bipartisan successor, Thomas Foley.

Table 4
Party Unity Votes in Congress, 1953–1988

Year	House	Senate
1953	52	n.a.
1954	38	47
1955	41	30
1956	44	53
1957	59	36
1958	40	44
1959	55	48
1960	53	37
1961	50	62
1962	46	41
1963	49	47
1964	55	36
1965	52	42
1966	41	50
1967	36	35
1968	35	32
1969	31	36
1970	27	35
1971	38	42
1972	27	36
1973	42	40
1974	29	44
1975	48	48
1976	36	37
1977	42	42
1978	33	45
1979	47	47
1980	38	46
1981	37	48
1982	36	43
1983	56	44
1984	47	40
1985	61	50
1986	57	52
1987	64	41
1988	47	42
1989	55	35
1990	49	54

SOURCE: N. Ornstein, T. Mann and M. Malbin, *Vital Statistics on Congress, 1991–92*, p. 198, based on *Congressional Quarterly*.

It may seem almost a tautology to say that strong parties will foster cooperation across the branches of government when the branches are in the hands of the same party, and that they will foster disagreement and conflict when the branches are in different hands. But to treat that point as a tautology would mask some of the important developments that have taken place over the past two decades. In the past, divided control would be an anomaly, the branches would conflict, issues would be drawn for the next election, the election would more or less resolve the issue, and the subsequent government would again be under unified control.

Table 5
Open Versus Restrictive Rules 95th–101st Congress

Congress (Years)	Total Rules Granted	—Open Rules—		—Restrictive Rules—	
		Number	Percent	Number	Percent
95th (1977–78)	211	179	85	32	15
96th (1979–80)	214	161	75	53	25
97th (1981–82)	120	90	75	30	25
98th (1983–84)	155	105	68	50	32
99th (1985–86)	115	65	57	50	43
100th (1987–88)	123	66	54	57	46
101st (1989–90)	104	47	45	57	55
102nd (January– August 1991)	27	13	48	14	52

SOURCES: *Rules Committee Calendars and Surveys of Activities, 95th–101st Congresses;* "Notices of Action Taken," Committee on Rules, 102nd Congress, throught Aug. 1, 1991. Table prepared by the Minority Staff, Committee on Rules, U.S. House of Representatives.

The situation now is different. Divided control has become normal and not just an anomaly. National issues are rarely decided in congressional elections. Instead, incumbency—always a plus—has become less a phenomenon rooted in the party composition of congressional districts and more one that rests on the personal support engendered by the individual incumbent.[6] Under these electoral conditions, we have to begin questioning the effects of institutionalized partisanship.

It should be obvious from the coincidence of dates, if nothing else, that the increased partisanship in the House during the 1980s did not result from long-standing, slow-developing changes in the electorate. The changes may have presupposed the nationalization of Southern Democrats, but that nationalization does not, by itself, explain why members of Congress were willing to strengthen their leaders' hands at the partial expense of their own ability to pursue their personal objectives as free-lancers. What happened was really very simple: House Democrats suddenly found themselves confronted by a conservative Republican President who was challenging some of their most basic policy assumptions. At the same time, they were also facing a Republican Senate that had changed hands in a stunning election in which GOP victories were widely interpreted as expressions of a Presidential mandate. Suddenly, House Democrats were feeling alone and threatened. They strengthened their party within Congress to protect themselves and the policies about which they cared.[7] Thus, divided control of the government—the same divided control that presupposes a weak party-in-the-electorate—became the key motivation during the 1980s for strengthening the levers of party in the legislature.

As a first and fairly straightforward step to review the effects of strengthened partisanship in the institution, let us consider *Congressional Quarterly's* Presidential Support scores for members of Congress. These scores represent the percentage of votes members cast in accordance with a clearly expressed position of the President. CQ has been computing these scores since 1954.

The Presidential Support scores in Table 6 show that the Administrations of Presidents Reagan and Johnson consistently show

[6]Alford, J. & Brady, D. 1989. "Personal and Partisan Advantage in U.S. Congressional Elections, 1846–1986," in Dodd, L. & Oppenheimer, B. *Congress Reconsidered*, 4th ed. (Washington, D.C.: CQ Press, 1989), 153–69.

[7]For an interesting discussion of this transition from the perspective of the Speakership, see Ronald Peters' impressive historical study of the office, *The American Speakership: The Office in Historical Perspective* (Baltimore, Md.: Johns Hopkins, 1990), ch. 5.

the largest differences between Republican and Democratic support scores than any of the other Administrations followed by CQ. Next after Reagan and Johnson come Kennedy and Bush. The Eisenhower, Nixon, Ford and Carter Administrations showed less partisan voting patterns in Congress.

However, the four relatively partisan Administrations were not all partisan in the same way. There was a crucial difference between Kennedy and Johnson, on the one hand, versus Reagan and Bush, on the other. The unusually high differences between Democrats and Republicans during the Kennedy and Johnson years stemmed not so much from the opposition of Republicans as from the strong positive support both of these Presidents received from their own party. Because that party was also the majority party in Congress, the high level of support helped both Presidents to govern.

During the Reagan and Bush years, in contrast, we do not see an especially high level of support from the President's party. Instead, we see extraordinarily low support scores from the Democratic opposition. In the 29 years between 1954 and 1982, there were only four years in which the House party opposed to the President had scores that averaged below 40 per cent (1963, 1973, 1976 and 1979.) But beginning in 1983, House Democratic support scores were below 40 percent every year from the middle of President Reagan's first term through the first two years of the Bush Administration. (That is the most recent year available from *CQ* at this writing.) Similarly, the Senate opposition party never fell below 40 percent from 1954 through 1982 over those same 29 years, but they were below 40 percent during four of the most recent eight years (1985–87 and 1990).

What these numbers suggest is that the majority party in Congress increasingly has been behaving over the past decade as if it were a classic opposition party with a duty to oppose the government in power. The problem with this kind of a self-perception is that the President is not a Prime Minister, and the majority party in Congress cannot be equated with a parliamentary opposition. Congress is a part of the government, not a shadow that sits on the outside. Unless Congress and the President find some way to work together, the government cannot be effective.

As a general rule, strong partisanship, persistent divided control and effective government do not go together. As more issues have become partisan, and partisan differences have become identified with institutional ones, disagreements too often have turned into major battles across the institutions of government. Benjamin Ginsberg and Martin Shefter have written a recent book in which

Table 6
Support for the President's Positions on Roll Call Votes,
1953–1990 (percent)

Presi-dent & Year	House Demo-crats	Repub-licans	Dif-ference	Senate Demo-crats	Repub-licans	Dif-ference
Eisenhower						
1954	54	n.a.	n.a.	45	82	37
1955	58	67	9	65	82	17
1956	58	79	21	44	80	36
1957	54	60	6	60	80	20
1958	63	65	2	51	77	26
1959	44	76	32	44	80	36
1960	49	63	14	52	76	24
Kennedy						
1961	81	41	40	73	42	31
1962	83	47	36	76	48	28
1963	84	36	48	77	52	25
Johnson						
1964	84	42	42	73	52	21
1965	83	46	37	75	55	20
1966	81	45	36	71	53	18
1967	80	51	29	73	63	10
1968	77	59	18	64	57	7
Nixon						
1969	56	65	9	55	74	19
1970	64	79	15	56	74	18
1971	53	79	26	48	76	28
1972	56	74	18	52	77	25
1973	39	67	28	42	70	38
1974	52	71	19	44	65	21
Ford						
1974	48	59	11	45	67	22
1975	40	67	27	53	76	23
1976	36	70	34	47	73	26
Carter						
1977	69	46	23	77	58	19
1978	67	40	27	74	47	27
1979	70	37	23	75	51	24
1980	71	44	37	71	50	21
Reagan						
1981	46	72	26	52	84	32
1982	43	70	37	46	77	31

Table 6
Continued

Presi-dent & Year	House Demo-crats	Repub-licans	Dif-ference	Senate Demo-crats	Repub-licans	Dif-ference
1983	30	74	44	45	77	32
1984	37	64	27	45	81	36
1985	31	69	38	36	80	44
1986	26	69	43	39	90	51
1987	26	64	38	38	67	29
1988	27	61	34	51	73	22
Bush						
1989	36	69	33	55	82	27
1990	25	63	38	38	70	32

SOURCE: *Congressional Quarterly Almanac,* various years.

they portray warfare across the branches as today's normal mode of operation.[8] The classic 1980s example would be the issue of whether to supply U.S. assistance to the Nicaraguan rebels of the time, known as the Contras.[9] Almost all of the Democrats in Congress opposed Contra aid; most of the Republicans supported it, and the balance of power was held by a shifting group of about 20–30 members, mostly Southern Democrats. Because the swing group did shift, U.S. policy toward the Contras also shifted almost every year and both branches were prepared to stretch the limits of their institutional power to prevent the other side from working its will irrevocably. The Iran-Contra Affair was by no means inevitable, but it was consistent with an atmosphere that was filled during the 1980s with thousands of lesser institutional battles between the two sides of Pennsylvania Avenue.

However, it would be seriously misleading to portray the relationship between Congress and the President since 1981 as if it were nothing but partisan battling. There was bipartisan support for the defense buildup during the early 1980s, for the Tax Re-

[8]Benjamin Ginsberg and Martin Shefter, *Politics By Other Means: The Declining Importance of Elections in America* (New York: Basic Books, 1990).

[9]See Michael J. Malbin, "Legislative-Executive Lessons From the Iran-Contra Affair," in L. Dodd and B. Oppenheimer, eds., *Congress Reconsidered,* 4th ed. (Washington, D.C.: CQ Press, 1989), 375–92.

form Act of 1986, and for a host of other major initiatives.[10] That should be no surprise. Recent Republican Presidents have needed the votes of at least some Democrats to get any part of their program through Congress.

It might seem as if we are heading toward a conclusion that would be the polar opposite of the opening quotation by Burns, Peltason and Cronin. That is, it might seem as if we are saying that all partisanship is bad for the country during divided government and, conversely, cross-party coalition building is good. But such a conclusion would be every bit as simplistic as the earlier one. The real problem comes not from partisanship in the legislature *per se,* but from the persistent lack of connection between partisanship inside the institution and the personalized support for incumbency in the electorate.

That is what makes the tactics and concerns of House Republicans so interesting. The House Republicans want to force the Democrats into taking public positions on tough votes that will then have to be defended in the next election. But one reason the Democrats have come to support a stronger leadership inside the institution is precisely the leadership's power to use restrictive rules for floor debate to protect them from having to make such a public defense. In other words, it is in the interest of the majority party in Congress to divorce what is happening inside the legislature from the subsequent accountability of election campaigns.

Republicans are divided about how to respond. The more aggressive House Republicans identified with the Conservative Opportunity Society believe they will gain seats by using their behavior inside Congress to promote congressional elections based on national issues. Republican Presidents, and their congressional allies, sometimes say they want to act vigorously to gain more Republicans in Congress, but they just as often seem to fear that forcing confrontation across the board will make the President unable to govern. Even considered in narrow electoral terms, such a failure to govern could well end up backfiring against the President's party in Congress. The future is likely to produce more of the same kind of mixed partisanship—stronger party-in-government,

[10]David R. Mayhew, "Does It Make a Difference Whether Party Control of American National Government is Unified or Divided?" (paper presented at the 1989 annual meeting of the American Political Science Association, Atlanta, Georgia, Aug. 31–Sept. 3, 1989); Jeffrey Birnbaum and Alan Murray, *Showdown at Gucci Gulch* (New York: Random House, 1987); Timothy J. Conlan, Margaret T. Wrightson and David R. Beam, *Taxing Choices: The Politics of Tax Reform* (Washington, D.C.: CQ Press, 1990).

weak party-in-the-electorate—as we have seen for the past decade. We might not wish for more of the same. We might prefer either to see a stronger party-in-the-electorate or a weaker party-in-the-legislature. But wishes alone are not going to change public officials' interests and goals or the modern forms of political communication that have combined to produce the present situation. To change the character of contemporary partisanship would either require Democrats to do a better job campaigning for the Presidency, or Republicans to do a better job campaigning for Congress, or an overwhelmingly important set of events to reshape the political landscape. Meanwhile, the country seems to be forced into a politics of muddling through. That will be enough to produce changes on individual policies—often major ones. The hard question is whether it will be enough to sustain effective policies over time.

The Post New Deal
Democratic Party

Elaine Ciulla Kamarck

The End of an Era and the Collapse of the Old Politics

The election of Ronald Reagan marked the end of an era in American politics—an era in which politics had been organized around support for and opposition to one great and innovative era in American history—the New Deal. As an organizing principle, the New Deal was so powerful that it defined American politics for almost 50 years. During this time the Democratic Party was organized around the preservation and expansion of the New Deal and the proposition that government had a critical role to play in the life of its citizens. In contrast, the Republican Party was organized primarily around opposition to New Deal programs and in support of free market principles over government assistance as the best way to aid individuals.

Then, in the 1980 election, the New Deal coalition that had been the bulwark of the Democratic Party crumbled, never to be reconstructed, as Ronald Reagan beat Jimmy Carter and in the process defeated some of the most liberal members of the United States Senate. The roots of this collapse are both cultural and economic. On the cultural side the modern leaders of the New Deal coalition had allowed the Democratic Party to become estranged from their core constituents in the middle and lower middle classes.[1] And on the economic side, profound structural changes in the economic life of the nation and the world gave rise to serious apprehension over the governing premises of the New Deal coalition.

In some senses the precursor to the cultural collapse of the New Deal coalition was Adlai Stevenson, Governor of Illinois and twice the unsuccessful Democratic candidate for the presidency. According to Michael Barone:

[1] See William A. Galston and Elain Ciulla Kamarck, *The Politics of Evasion* (Washington, D.C.: Progressive Policy Institute, 1989), Section I.

Stevenson was the first leading Democratic politician to become a critic rather than a celebrator of middle-class American culture—the prototype of the liberal Democrat who would judge ordinary Americans by an abstract standard and find them wanting.[2]

But if the warning signals for what was to happen to the Democrats were present in the campaigns of Stevenson in the 1950s, the cultural death knell for the New Deal coalition was rung in the 1960s, a complex decade in which issues of race, feminism and the counterculture became inextricably mixed up with the politics of the Democratic Party. In recounting the political history of the sixties E.J. Dionne, Jr. summarizes the effect of cultural politics on the Democratic Party as follows:

Liberals suffered in part because they were no longer perceived as speaking for the public interest, but for a series of particular interests—labor, peace activists, blacks, women, gays, teachers, cities, government employees, among others. . . . What many liberals drew from the New Left. . . . was its latter-day mistrust of working class people and their values, its fundamental mistrust of the United States' role in the world, and the emphasis of many in its ranks on the relative importance of culture over economics.[3]

Nevertheless, the Democratic Party may have survived the cultural commotion of the 1960s had the cultural upheavals not been followed by the peculiar economics of the 1970s. Two things happened in that decade that were to further weaken the base of the New Deal coalition. First was the appearance, simultaneously, of high unemployment and inflation; a situation that Keynesian economics had assumed to be impossible. Second was the beginning of stagnant economic growth and actual downward mobility for the very people who used to be the bulwark of the Democratic Party—working class laborers without a college education. The adjusted wages of white males with a high school education went steadily downward in the 1970s as did the average real weekly earnings for non-supervisory workers—80 percent of the workforce—which fell 16 percent from 1973 to 1989.[4]

This dramatic loss of earning capacity has been masked somewhat by the fact that during that same time women went to work

[2]Michael Barone, Our Country: The Shaping of America from Roosevelt to Reagan (New York: The Free Press, 1990), 286.

[3]E.J. Dionne, Jr., Why Americans Hate Politics (New York: Simon and Schuster, 1991), 142–144.

[4]See Robert J. Shapiro, "The Family Under Economic Stress," in Elaine Ciulla Kamarck and William A. Galston, eds., Putting Children First: A Progressive Family Policy for the 1990s," (Washington, D.C.: Progressive Policy Institute, 1990).

and helped maintain family income and middle class lifestyles. Nevertheless, the most salient economic fact for the fortunes of the Democratic party was that it could no longer guarantee continual upward mobility for working class families while, at the same time, it was becoming culturally estranged from them. The loss of middle and working class upward mobility led to the emergence of a tax revolt in the late 1970s that continues unabated today.[5]

Underlying the cultural and economic difficulties Democrats faced were changes in the structure of the economy, changes which had the immediate effect of weakening perhaps the most important component of Democratic, liberal strength—the American Labor movement. As the economy transformed itself from an industrial age economy to a service economy to an information economy the ability of the labor movement to prosper deteriorated rapidly. In 1954 fully 35 percent of American workers were represented by unions. By 1980 this number had slid to 23 percent and in 1988 the proportion of the workforce that was unionized fell to 17 percent.[6] Furthermore, labor unions have been unable to gain a foothold in the newer, hot, high tech industries of the information age economy. As Thomas Edsall has pointed out, "[T]he decline of the political power of labor resulted in an inability to provide a solid foundation of political support for the network of protective social legislation and regulation enacted into law in the fifty years since the New Deal."[7]

But the final and perhaps most devastating nail in the New Deal coffin was the collapse of the public consensus around the governing assumptions of the Democratic Party. Aided by an aggressive and sophisticated conservative movement, the public perception of government spending in the late 1970s worsened in ways guaranteed to undermine the liberal consensus of the 1960s. The first wave of New Deal programs—the minimum wage, social security, unemployment compensation, and later on, the G.I. Bill, the mortgage deduction and Medicare—were broad based programs with universal appeal. Most of them derived their popularity from the fact that they were, in some way, earned; for instance, citizens paid into social security and they paid, with military service, for their G.I. benefits. These programs now constitute the

---

[5] Witness the defeat in 1990 of Governors who raised taxes and the meteoric decline in Bush's ratings when he abandoned his anti-tax pledge in the fall of 1990.

[6] Paul Starobin, "Unions Turn to Grass Roots to Rebuild Hill Clout," *Congressional Quarterly*, September 2, 1989, 2251.

[7] Thomas Byrne Edsall, *The New Politics of Inequality* (New York: W.W. Norton and Co., 1984), 163.

status quo in American politics and therefore they no longer form the basis for division among the parties.

With the creation of a welfare state that served a chronically poor and dependent population, however, the New Deal *impulse* (as distinguished from the actual programs) began to lose much of its political support. Because nothing was expected of the welfare mother (and even less of the welfare father) in return for government support, these programs could not possibly enjoy the broad based legitimacy afforded the large social programs of the earlier era. Not only did this approach to the poor fail to solve poverty; more importantly it injected a new and virulent skepticism into the long held belief that government had a positive role to play in bettering the life of all its citizens. In the minds of many voters government ceased to be the provider of economic opportunity for all and became instead the instrument of unearned handouts for some.

But if the New Deal era had ended after nearly 50 years, the Reagan era ended in less than ten. Unlike some of his more ardent followers, Ronald Reagan had no intention of reversing the first New Deal. In spite of attempts by David Stockman and a hard corps of true blue conservatives, the political consensus to dismantle the existing middle class welfare state did not exist.[8] The middle class entitlement programs born in the New Deal era were now the status quo and politically untouchable even by the most conservative President to head the party for nearly half a century.

Reagan did manage to put an abrupt halt to government experimentation and growth in a broad range of social programs for the poor and he certainly changed the prevailing conventional wisdom in the electorate in ways that would make it even harder, if not impossible, for a New Deal Democratic party to reassert itself. But unlike his hero Roosevelt, Ronald Reagan never developed an alternative paradigm for what government could be. He created short term economic growth through the stimulus of large deficits, but he did not follow through on the conservative revolution advocated by his budget director David Stockman and others, nor did he create a new, conservative paradigm of government. Reagan husbanded his political resources for no particular theory of government and, while his strong personal beliefs were a source of the perception that he was in fact a strong leader, there was no parallel governmental theory or paradigm. As Jack Pitney points out in his chapter on the Reagan coalition in this volume, Repub-

---

[8] See David A. Stockman, *The Triumph of Politics: Why the Reagan Revolution Failed* (New York: Harper and Row, 1984), Chap. 7.

lican politics in 1984 and 1988 especially concentrated on the creation of "wedge" issues at the expense of "magnet" issues and left America a presidential electoral coalition not paralled by a governing coalition.

The Reagan Administration was the real moment of truth for the Republican Party. When the opportunity and the mandate was in hand—in 1984 and again in 1988—they blinked. Republicans had come to be just as addicted to big government as the Democrats. Their only difference was to promise not to do more of it. But the unfinished agenda of the liberal state included in it the still difficult problems of black Americans. The Republican attack on government was very specifically an attack on the one group in the electorate that still relied on extensive government. Even without the skillfully exploited "wedge" issues of Willie Horton or racial quotas, the Republican halt to the New Deal was bound to work against the interests of black Americans in particular.

This brings us to the political present; one that is characterized by two political parties with two obsolete visions of government. The Republicans manage to win presidential elections because they have an optimistic view of America's future and a sense of America's place in the world that comports more closely with the way most Americans view their destiny. Their theory of domestic prosperity however, is vacant, old fashioned, laissez faire, and fails in its ability to deal with still unfinished social business, in particular the high poverty rates of black Americans. As countless columns and cartoons have shown, George Bush, master of the New World Order, is completely devoid of a domestic policy, let alone anything as coherent as a paradigm.

Meanwhile, traditional Democrats talk in terms of programs, policies and centralized government bureaucracy that no one in the electorate has believed in for a decade. In his book *Why Americans Hate Politics*, Dionne notes that "liberalism and conservatism prevent the nation from settling the questions that most trouble it." Both parties, says Dionne, have been captured by an upper middle class elite that have taken America away from a "politics of remedy." The result is that, in the words of Paul Taylor, a political reporter who covered the 1988 election,

[V]ast number of voters are dropping out of the market altogether: the dialogue doesn't interest them. At the close of our most recent national town meeting, a record 91 million adult Americans had nothing to say.[9]

[9]Paul Taylor, *See How They Run: Electing a President in an Age of Mediaocracy* (New York: Alfred A. Knopf, 1990), 267.

Low voter participation, record high political cynicism, and distrust of government lead to the need for an entirely new paradigm of government and politics.[10] A recent series of focus groups found that Americans felt that their relationship with the political process has been "severed."

The points at which the political system seems to break down are in the way the political agenda is set, in the way policy issues are formed, and in the way these issues are debated.[11]

To fully understand the collapse of the New Deal coalition and the outlines of a Post New Deal Democratic Party, the story of cultural alienation and slow economic growth must be seen along with the collapse of faith in government's ability to solve problems. The remainder of this chapter is devoted to an analysis of this loss of faith and to how understanding those causes can lead to a new Democratic Party.

THE CRISIS OF ACCOUNTABILITY OR K-MART QUALITY AT SAKS FIFTH AVENUE PRICES

If the average American shopper goes to buy a dress at K-Mart, she can expect a certain level of quality and design and a low price. If she goes to buy a dress at Saks Fifth Avenue, she expects a much higher quality, a much better design, and a much higher price. What she or any other consumer will rebel against over time is K-Mart quality at Saks Fifth Avenue prices and that is exactly what many voters feel they have been getting from their government in the past few decades.

The secret to the collapse of the old politics can be found in the failure of the old government, a failure which is, more often than not, linked to Democrats and not to Republicans in the minds of the voters, even though failed government has been practiced by both parties. The first failure is of accountability. People in government simply don't seem to pay for incompetence or, in some cases, outright criminal behavior.[12] Poor collection of information

---

[10]See Ibid, Chap. 9, for a good discussion of the voters loss of faith in the system. For instance, trust in government fell from a high of around 80 percent in the late 1950s to about 33 percent in the lates 1970s.

[11]"Citizens and Politics: A View From Main Street America," prepared for the Kettering Foundation by the Harwood Group. (Dayton, OH; The Kettering Foundation, June 1991), 11.

[12]In New York City schools teachers, principals, and custodians who commit crimes have their jobs protected. See Andrew Stein, "Teaching Sleazy Lessons," *The New York Times*, June 3, 1989.

in the student loan program allows millions of dollars to go to those who have defaulted on previous loans. In Cuyahoga County, Ohio, County Commissioners found, to their dismay, that they could not fire corrupt and unethical welfare workers.[13] And in New York City where convicted criminals are allowed to keep their jobs in the education system, a subway fire killed several people because the fans that should have prevented the lethal smoke from entering the tunnel had sat in an Ohio warehouse for thirteen years. No one was fired.[14]

Lack of accountability is everywhere and at every level of government. During the decade of the 1980s, government employment grew at a rate that outstripped population growth. Public sector unions grew more quickly than any other union sector.[15] But in spite of this increase in public service few average citizens perceived an increase in the quality of public services, especially in the two areas which mean the most to citizens—safety and education. During this time non-elected governmental officials came to be protected by a civil service system which was designed in the late 1800s to protect citizens from incompetence. But by the late 1900s the system as often as not did just the opposite—it protected the civil service from their own incompetence.

In 1991, a year of record financial distress on the part of state and local budget officers, 29 states cut their budgets but only nine laid off employees. The reason? Firing incompetent civil servants is nearly impossible; iron clad seniority rules and practices called "bumping" (in which a laid off employee can displace someone with fewer years of service) mean, according to the author David Osborne, that "[y]ou get people in jobs they don't want and aren't good at."[16] Thus layoffs, aside from being politically damaging can, in fact, make the problem of governmental non-accountability worse.

The crisis of accountability is no less severe among elected officials, especially legislators, among whom the avoidance of accountability has reached the level of art. Protected by large election bank accounts, large staffs and expensive consultants

---

[13]Conversation with Commissioner Timothy Hagan, March 1990.

[14]See Jim Dwyer, "Failure of the Fans," *Newsday*, December 30, 1990.

[15]In 1959 public employees counted for 8 percent of all unionized workers; by 1974 they accounted for 38 percent of all unionized workers; and by 1987 public employees accounted for 47 percent of all unionized workers. (Sources: AFL-CIO and the Department of Labor, Bureau of Statistics.)

[16]"Laughing at the hangman: Civil Service unions employ secret weapons to spare them big layoffs as budgets are slashed," *U.S. News and World Report*, June 17, 1991, 28–29.

expert at obscuring the issues of governance on which they should be held accountable, individual congressmen at record high levels manage to avoid defeat while the reputation of their institution reaches record low levels.

The crisis of accountability is complicated by a persistant misunderstanding and failure to act on the financial crises that face many levels of government. By 1991 nearly every state in the union was coping with the severe budget deficits that the federal government in Washington had dealt with for a decade. Slow economic growth and budget deficits have provided politicians of both parties with an excuse for stasis. The reactions of both political parties to the fiscal crisis of government at all levels has been nothing short of disgraceful. Republicans hold onto a stubborn belief in ever lower taxes; the reaction to Bush's reversal on his tax stand in the fall of 1990 was most vehement from the right. Democrats, on the other hand, refuse to think seriously about reducing the size or scope of government.

While the political parties are involved in inept responses to the crisis, ordinary Americans have come to the conclusion that, in government, money doesn't equal success. In any city or county in the country, a casual newspaper reader can find stories that attest to increasing inefficiency in government. In New York City the city workforce increased by 50,000 in the decade of the 1980s while population remained constant. Similarly, employment in the school system rocketed by 40 percent while the number of students remained constant.[17] Nationally, increases in educational spending at all levels have not resulted in increases in test scores. In fact the money has not even gone to increase substantially the number of teachers; most of the money has gone to administration. A look at education spending led the author Peter Brimelow to conclude that American public education shares many characteristics with Soviet-style socialism.[18]

At the national level money reserved for the cleanup of toxic waste dumps is spent on legal fees.[19] And nearly one-third of the $200 million spent by the federal government since 1988 to clean up the nation's worst toxic waste sites has been spent not in actual cleaning but in the administrative expenses of private contractors.[20]

---

[17]Dan Cordtz, "Managing New York," *Financial World*, February 19, 1991.

[18]"American Perestroika," *Forbes*, May 14, 1990.

[19]Paul Craig Roberts, "Superfund's Costly Failure," *The Washington Times*, September 3, 1990.

[20]Michael Weisskopf, "The Supermanagement of Superfund," *The Washington Post National Weekly Edition*, August 5–11, 1991, 10.

The ineffective expenditure of large sums of money is not unique to E.P.A. In 1964 NASA (National Aeronautics and Space Administration) had 1,477 employees per space mission launched, by 1974 that number had risen to 1,625, in 1984 there were 1,823 and in 1990 there were 2,953 employees per launch. Gregg Easterbrook, the author of an article on NASA, points out that this bloating occurred during "a period when computers have revolutionized the efficiency of technical operations and knowledge of space flight has increased. . . . Imagine any private company trying to compete with twice as many workers per product as in 1964."[21]

But while government spending without regard for results goes on in all segments of government, its political consequences have been most serious in the case of the poor which may account for the current unpopularity of welfare far more than some sudden drop in the compassion levels of Americans between the late sixties and the nineties. A study conducted at the Center for Urban Affairs and Policy Research at Northwestern University calculated that if the $4.85 billion spent by Cook County, Illinois in 1984 for anti-poverty programs and transfers were to be divided by Cook County's 1984 poverty population, each poor person would have an average of $6,209, or over $18,000 for a family of 3.[22] In other words, they would not be poor. Most of the money spent on poverty goes not to poor people but to services provided by non-poor people for them. Of the amount spent only 34.5 percent went directly to the poor in the form of cash assistance.[23] The problem with this level of spending as far as the public is concerned is that it doesn't appear to solve the underlying problems of poverty.

Stories of the ungainliness of the poverty bureaucracy abound. In one Louisiana public housing project there is a 31 percent vacancy rate, an 11 percent uncollected rent rate, and hundreds of stories like the one where a woman spent ten years waiting for a broken window to be fixed. And yet the housing authority spent $4.7 million operating the project, with most of the federal money going (or not going) to maintance or utilities.[24] Job training money from the federal government has not appreciably improved the skills of a group of people who are, every year, less and

---

[21]"The Case Against NASA", *The New Republic,* July 8, 1991, 18.

[22]Diane Kallenback and Arthur Lyons, *Government Spending for the Poor in Cook County, Illinois: Can We Do Better?* (Evanston, IL: Center for Urban Affairs and Policy Research, Northwestern University, 1989).

[23]Ibid.

[24]Series by Jon Eig "Decaying Homes, Blighted Hopes," June 18, 1990; "Desire pays price for short-cuts," June 19, 1990; and "Try to build it up or tear it down," June 20, 1990; in *New Orleans Times Picayune.*

less able to compete in the information age economy.[25] In city after city, money spent on welfare programs has only maintained poverty, not solved the difficult problems such as generational repetition in the underclass. No wonder that many Americans now share the feelings expressed by Ronald Reagan's famous quip, "We had a war on poverty and poverty won."

When productivity drops in the private sector, companies lose market share. Eventually they change the way they do business or they go broke, or both. As the above examples show, the standard of productivity, so central to the successful operation of a healthy economy, has been, until recently, missing from discussions about government and its effectiveness. But, as Morely Winograd and Doug Ross have pointed out, when voters apply that standard to government, the result is a contradiction understandable in market terms but not, previously, in political terms.[26]

Ever since the tax revolt began in the late 1970s, traditional Democrats have been refusing to understand the message coming out of seemingly contradictory poll findings: the public wants good government services and they don't want to pay more taxes. The message is simple: people will not pay more taxes for the lousy government they feel they have been getting. According to Winograd and Ross, the voters are acting in the political marketplace like the intelligent consumers that they are in the commercial marketplace. In the marketplace they refuse to pay Saks Fifth Avenue prices for K-Mart quality clothes; the same applies to their behavior in politics and government.

The crisis of accountability in government has not had the same negative effects on the Republican Party as it has had on the Democratic Party. Republicans have always believed (but not always acted) as if government was *not* the answer. As government collapses, more and more classic conservatives are in the posture of saying "we told you so."

Democrats, however, have been the party of government; as it has collapsed many leaders have found themselves in the position of having to defend a system that simply does not work anymore. To make matters worse, a complex system of interest groups has grown up around the provision of government services by government employees, and these groups have had a disproportionate impact on the Democratic Party as other groups have left the party, thus shrinking its funding and primary election base. And

[25]See Katherine Boo, "Beyond Beauty Schools," *Washington Monthly*, March 1991.
[26]"Americans Need Better Leadership and the Democrats are Prepared to Offer New Choices," *Detroit Free Press*, May 3, 1991.

finally, the most important of all Democratic constituencies—black voters—found, in the last several decades, that their ticket into the middle class was through government employment.[27] Thus within the Democratic Party, there is powerful resistance to changing large aspects of the way we do business in government, even as the need for change grows more and more urgent.

The solution to the crisis of accountability is no different than it is in the non-governmental sector: government has to change the way it does business. In the words of the author David Osborne, we need to "reinvent" government. And yet, in the current political stalemate neither party has the incentive to do it. Republicans are content to make the critique of government in the hope that failure of government will lead to a Democratic meltdown at the nonpresidential levels; and Democrats are locked into defense of the status quo in government.[28] The crisis of accountability continues.

THE ABDICATION OF INDIVIDUAL RESPONSIBILITY OR THE JOE KLEIN QUESTION

During the 1989 mayoral campaign in New York City, Joe Klein, columnist for New York Magazine and one of the city's most influential commentators, asked the mayoral candidates the same question at every relevant opportunity: "What does the government owe the 15 year old pregnant welfare mother and what does she owe the government?" The answer to the first part of the question was always, as Klein tells it, comprehensive. In contrast, the second half of the question produced generally puzzled looks and no answers.

The inability of Democratic politicians to answer this question is another important aspect to the loss of faith in government. The emergence of an intractable underclass (a group that did not and, more importantly, could not, take part in any of the economic expansion of the 1980s) which had distinctive, often self-destructive and, to the larger society, immoral patterns of behavior, has led to a disappearance of the concept—the "deserving poor."

Once again the political world responded to this new form of poverty in a polarized and irrelevant manner, and dismissed the

[27]See Nicholas Lemann, *The Promised Land* (New York: Alfred A. Knopf, 1991.)

[28]Bush Administration officials like Housing and Urban Development Secretary Jack Kemp are leading an "empowerment" movement which concentrates on new ways of dealing with poverty. But these officials and their "new paradigm" counterparts have had little success so far in the Bush Administration. See Jason De Parle, "Kemp's Proposals on Poverty Given Sympathy, Not Action," *The New York Times*, July 1, 1991, A1.

observations and values of average voters. Conservatives crowed again over the failure of government and wrote that the welfare state was, in fact, responsible for the formation of a large underclass. They used this line of analysis to argue that the welfare state should be dismantled.[29] Liberals, on the other hand, ignored problems of individual responsibility among the chronically poor, preferring instead to criticize the inadequate responses of the state and the continuing virulent reality of American racism.

But the liberal tendency to pronounce the state at fault for the problems of the poor and to blame racism for everything was doomed to come into conflict with the long standing American belief in the efficacy of individual effort. Belief in individual effort was reinforced during the decade of the eighties by a renewed interest in immigration. Asian immigrants, in particular, proved capable of making amazing progress in spite of language and racial barriers.[30] The success of the Asians, many of whose children became valedictorians of their high school classes after only one generation in this country, shed new doubt on the contention that the black poor were poor because of the racist system. In city after city, Asians came, suffered racial slurs, lived in the same poor housing, sent their kids to the same bad schools, and prospered. Even black immigrants proved able to make economic progress when American underclass blacks could not.[31]

In 1986 Americans celebrated the 100th anniversary of the Statue of Liberty and passed a new immigration act, opening up America to immigrants from around the world once more. By the end of the decade immigration had more than doubled and many of those immigrants were people of color.[32] The renewal of immigration led Michael Barone to comment:

Their success undercut the arguments often made in the 1960s and 1970s that the country provided no avenues of upward mobility for the

[29]See Charles Murray, Losing Ground (New York: Basic Books, 1986).

[30]Asian immigrants accounted for 12.9 percent of all immigrants in the decade of the sixties and for 35.2 percent of all immigrants in the decade of the seventies. The World Almanac and Book of Facts, 1989, 541.

[31]According to James Fallows, "[B]lack skinned immigrants from the Caribbean and Africa are generally successful, like other immigrants, and more successful on average than native-born American blacks. By some measures of educations and income they are more successful on average than native-born whites." More Like Us (Boston: Houghton, Mifflin, 1989), 119.

[32]Immigration in 1979 was 460,348. By 1989 it was 1,090,924, according to the Immigration and Naturalization Service.

poor; their general acceptance undercut the idea that Americans were bigoted and cruel. . . . [33]

By the end of the 1980s the continuing saga of black under-class poverty stood in sharp contrast to America's renewed experience with immigrants. Inevitably, discussion began to turn to the role of individual responsibility among the chronically poor. What was once the refrain of hardhearted conservatives began to be frankly admitted by those who worked most closely with the poor. Sister Connie Driscoll runs one of the most admired homeless shelters in the country in the Woodlawn section of Chicago. In a lengthy interview in the Chicago weekly the *Reader*, Sister Connie describes the people she helps as follows:

Foolish and ill-informed choices are an aspect of the homeless problem that 'people wouldn't talk about before. They wouldn't talk about the fact that in all of this population there was such a serious problem with drugs and alcohol and a lack of personal responsibility and accountability. They just kept screaming that it was all housing, and as soon as we build houses for everybody in the United States, everybody's going to live happily ever after.'[34]

The black columnist William Raspberry has become an eloquent proponent of greater honesty on this topic. In a recent column he writes:

While we're busy with school reform, school choice, Afrocentric education and a few dozen other experiments designed to help the children most in need of help, I wish we'd find time to teach them what we already know: When it comes to your life chances—your prospects for getting on in the world—what you do matters a great deal more than what is done to you.[35]

Finally, an important book by Nicholas Lemann traces the history of black sharecropper families from their Mississippi roots to their Chicago Ghettos. It is difficult to read the history of Ruby Daniels' family chronicled in that book without concluding that

[33]Barone, *Our Country*, 656.

[34]Bryan Miller, "From the Shelter," *Reader, Chicago Weekly,* July 20, 1990, vol. 19, 20.

[35]"Social Traps, Individual Effort", *The Washington Post*, March 4, 1991. In an earlier column Raspberry cites the work of Chester Finn and says, "If there is a theme to Finn's response it is that most of the awful things that happen to those who constitute the American 'underclass' are less the result of inadequate government intervention than of their own disastrous behavior." See "Disastrous Behavior," *The Washington Post*, August 8, 1990.

while many of their problems were the result of segregation, discrimination and other negative consequences of state actions, their problems were often the consequence of individual choices and behavior.

Yet social programs in the past three decades have been built and defended without regard to the behavior of their clients. The concept of the "earned benefit," so critical to the long standing popularity of programs like Social Security and the G.I. Bill is, by and large, missing from programs for the poor. Attempts to introduce this concept into poverty programs via programs like workfare, for instance, were vigorously opposed by the liberal establishment until late in the decade. By not recognizing the importance of individual responsibility in the promotion of individual welfare, the defenders of the social welfare state managed to put themselves on the opposite side of the dominant American experience—the immigrant experience—where individual initiative is preeminent.

Because conservatives succeeded in linking the social disintegration of the underclass to the welfare state and arguing, consequently, for its dismantlement, liberals in the eighties were put on the defensive when, in fact, the times called for a much different strategy—one that focused on creativity and change. This contributed further to the profound lack of faith in government and politics which is so characteristic of voters in the post New Deal era.

Taken together, the twin failures of liberal government—the crisis of accountability and the abdication of individual responsibility—have led to a crisis in liberal politics epitomized by Michael Dukakis, who, at the 1988 Democratic Convention attempted to shed the liberal label by claiming that the election was not about ideology but about competence. Other liberal politicians have tended to try to cope by hiding behind a mask of governmentese in order to obscure what is really going on in government. In the words of Barbara Whitehead, the social historian, "conference table talk" has replaced "kitchen table talk" in the public dialogue—leading more and more people to suffer the sense of disconnection from politics that is expressed in the following quote from one of the participants in the above mentioned Kettering study:

Policymakers are speaking a different language. It's one of avoidance; its one of 'it needs further study'—something that doesn't mean anything. They can have all of these debates on television, but when the policymaker is finished talking, you still don't know where he stands.[36]

[36]Kettering, 11.

THE POST NEW DEAL DEMOCRATIC PARTY

For the past decade, while the roots of the Democratic Party's failure were increasingly evident—leaders of the Party persisted in what I and my co-author William Galston have called the politics of evasion. The politics of evasion consists of a series of myths about the electorate—myths invoked by party leaders to avoid having to contend with the serious ideological crisis of the post New Deal Democratic Party. Yet with every passing study of the electorate it becomes clear that the problems of the Democratic Party are not due to short term forces in effect at the presidential election. The longer term trends are as follows:

1. Democrats are no longer the majority party in the electorate.
2. Democrats command only about one third of the electorate with another third favoring the Republicans and yet another third identifying as Independents.
3. Since younger voters are more Republican and the oldest voters are the most Democratic, the Republican share of the electorate is bound to increase, not decrease.[37]

Even more disturbing to Democrats is the fact that poor Republican performance in the economy has not helped them. After more than a year of recession, 44 percent of those polled said that Republicans are more likely to keep the country prosperous and only 29 percent say that Democrats could keep the country prosperous.[38] This finding occured in other polls as well.[39] The disturbing conclusion is that the Republican edge on handling the economy had not eroded following a year of recession—a resounding vote of no confidence in the Democratic Party.

These findings and others like them have created a steady drum beat of bad news for the Democrats at the presidential level and anxiety about the prospect that Republican presidential successes might some day translate into Republican successes at the Congressional, state, and local levels, thus completing the partisan realignment that has eluded the Republican Party. Against this

---

[37]Adam Clymer, "Poll Finds GOP Growth Erodes Dominant Role of the Democrats," *The New York Times*, July 14, 1991.

[38]Ibid.

[39]In response to the question "Who is better able to handle the nation's economy?"—49 percent of respondents in March 1991 answered the Republicans and only 32 percent said the Democrats. These numbers were not substantially different than the responses to this same question in January of 1990 when 52 percent rated the Republicans as better able to handle the economy and only 33 percent said the Democrats could. Source: *The Washington Post/* ABC Poll, March 22, 1991.

backdrop, some Democrats, notably members of the Democratic Leadership Council and its think tank the Progressive Policy Institute, began to talk about a new program for the Democratic Party. In May of 1991 they adopted a pre-election year platform at the Democratic Leadership Council's first ever convention in Cleveland. The Democratic version of the Republican "new paradigm" is called the New Choice and was the first step in an effort to redo the fundamental ideology of the Democratic Party. But unlike the Republican "new paradigm" which exists as a function of think tanks and some very creative conservatives in the Bush Administration, the Democratic "new choice," while somewhat less clearly defined, exists as a governing strategy for a variety of state and local Democratic elected officials thus guaranteeing that, as these people move to define the national party, a new Post New Deal party will emerge.

What will the Post New Deal Democratic Party look like? First of all it will derive its strength and creativity from state and local governments across the country where Democrats still win elections and the Democratic Party as a governing force is not in disgrace. Ironically, this Democratic Party (as distinct from its Congressional wing) is the product of the Reagan era in which responsibility and leadership for many domestic problems was shifted from the federal to the state and local level.[40] Secondly, it will be shaped by three dominant themes:

the need to embrace the new global economic imperative; the need to reinvent government; and the need to re-establish the social contract along the lines of reciprocal obligation.

The remainder of this chapter explores those three themes.

THE GLOBAL IMPERATIVE

Global competition and rapid economic change set the context for the future American economy. Investment capital now flows freely among many nations thus evading the ability of governments to control or influence its use. Similarly, new technologies move around the globe with lightening-like speed, meaning that no nation can sit on its technological lead for very long. In *The New Realities* by Peter F. Drucker, the shift to the global economy is summed up as follows:

---

[40]The best account of the new energy in statehouses can be found in David Osborne, *Laboratories of Democracy* (Boston: Harvard Business School Press, 1990).

Where none of the traditional factors of production—land, labor and money—determine competitive advantage any longer, trade is increasingly being replaced by investment as the world economy's driver.[41]

The changes in the world's economy are forcing equally dramatic changes in our conception of what governments should and should not do to insure domestic prosperity. While some of these changes require Democrats to shed some old impulses, others involve an affirmation of some policy directions that are already present in the party. In an important book on competitive advantage, the economist Michael Porter takes a look at a series of industries and tries to figure out what contributes to international competitive advantage.[42] True international competitive advantage is not, Porter concludes, the result of actions by governments. It is the result of actions of individual companies working in a context that is set, in part, by government. The critical factors are the skills, talent and imagination of a nation's workers and managers; government actions often don't matter or can frequently impede the achievement of competitive advantage.

In the global economy some of the traditional economic habits of the old Democratic Party and the old Republican Party are often counterproductive. The achievement of international competitive advantage is a painful process, according to Porter, because it flows from a vigorous domestic competition. And yet it is vigorous competition which traditional Republican businessmen pay homage to, while simultaneously seeking all manner of governmental actions to protect them from competition.[43] Traditional Democrats, on the other hand, support labor initiated policies to soften the blows of competition that threaten jobs for their members.

The Democratic Party began to kick its old habits and accept the imperatives of the global economic order in the spring of 1991. In spite of an all out effort by the AFL-CIO to block passage of "fast track" negotiating authority for a free trade pact with Mexico, "fast track" passed through Congress with the support of

---

[41]Peter F. Drucker, "The New World According to Peter Drucker," *Business Month*, May, 1989, 56.

[42]Michael E. Porter, *The Competitive Advantage of Nations* (New York: The Free Press, 1990).

[43]To their credit, libertarians have frequently called Republicans on this. In his review of the libertarian movement, E.J. Dionne, Jr. states, "Libertarians have been among the most consistent critics of business organizations that preached free enterprise loudly and then quietly accepted the benefits of government subsidies or regulatory actions that hurt their competition." *Why Americans Hate Politics*, 281.

some Democratic members and with the tentative support of Majority Leader Congressman, Richard Gephardt. Gephardt's support was particularly important because in his 1988 presidential campaign he had emerged as the party's leading Japan basher and, by implication, the party's most high-profile advocate of protectionist policies.

Having moved, however cautiously, towards acceptance of the new global order, the Post New Deal Democratic Party must now develop policies consistent with its past and its values. Only then will it be able to attract and retain the loyalties of average workers in the new economy. The first step will be to shift the focus of attention from the protection of jobs to the protection of a worker's ability to move out of an old job and into a new one.

Labor unions have traditionally organized by industry and within industry by job classification. Neither, however, is particularly appropriate to a rapidly changing economy in which some industries and many jobs don't last a decade, let alone a lifetime. If the labor movement and the Democratic Party are to survive as champions of working men and women they must do so by offering the only thing that brings security in the global economy—some means of upgrading skills and aiding workers in both geographic and job mobility. Focus on the worker and his or her skills is far more appropriate to the modern economy than industry and job centered approaches.

Innovative thinkers, such as the sociologist Michael Sherradan, have already begun to develop the forerunners of the kind of programs that are worker centered. In a recent book, *Assets and the Poor,* Sherradan calls for the creation of Individual Development Accounts, savings instruments that could be used by the poor and the working poor (with or without government matches) for self-employment or education and training.[44] A similar model was developed by former Michigan Governor Jim Blanchard and his Commerce Director Doug Ross. The Michigan Opportunity Card was to be a bank card-like instrument which would entitle the bearer to a certain amount of state supported adult education and training services.

In addition to skill specific programs, there are a variety of programs in place which would stimulate entrepreneurial behavior. In Washington State unemployment compensation can be

---

[44]Michael Sherradan, *Assets and the Poor* (New York: M.E. Sharpe, Inc., 1991).

paid in a lump sum to aid in the start up of a small business.[45] In many states there are now thriving microenterprise projects which make small loans and provide invaluable networks to average Americans who want to go into business for themselves.

The importance of sharpening workers' skills and aiding small entrepreneurs is matched by the importance of getting workers into the workplace to begin with. Post New Deal Democrats need to focus on the forgotten half of American society—young people who do not go on to college. These people work hard, but compared to their counterparts in other countries, they don't work smart.

Poor high schools and rip off, for profit, vocational schools are not the answer. One promising alternative can be found in comprehensive apprenticeship programs that are carefully integrated into basic high school curriculums in concert with actual employers and actual job experience. Similar programs have proved successful in countries like Germany where the non-college work force consistently outperforms the American non-college work force. Americans have (correctly in my view) objected to any form of tracking which could be used to funnel minorities into non-college tracks, but the crisis of the non-college-educated worker's earning potential in America demands that we accept the fact that not everyone wants to go to college. The state of Oregon has recently passed a bill that would create dual track high schools designed to increase the job skills of non-college bound youth and to lower the drop out rate. The bill addresses the problem of tracking by building in guarantees that students will be able to move out of one track and into another.[46]

Acceptance of the global imperative should lead the Post New Deal Democratic Party back to its oldest base—American workers—not by protecting their jobs or their industries but by providing them with the means of upward mobility. The global imperative should also lead the Democratic Party into an even stronger alliance with a relatively new piece of its coalition—environmentalists. In Porter's new paradigm of competitive advantage, government policies that protect industry from competition and thus the need to change are, in the long run, detrimental to their

[45]The program is run under a state suprevised experiment from the Federal Department of Labor. See Peter T. Kilborn, "Novel Program for the Jobless Aims to Create Entrepreneurs," *The New York Times,* May 16, 1990, A1.

[46]William Celis, 3d, "Oregon to Stress Job Training In Restructuring High School," *New York Times,* July 29, 1991, A1.

ability to compete. But government actions that force change and therefore innovation, while painful in the short run, are helpful in creating competitive advantage in the long run. "Stringent standards for product performance, product safety, and environmental impact contribute to creating and upgrading competitive advantage."[47] Thus the Porter paradigm points to the economic utility of government policies that promote strict environmental and strict health and safety standards. Democrats have traditionally advocated these standards for reasons of the public good; to the extent that these standards force technological innovation and therefore productivity increases, they contribute to the economic good as well.

THE REINVENTION OF GOVERNMENT[48]

The central political innovation of the New Deal was the use of government to bring about large scale improvements in the lives of ordinary citizens. Activist government at the federal level became a central and defining feature of the Democratic identity, even when it ceased, in some cases, to be the most efficient way of promoting the public good. The Post New Deal Democratic Party will coalesce around the proposition that activist government need not be synonymous with bureaucratic government and that the purpose of government should be the expansion of individual opportunity, not the expansion of government.

Variations on this theme—loyalty to *activist* government as distinct from *big* government or *more* government—can be heard in the pronouncements of a cross section of new Democratic leaders at the state and local level. In Chicago, for instance, a town known for the precept "Why hire one city worker when four can do the job," Mayor Richard Daley's May 6, 1991 inauguration speech contained the following warning:

But we should never forget that our mission is to serve people, not to perpetuate needless bureaucracy.

In Texas the new thinking is expressed by State Comptroller John Sharp, a protege of Governor Ann Richards, who, upon presenting a $4 billion savings plan to the State, commented:

---

[47]Porter, *Competitive Advantage*, 647.

[48]This term has been coined by the author David Osborne and appears in the title of his book *Reinventing Government: In Search of Excellence in the Public Sector*, (Reading, MA: Addison Wesley, 1991).

We're people who think government is a good thing. . . . and that there
are ways to make it more efficient. . . . This state is sick and tired of bureaucrats with a handful of gimme and a mouthful of bull.[49]

In Florida Governor Lawton Chiles and his Lt. Governor Buddy
MacKay have announced that they intend to redesign the government. Their first step was to sunset Florida's entire civil service job
classification system at the end of 1992, thus beginning the transformation of a system based on seniority to a system based on performance. Next will come a downsizing of state government and a
transfer of power to local government with a mandate to design
and coordinate services that stress prevention and cost savings.[50]

Dissatisfaction with the public sector has led to a renewed interest in the privatization of public services—a Republican concept that has long been anathema to the Democratic Party and to
the labor movement, in particular the public employees' unions.
Privatization began in the new rapidly growing cities of the South
and the West—cities that, even when they were governed by Democrats, did not have the machine and union traditions of older,
Northern cities. And yet even these older cities, forced by fiscal crisis, are contemplating or experimenting with privatization.[51]
Mayor Daley of Chicago has embarked upon a thoroughgoing
program of privatizing as many city services as he can. He has fi-
nessed the union problem by promising that the city would contract with only union companies.[52] In doing so, he has correctly
identified the problem as the lack of competition, not unions per
se. Ed Rendell, the Democratic candidate for Mayor of Philadelphia, won a Democratic primary on a program of restructuring the entire city government—including privatization.[53] And

[49]David Maraniss, "With 'Bubba' in Mind, Texas Democratic Leaders Advance on
Deficit," The Washington Post, July 15, 1991, A1.

[50]Neal R. Pierce, "Cutting Government Down to Size," National Journal, July 6,
1991, 1700.

[51]See for instance, Michael deCourcy Hinds, "Cash-Strapped Cities Turn
to Companies to Do What Government Once Did," The New York Times, May 14,
1991, A12.

[52]See, David S. Broder, "Private Firms, Public Service," The Washington Post, July
10, 1991, A21.

[53]Note the following comment: "But I plan to explore privatization across a
whole range of City services, including: legal and debt collections services; data
processing and computer services; building and grounds maintenance; custodial
services; fleet management and maintenance; vehicle towing and storage; road and
street maintenance; tree trimming and planting and streetlight operation, to name
just a few." Testimony of Edward G. Rendell before New York City Council President's Hearing on Restructuring Municipal Government, June 13, 1991.

Andrew Stein, President of the New York City Council and mayoral hopeful, wrote in *The New York Times*, "City Government must no longer be accorded the status of protected monopolies."

The popularity of privatization comes in response to the realization that governments are monopolies and, as such, have all the flaws that private sector monopolies have. E.S. Savas, one of the best known students of privatization, comments that monopolies subject citizens to "endless exploitation and victimization because so-called public servants have a captive market and little incentive to heed their putative customers."[54] But, as Steven Kelman points out in an article in *The American Prospect*, a journal devoted to rethinking liberalism, the privatization approach writes off government as hopeless and "underestimates the potential for renewal from within public organizations. Examples of innovation and improvement, however, are readily at hand."[55]

Those examples inspire the work of David Osborne, founding father of the movement to reinvent government, whose book on the topic has the distinction of having transformed governments even before its publication. Osborne, along with others, has consulted with Governor Chiles of Florida and with Governor Weld of Massachusetts. He is author of the term "reinventing government" and also of the term "entrepreneurial government." His approach involves the use of market-type mechanisms to improve government's accountability. For instance, he advocates, wherever possible, that we "inject competition into public service" and then illustrates instances where the injection of private competition has improved the public sector's delivery of services. Other Osbornian mandates include: "Tie spending to results. . . . Let people choose among many service providers. . . . Use goals, not rules and budgets, to drive your organization. . . . Decentralize authority. . . . Whenever possible, use market mechanisms rather than administrative mechanisms."[56] The beauty of Osborne's work is that he distills the principles of entrepreneurial government from experiments and innovations in actual government. Thus they are a far cry from the type of dry "Let's make the government run like a business" arguments that have so under-inspired the Republican party's approach to these problems.

[54]Quoted in: Steven Kelman, "The Renewal of the Public Sector," *The American Prospect* Summer 1990, 52.
[55]Ibid.
[56]David Osborne, "Ten Ways to Turn D.C. Around," *The Washington Post Magazine*, December 9, 1990.

The movement to "reinvent" government is destined to become the hallmark of the Post New Deal Democratic party because Democrats, unlike Republicans, still retain faith in government. So far this movement is, however, rooted in state and local governments where those who have been doing the reinventing tend to be Democrats and where, not surprisingly, Democrats still win elections. As more and more practitioners of state and local entrepreneurial government become part of the Federal Government, they will reinvigorate the presidential and congressional party as well. Freshman Congressman Rob Andrews of New Jersey, newly arrived from the post of County Commissioner where he had run a classic Osbornian government, surprised the Equal Employment Opportunity Commission lobbyist by proposing that instead of giving the agency more money for overhead, Congress should amend the enabling legislation so that when the EEOC successfully settles or wins a claim for employment discrimination, it could collect attorneys fees from the losers. No one had ever made such a suggestion before.[57]

By vigorously championing the reinvention of government and then implementing those changes, the Post New Deal Democratic Party will show a skeptical electorate that they can be trusted with the federal government once again.

THE PRINCIPLE OF RECIPROCAL OBLIGATION

Most Americans hold simple, basic values—especially hard work and individual responsibility—and they recognize that these values are important to our greatness as a nation. When government, however well intentioned, undermines those values, it does not serve the national interest. When government, however well intentioned, does not expect anything from its citizens in return for its largesse, we undermine the public's commitment to an activist government.

To understand the importance of these principles to our politics one need only go back to one of the most popular and valuable programs of all time—the G.I. Bill. No one ever begrudged the returning soldier (black or white) his free college education; after all, that person had served his country and his country owed him. Similarly, Social Security retains its place as another of the most popular programs of all time because people paid into it, elevating it from a handout to an earned benefit. The final

[57]See Congressman Andrews' floor statement, February 22, 1991.

theme in the creation of a Post New Deal Democratic Party will be the introduction of reciprocal obligation to the design of social programs.

This principle is central to the rebirth of the Democratic Party for two reasons. The first is that, as we have seen in the politics of the past decade, it is impossible to forge a political consensus around policies which involve the redistribution of wealth from those who work to those who don't. Secondly, and of equal importance, is the fact that the notion of reciprocal obligation goes hand in hand with the creation of a responsible and caring community.

Reciprocal obligation forms the basis for a series of recently popular proposals that involve trading service for education. This concept is growing in popularity because it is a way to provide greater social services and a means to finance education. Once such idea is the Police Corps, developed and championed by Adam Walinsky. In it students who receive grants to study an undergraduate ROTC-type course in police work would then repay them with a set number of years of service in city police departments. This plan was introduced in the Congress in 1990. A full scale national service program is also under consideration in Congress and a small experimental program has been funded. One version of national service would replace existing college loans and direct grants from the government with the following compact: young people who serve their country in a military or non-military capacity would receive automatic tuition vouchers for the college of their choice.

Small service for education programs abound. One of the best exists in Boston. City Year gives $100 a week stipends and college scholarships of $5000 to each person who completes a year of service among the poor and needy in Boston. In Atlanta, a program between Clark Atlanta University and University Homes (a public housing project) will place 40 social work graduates and their families in public housing for a year. The families will receive inexpensive housing and course credits and will provide the other residents of the projects with positive role models and educational help.

The concept of service for education can be extended to a wide variety of services. In an article called "The Crisis Corps: A Plan to Start Turning New York Around," Joe Klein suggested requiring a year's service as a building inspector as a condition for becoming a licensed architect or engineer in New York State. This would greatly improve existing inspections; for one thing the inspectors would move through the system "too quickly to become jaded or corrupt. They would provide markedly better service at markedly lower cost."[58]

Another set of newly emerging programs focuses on ways that the state can reinforce parental responsibility for their children's behavior. In Wisconsin under "Learnfare," welfare families forfeit a portion of their benefits if their teenage children skip school.[59] In Illinois parents were threatened with jail and with a $500 fine under a state law that holds them responsible for their child's attendance at school.[60] In Arkansas parents who do not attend important parent-teacher conferences face civil penalties and fines. In Atlanta a curfew for teenagers went into effect in November of 1990 and parents were subject to jail and fines if their teenagers were found violating the curfew.[61] And in Los Angeles, the City Attorney Parenting Program requires reluctant parents who are found guilty of failing to exercise care for their minor children—usually by allowing them to become involved in gangs—to participate in parent education programs or face criminal prosecution.[62]

One final and particularly thorny question of reciprocal obligation is raised by the persistence of the welfare underclass. There is a growing sense that people in the welfare system can and should be held to certain standards of behavior. According to the sociologist Lawrence Mead of New York University, "A program that is simply an entitlement without a work requirement is not only likely to be unpopular, it fails to deal with the serious behavioral problems of the poor."[63] The most recent welfare reform act passed by Congress contains a mild version of a workfare requirement. In Wisconsin, the "Parental and Family Responsibility Initiative" seeks to deal with the thorny problems of teen pregnancy and the lack of marriage by removing disincentives in the welfare system that prevent young couples from marrying and working. It also seeks to encourage male responsibility for the children they

[58]Joe Klein, "The Crisis Corps: A Plan to Start Turning New York Around," *New York Magazine*, May 14, 1990.

[59]Lee Smith, "Getting Junkies to Clean Up," *Fortune Magazine*, May 6, 1991.

[60]"Truant Student's Parents Are Threatened With Jail," *The New York Times*, November 21, 1990, A1.

[61]Ronald Smothers, "Atlanta Sets a Curfew for Youths, Prompting Concern on Race Bias," *The New York Times*, November 11, 1990, A33.

[62]James K. Hahn, "City Attorney Parenting Program Procedures," (Los Angeles: City Hall, Gang Prosecution Section).

[63] Warren Brookes, "Tax cuts to rescue families?" *The Washington Times*, July 8, 1991, D1.

sire by "permitting judges to order unemployed non-custodial parents to participate for forty hours a week in education, work and parenting classes. . . . All unemployed non-custodial fathers in the pilot counties will be ordered by the judge to 'seek work' by reporting to the county JOBS program."[64]

While most service for education programs cater to the middle and working class youth who want to work for their education; service could also be required of all unemployed welfare fathers. As many job programs have shown, there is no training for a job that beats having an actual job and the discipline that implies. And as many experiments in tenant ownership and management have shown, the poor really can behave with the same level of responsibility as the middle class when the incentive structures are right.

Democrats have, for too long, been afraid to ask the poor to live by the same values by which the rest of us live. Conservatives have used the absence of values in public policy to build public sentiment against the welfare state and to argue for its abolition. Liberals need to insert values into public policy in ways that create a consensus for a new welfare state—one that moves away from maintenance and towards economic independence.

CONCLUSION: THE CONSTITUENCY PROBLEM AND THE NEED FOR SECOND STAGE POLITICS

Finally, the Democratic Party cannot move forward with a new politics by turning its back on the important constituencies that have been loyal to the Democratic Party. Conversely, however, these constituencies need to adapt themselves to the emerging world. Failure to do so on the part of black leaders has led to unprecedented weakness in public support for civil rights; failure to do so on the part of feminist leaders has meant that young women refuse to call themselves feminists even while they support a feminist agenda; and failure to do so in the labor movement has meant that it seeks, with increasing frequency, to compensate for its weakness in the marketplace with protection from the government.

To quote the feminist Betty Friedan, who coined the phrase "The Second Stage," the leaders of the major Democratic constituencies need to move to their own "second stage." For instance, America has only too recently rid itself of the legalized forms of racism from which it has suffered for so long. The second stage for

---

[64]Tommy G. Thompson, Governor, "Parental and Family Responsibility Initiative," (State of Wisconsin, February 1991), 2.

racial equality will not be fought on the tired turf of civil rights but on the questions of upward mobility in the economic sphere. In an economy which is increasingly dependent on women and of which women have now become an indispensable part—the feminist agenda has to understand, as Friedan argues, that the family is the new feminist frontier. And finally, in an economy in which the "creative destruction" of capitalism means that jobs disappear on a regular and increasingly frequent basis—the labor movement needs to shift its focus and become the protector of flexible, innovative, well trained workers, not the protector of outmoded jobs in outmoded classifications.

The Post New Deal Democratic Party will not result from the aggregation of a series of group demands. Rather, it will grow out of simple beliefs and principles true to the American heritage; and it will be backed up by a set of policies that are as innovative and universal in their values as the policies of the New Deal. When the Democratic Party emerged to dominate a half century of American political life it did so because it was experimental and provocative. With any luck the new Democratic Party will take this one lesson from the old.

Frames, Wedges, Magnets, and Silver Bullets: Republican Strategies

John J. Pitney, Jr.

DURING THE 1980S, REPUBLICANS WON THREE PRESIDENTIAL ELEC-
tions and wiped out the Democrats' longstanding lead in party
identification.[1] Yet in Congress and the statehouses, the GOP
never went much beyond its 1980 showing, and it finished the
1990 election weaker than ten years before:[2]

	1980	1990
House Seats	192	167
Senate Seats	53	44
Governors	23	20
State Legislative Chambers	35	23

Republicans blame a rigged gameboard. While their national
committees raised and spent over a billion dollars during the
1980s,[3] Republicans say, Democratic incumbents milked far more
advantage from the franking privilege and other taxpayer-
financed advantages. This argument explains individual elections,

[1] Historical data from: Helmut Norpoth and Michael R. Kagay, "Another Eight
Years of Republican Rule and Still No Partisan Realignment?" paper presented at
the annual meeting of the American Political Science Association, Atlanta, August
31–September 3, 1989. The 1990 figure is from CBS poll reported in: *New York
Times*, January 21, 1990, 24.

[2] Data from: *The American Enterprise*, January/February 1991, 95.

[3] Ed Rollins [then Co-Chairman of the National Republican Congressional Com-
mittee], address to Republican Communication Association, Washington, DC, December 14, 1990.

not long-term trends. If incumbency had been the Republicans' main barrier, they would have overcome it in time, since all undefeated incumbents eventually retire or die. In the case of state legislatures and the U.S. House of Representatives, Republicans point to an additional culprit: unfair districting. Although this argument has more force than many scholars acknowledge—the direct and indirect effects of gerrymandering have indeed cost the GOP a significant number of seats[4]—utterly fair districts would still have left House Republicans in the minority. The last time an absolute majority of voters supported GOP House candidates was 1946.[5]

So what else can explain GOP disappointments? Says Republican strategist Eddie Mahe, "a lot of seats were lost by dumb Republican candidates or campaigns."[6] Experienced office-holders, staffers, or political activists tend to make the most successful candidates; and according to Rich Bond, Republicans are often "outpointed on name identification, government experience, and image to boot."[7] Republican candidates have also suffered because different issues have driven presidential and non-presidential races. When choosing a chief executive, Americans think about broad issues of economic management, where Republicans have had an edge. When voting for other offices, people think more of domestic issues such as Social Security, where Democrats had a strong advantage through the decade.[8]

The candidate problem is linked to the issue problem. Ronald Reagan ended the malaise of the late 1970s and curbed the federal government's growth, but Reagan-era Republicans faltered at the next step. As Newt Gingrich says, they "failed to offer real alternatives to the failed bureaucracies of the welfare state."[9] With a negative approach to public policy, they had trouble signing up good people for their "farm clubs," the nitty-gritty state and local offices that supply congressional candidates. "The Republicans

---

[4]Leroy Hardy and Alan Heslop, *Redistricting Reform: An Action Program* (Claremont, California: Rose Institute, 1990), 15–30.

[5]Norman J. Ornstein, Thomas E. Mann and Michael J. Malbin, Vital Statistics on Congress 1989–1990 (Washington: CQ Press, 1990), pp. 47–48; *CQ Weekly Report*, February 23, 1991, 487.

[6]Rhodes Cook, "Self-Inflicted Wounds Cost GOP Majority in '80s," *CQ Weekly Report*, March 3, 1990, 687–691, at 687.

[7]Ibid., 690.

[8]Gary C. Jacobson, *The Electoral Origins of Divided Government* (Boulder, Colorado: Westview Press, 1990), 112–120.

[9]Newt Gingrich, "The Life of the Party: Republicans Must Build New Coalitions to Win," *Policy Review* 51 (Winter 1990), 6–8, at 6.

hate government," explains the Democratic majority leader of the Wisconsin state senate. "Why be here if you hate government? So they let us run it for them."[10] "We have no Republicans that take city government seriously," says GOP pollster Lance Tarrance. "We have no Republicans except in the boroughs, those Republican suburbs, taking county government seriously, and that's because they have to because they are all out there."[11] These comments overstate the case: one can find Republicans with an interest in state and urban policy.[12] Nevertheless, Democrats surely have far greater interest.

Republicans could have fared better. And they could still make gains in the years ahead by embracing a public philosophy that seriously addresses domestic issues through market-oriented and non-bureaucratic means. Before detailing the failures of the 1980s and prospects for the 1990s, we must first discuss the vernacular of political issues: terms such as "frames," "wedges," "magnets," and "silver bullets."

THE VOCABULARY OF ISSUES

Frames

To "frame" the issues is to determine which topics dominate the campaign and how those topics are defined. Whoever frames the issues has the upper hand.[13]

Abortion illustrates the power of issue-framing. Americans have mixed feelings about the subject: while they disapprove of most abortions, they also dislike government intervention in private lives. When the question focuses on the circumstances of the abortion, Americans take the "pro-life" side. When the focus shifts to individual decision, the advantage goes to the "pro-choice" side. In a September 1989 CBS poll, 69 percent agreed with the statement "I don't think the government has any business preventing a woman from having an abortion." Yet in the same poll, 53 percent said that abortion should "be legal only in such cases as rape, incest, or to save the life of the mother" or should "not be permitted

[10]Alan Ehrenhalt, *The United States of Ambition* (New York: Random House, 1991), 126.

[11]Quoted in: Elaine Ciulla Kamarck, ed., *The Future of the Republican Presidential Coalitions* (Washington: Progressive Policy Institute, 1990), 23–24.

[12]Edward L. Lascher, Jr., "The Case of the Missing Democrats: Reexamining the 'Republican Advantage' in Nonpartisan Elections," typescript, Harvard University, 1991.

[13]William Riker, *The Art of Political Manipulation* (New Haven: Yale University Press, 1986), esp. 142–151.

at all." And two-thirds of the respondents supported viability testing and parental consent.[14]

In the 1989 Virginia gubernatorial race, Douglas Wilder framed the issue as a woman's right to choose. His well-produced television advertisements avoided any comment on the desirability of abortion itself and instead stressed Virginia's tradition of personal freedom (emphasized by pictures of the Jefferson Memorial). His Republican opponent failed to respond until the end of the campaign, thus allowing Wilder to control the debate.[15] The issue helped Wilder win the election.

In seeking to frame the issues, one must find terms of debate that will yield the most political advantage. This is hard work. Policy activists often have arcane interests that matter little to the electorate (e.g., committee ratios in the House of Representatives), so it takes political discipline for them to put the voters' concerns ahead of their own pet issues. It takes moral discipline to respond to those concerns while holding to one's principles. And it takes artistry to wed these disciplines in a way that wins elections. Candidates who go too far in pursuing their private agendas will bore and confuse the voters. Candidates who merely parrot the polls will not only lose their integrity, they will still lose political ground, since voters distrust weathervane politicians. The trick is to define the choices so that a principled alternative engages the voters' interest and wins their support.

Wedges

A "wedge" issue splits the opposition, causing a large share of its supporters to switch sides or withdraw from battle. Wedge issues have acquired a bad odor as critics of negative campaigning have attributed the concept to amoral political consultants. In fact, though, politicians have always used wedge issues—and often for honorable ends.

In the 1858 Illinois Senate contest, Abraham Lincoln asked Stephen A. Douglas: "Can the people of a United States Territory, in any lawful way, against the wishes of any citizen of the United States, exclude slavery from its limits prior to the formation of a State Constitution?"[16] This question framed an effective wedge is-

[14]Rosita M. Thomas and Rinn-Sup Shin, *Abortion: National and State Public Opinion Polls* (Washington: Congressional Research Service, 1989), 5–9.

[15]Morton C. Blackwell, "Don't Let Proponents Define Abortion Issue," *Human Events*, December 2, 1989, 10–11.

[16]Robert W. Johannsen, ed. *The Lincoln-Douglas Debates* (New York: Oxford University Press, 1968), 79.

sue: no matter which way Douglas answered, he was sure to lose support. If Douglas answered yes, then he would please free-soil Illinois Democrats, thus improving his prospects in the 1858 Senate election. At the same time, a "yes" would also anger Southerners who sought to extend slavery, thereby hurting him in the presidential race two years later. Conversely, a "no" would placate Southerners at the risk of Illinois support that he needed to hold his seat. He answered yes, a reply that contributed both to his 1858 victory and his 1860 defeat at the hands of the man who posed the question.[17]

Wedge issues make powerful weapons, but they cannot alone sustain a realignment of the electorate. Disrupting and discrediting the opposition is not the same as creating loyalty to one's own side. That task requires "magnet" issues.

Magnets

A "magnet" issue is a positive policy stand that attracts voter support and inspires people to take part in politics. The Lincoln era offers another illustration. While slavery pervaded the 1860 campaign, Republicans sought to keep other issues on the agenda as well. Their platform backed federal aid for building a transcontinental railroad, demanded enactment of the homestead act, and decried any view of homesteading "which regards the settlers as paupers or suppliants for public bounty."[18] During Lincoln's tenure, a Republican Congress passed the homestead and railroad measures, and set up a system of land-grant colleges.[19] These forward-looking positions helped Republicans win extraordinary support from voters under twenty-five. According to historian William Gienapp, younger voters flocked to the Republican Party because of its "fresh and youthful spirit, the persuasiveness of its appeal, and the Democratic Party's image as a tired, badly divided and hopelessly corrupt organization."[20] For the rest of the century, this generation would supply the party with many of its leaders and rank-and-file voters.

During the 1930s, Franklin Roosevelt endowed the Democratic Party with its own magnet issues: Social Security, labor

---

[17]Riker, 5.

[18]Donald Bruce Johnson, ed. *National Party Platforms,* vol 1. (Urbana Illinois: University of Illinois Press, 1978), 33.

[19]James M. McPherson, *Abraham Lincoln and the Second American Revolution* (New York: Oxford University Press, 1990), 40.

[20]Quoted in: William E. Gienapp, "Who Voted for Lincoln?" in *Abraham Lincoln and the American Political Tradition,* ed. John L. Thomas (Amherst, Massachusetts: Amherst University Press, 1966), 50–97, at 70.

rights, job creation, and rural electrification, to name a few. These issues exerted a powerful attraction on the voters: more than half a century later, Americans who came of age during the New Deal remained the Democratic Party's staunchest supporters.[21]

This realignment did not happen all at once. After the Democrats scored massive victories in the early 1930s, their strength in Northern nonpresidential races then ebbed because state and local Democratic parties kept fielding machine-run hacks. Throughout the 1940s and early 1950s, Republicans stayed competitive at the grass roots. Meanwhile, however, the New Deal had inspired a generation of issue-oriented Democratic activists to enter politics. These programmatic liberals inched into influence and spearheaded the Democratic resurgence of the late 1950s.[22]

To a lesser extent, John Kennedy's New Frontier brought its own batch of Democratic activists into politics.[23] Vietnam and the perceived failure of the Great Society, however, diminished its long-term impact.

Silver Bullets

Candidates and political aides often believe that a particular magnet or wedge will provide their "silver bullet," a device that settles elections all by itself, either by destroying the opposition or making one's own side irresistible. Outside of Wolfman movies however, silver bullets are rare. Lincoln's Freeport question drew blood, but Stephen Douglas's problems with slavery and sectionalism went beyond one exchange at one debate.[24] Likewise, no single element of the Roosevelt agenda realigned the electorate; rather, it was a range of positions that attracted voters and activists.

Issues have the greatest long-run impact when they are rooted in reality instead of puffery, in policy instead of public relations. Lincoln's stand on slavery moved the electorate because the issue involved high stakes and because he had spent years carefully

[21]Polls conducted in the late 1980s and early 1990s found the following: Among voters who turned 18 between 1931 and 1934, Democrats had a 16-point lead in party identification. By contrast, voters who turned 18 after 1987 gave the GOP a 12-point edge. Gallup polls cited in: *Christian Science Monitor*, April 5, 1991.

[22]James L. Sundquist, *Dynamics of the Party System*, rev. ed. (Washington: Brookings, 1983), 262–268.

[23]William Schneider, "JFK's Children: The Class of '74," *Atlantic Monthly*, March 1989, 35–58.

[24]James M. McPherson, *Battle Cry of Freedom* (New York: Ballantine, 1989), 183–184.

building his record. The New Deal won millions of Democratic loyalists because it poured concrete on the roads and put money into people's pockets. A policy-oriented approach requires commitment and effort, so political professionals often shun it in favor of the search for the silver bullet. While conjured-up issues may work in a specific race, they have little durability. Says Clifford Brown, "a power base built on images, symbols and personal popularity is fragile. It can be wide, but it will be thin. It can be easily created, but it is easily destroyed. . . . The problem is that a focus on image tends to soften, not harden the loyalty of normally solid constituencies."[25]

REAGAN COALITION, NOT REPUBLICAN COALITION

The View from 1980

During the 1980 campaign, Republicans had no silver bullets, but they did make intelligent use of wedge issues. Reagan pried working-class Americans from the Democratic Party by framing the economic issue around one question: "Are you better off than you were four years ago?" Whereas Ford had run 18 points behind Jimmy Carter among blue-collar voters, Reagan ran even.[26] Carter's mishandling of Mideast policy enabled Reagan to stress his support for Israel. The traditionally-Democratic Jewish vote gave Carter a mere 6-point edge in 1980, compared with a 30-point lead in 1976.[27] An array of concerns ranging from civil rights to abortion helped Reagan pare socially-conservative voters from Carter's base. Among southern whites, the GOP presidential lead jumped from 6 points in 1976 to 27 points in 1980.[28]

The Republicans also had strong magnets. The Kemp-Roth tax cut had wide drawing power, as did the GOP proposal for a military buildup. In 1980, 49 percent of Americans said that we were spending too little on the military, while only 14 percent said that we spent too much.[29] These figures, which reversed a decade-long trend, reflected a consensus for an assertive defense against Soviet expansionism.

[25]Clifford W. Brown, Jr., *Jaws of Victory* (Boston: Little, Brown, 1974), 6.
[26]CBS/*New York Times* exit polls cited in: "The 1984 Election Results," *Public Opinion*, December/January 1985, 23–42, at 33.
[27]"The 1984 Election Results," 32.
[28]"The 1984 Election Results," 34.
[29]Gallup polls, cited in: Harold W. Stanley and Richard G. Niemi, *Vital Statistics on American Politics*, 2d ed. (Washington: CQ Press, 1990), 333.

Although this point is difficult to quantify, Reagan's ideological commitment probably enhanced his popularity. Voters like candidates who say what they believe—and Reagan's positions clearly arose from conviction, not calculation. Myth has it that supply-side economics was a gimmick foisted upon Reagan late in the 1980 campaign; in fact, he had long supported growth-oriented tax cuts.[30]

The 1980 election involved more than the person of Ronald Reagan: the GOP made gains at all levels, including its first U.S. Senate majority since the election of 1952. Republicans surged by uniting behind the general themes of the Reagan program, particularly the tax cut. This success led many Republicans to envision the long-sought realignment that would make them the undisputed majority party.

Yet a careful observer in 1980 should have spotted signs that the "sea change" would not happen easily. Republican House candidates won just 48 percent of the total popular vote, a solid showing, but below the share they got in 1968, the high-water mark of the post-Eisenhower era.[31] The GOP won the Senate only because it swept smaller states: nationwide, Democratic Senate candidates led by nearly three million votes.[32] The Republican congressional showing was best regarded as a starting point, not a resting point. Building upon this base would require political boldness and a presidential commitment to increase GOP strength on the Hill. And such a commitment, would be most likely to come from an Administration confident of reelection. But despite his huge margin in the electoral college, President Reagan won less than 51 percent of the total popular vote, leaving his advisers skittish about trading short-term political advantage for the long-term strength of the Republican Party.

Half Past Reagan

Notwithstanding the widely-shared memory that Reagan held the public spellbound for eight solid years, his first term gave Republicans reason to worry. After his early legislative victories, the recession of 1981–82 mowed down his approval ratings: by late

[30]Martin Anderson, *Revolution* (New York: Harcourt, Brace Jovanovich, 1988), 151–163.

[31]Ornstein, Mann, and Malbin, *Vital Statistics*, 47–48.

[32]Democrats won 51.0 percent to the Republicans' 47.7 percent. Steven Ellis, ed., *Republican Almanac 1989* (Washington: Republican National Committee, 1989), 6. See also: John T. Pothier, "The Partisan Bias in Senate Elections," *American Politics Quarterly* 12 (January 1984), 89–100.

January 1983, 56 percent *disapproved* of the job he was doing, while only 35 percent approved.[33] In 1982, Republicans lost effective control of the House by dropping 26 seats. The GOP kept the Senate, but only through victories in close races. Republicans won only 44 percent of the total Senate vote, and a switch of fewer than 35,000 ballots would have tipped the chamber to the Democrats.[34]

While the economic recovery later restored Reagan's political health, the bad months reinforced his handlers' caution. As a result, the Reagan political team focused on padding his reelection margin instead of helping GOP candidates for other offices. "As good a communicator as the president is, he really never, in my opinion, enjoined that issue of what it really means to have the numbers in the House," complained House Republican Leader Bob Michel after the election. "Shoot, you don't need but three sentences or four [in campaign appearances] but you've got to pound 'em hard. . . . Here the son of a buck ended up with 59 percent and you bring in 15 seats."[35]

Even more significant than the campaign's inattention to Republican candidates was its message to the voters. It aimed its wedge issues—particularly the danger of a tax increase—at the Mondale-Ferraro ticket rather than the Democratic Party as a whole. And it failed to lay out a clear agenda of magnet issues for the second term. The Reagan campaign framed the election as a choice between continuity ("It's morning again in America") and backsliding ("Why would we ever want to go back?"). While this frame gave voters good reason to keep Reagan in the White House, it gave them no reason to change things on Capitol Hill. Compared with 1980, Reagan boosted his popular-vote percentage by eight percentage points, yet House Republicans fell back a point. The CBS/*New York Times* exit poll showed the gap between Reagan and House GOP candidates occurring in every voter category:[36]

---

[33]Gallup poll conducted January 28–31, 1983. Cited in: George C. Edwards III, *Presidential Approval: A Sourcebook* (Baltimore: Johns Hopkins University Press, 1990), 97.

[34]Thomas E. Mann and Norman J. Ornstein, "Sending a Message: Voters and Congress in 1982," in *The American Elections of 1982*, ed. by Thomas E. Mann and Norman J. Ornstein (Washington: American Enterprise Institute, 1983), 133–152, at 137.

[35]Lee Byrd, "House GOP Leader Unthrilled by Reagan Landslide," Associated Press, November 8, 1984.

[36]Historical exit-poll data cited in: *New York Times*, November 11, 1988, A16; November 8, 1990, B7.

	Reagan Vote	GOP House
Men	62	52
Women	56	46
White	64	54
Black	09	08
Latino	37	31
East	52	46
Midwest	58	50
West	61	52
South	64	48

The figures from the South are especially telling because they highlight another result of the Republican Party's lack of magnet issues: recruitment trouble. In 36 Southern House districts, no Republican candidate even ran. (The GOP also forfeited 18 non-Southern seats.) In the races that the GOP did contest, it tended to run inexperienced candidates.[37] No wonder. In 1980, the Republican Party had framed itself as the vehicle of change. Now it was a holding operation. Why would a prospective candidate go through the time, trouble and expense of a grinding House campaign simply to serve as an agent of the status quo?

From Reagan to Bush

In 1985, the Reagan Administration did try to deploy a major magnet issue: tax reform. The final legislation may have indirectly helped the GOP by helping the economy; however, its direct political impact probably worked against the party. By inflaming regional and economic divisions, the issue pitted House Republicans against one another and against Reagan. The ensuing resentments lasted for years.[38] Just as important, the new law got jeers from the voters it was supposed to attract: most people thought that it made the tax system *more* complicated and unfair.[39]

[37]Linda L. Fowler and L. Sandy Maisel, "The Changing Supply of Competitive Candidates in House Elections, 1982–1988," paper presented at the annual conference of the American Political Science Association, Atlanta, August 31, 1989.

[38]John J. Pitney, Jr., "Republican Party Leadership in the US House," paper presented at the annual conference of the American Political Science Association, San Francisco, September 1, 1990.

[39]In *USA Today*/CNN poll conducted April 10–11, 1988, 85 percent said that the new law was more complicated than it needed to be, and 66 percent dubbed it "unfair." *USA Today*, April 14, 1988, B1. According to Gallup surveys taken two years later, only 12 percent said that it had made the system simpler. Frank Newport, "Tax Reform," *The Polling Report*, April 9, 1990, 2.

In 1986, the Republicans lacked a cause to stiffen their spine and hold their support. They lost the Senate majority and suffered further erosion in the House.

Two years later came the Bush campaign with its now-famous wedge issues, including the Massachusetts prison furlough program. Contrary to elite wisdom, these issues were indeed fair game, because they revealed a great deal about Dukakis's leadership.[40] But like the 1984 attacks on Mondale, Bush's wedges pointed only at the top of the ticket, not at the entire Democratic Party. And at the same time, the Bush campaign fell short on magnet issues. In response to a debate question, Bush said that his policy on homelessness was "full funding of the McKinney Act"—an answer that had meaning only for die-hard policy buffs.

In hindsight, Republicans could fault Bush for failing to run on messages that would build the party. Such criticism overlooks the campaign's setting. Unlike Reagan in 1984, Bush ran behind during most of the election year: only in mid-September did he pull ahead, and even then, his margin teetered.[41] Because the outcome remained in doubt until the end, it is understandable that the Bush campaign focused narrowly on winning the White House.

Whoever was to blame for the absence of magnet issues, the result was clear. With miserable recruitment—nearly one-fourth of the Democratic victors ran with no GOP opponent—the Republicans lost still more seats from their already-paltry base. Many Democrats won in normally-Republican areas, while few Republicans managed a parallel feat on Democratic turf. In 1988, 134 House districts gave Bush at least 60 percent of the vote. Of these districts, Democratic congressional candidates won 34: fully one-fourth. In 48 districts, conversely, Dukakis held Bush to less than 40 percent. Of these, Republican candidates took just one.[42]

---

[40]According to journalist Michael Barone, a moderate Democrat: "The [furlough] episode showed how Dukakis took a sensible and defensible policy (granting furloughs to prisoners about to be released) and carried it to ridiculous extremes (granting furloughs to prisoners never to be released.) It provided a valid basis for an inference that liberal Dukakis appointees would take sensible liberal policies and carry them to ridiculous extremes—with Dukakis's approval. . . . " Michael Barone and Grant Ujifusa, *The Almanac of American Politics 1990* (Washington: National Journal, 1989), xxxvi.

[41]Hotline/KRC tracking polls cited in: Gary Maloney, ed., *The Almanac of 1988 Presidential Politics* (Falls Church, Virginia: American Political Network/LTV, 1989), 72.

[42]Calculated from data in: Glen Bolger, "An Analysis of President Results by Congressional District," paper prepared for the National Republican Congressional Committee, May 9, 1989.

The first two years of the Bush presidency generated scant magnetism. The administration's major policy victories consisted mostly of sustained vetoes (e.g., the 1990 civil rights bill) or changes in bills supported by Democrats (e.g., market-oriented provisions added to clean-air legislation). Bush's best-remembered promise—"no new taxes"—died with the budget agreement of 1990. During that midterm election year, tax-induced disarray and yet another weak crop of candidates led the GOP to its third straight seat loss in the House. The "anti-incumbent tide" hurt Republicans more than Democrats: the average vote percentage for Republican incumbents fell eight points from 1988, compared with a three-point drop for Democratic incumbents.[43]

In the bitterness of defeat, the temptation is to curse a single, simple error: the silver bullet that was never fired. Close examination, however, reveals that the GOP's failure cannot be reduced to one specific issue.

THE MISSING SILVER BULLETS?

Tax and Budget

Many Republicans believed that Bush had given up a silver bullet with 1990 budget agreement. In fact, the tax issue had less magic than they thought. Reagan acceded to several increases during the 1980s, starting with the Tax Equity and Fiscal Responsibility Act of 1982, the largest peacetime tax hike in history. Most of these measures also had substantial support from congressional Republicans. The voters of the 1980s thus had no plausible reason to think that a vote for the GOP was an ironclad vote against new taxes. In 1988, two-thirds believed that Bush would eventually give in on his "Read my lips" pledge.[44] Voters may have considered Democrats even more tax-prone than Republicans, but most congressional Democrats avoided Walter Mondale's tactic of explicitly promising higher taxes. As a result, the decade saw only a few incumbents lose their seats over the issue.

If Republicans had consistently refused to consider any tax increase at all, the issue would have had more effect—but in whose favor? Such an absolute stand would have required a massive reduction in federal spending. If that reduction had merely consisted of scrapping or shrinking existing programs, it might have

[43]Glenn R. Simpson, "A Closer Look at Election Figures Shows More Democratic Strength," *Roll Call*, November 19, 1990, 19.

[44]CBS/*New York Times* poll conducted November 11–16, 1988. Cited in: "The 1988 Election Results," *Public Opinion*, January/February 1989, 21–33, at 33.

hurt the GOP. Big cuts would inevitably have struck Medicare, Social Security, and other programs that help the Republican Party's middle-class supporters.[45] Voters might have accepted the pain and rewarded the GOP for its steadfastness, but it is also possible that they would have punished Republicans for slicing programs they liked. Although Social Security benefits continued to rise, even the mere consideration of cuts cost the GOP a number of seats in the 1982 midterm.

It might have been possible to achieve major savings through fundamental *restructuring* of government programs, but radical reforms (e.g., replacing Medicare with health-care savings accounts) entailed political risks that scared most Republicans.

Social Issues

"Social issues" comprise a variety of concerns that evoke deep feelings. In 1990, Jesse Helms used one such issue—the 1990 Civil Rights Bill—to upset a black challenger whom he accused of supporting racial quotas. Some immediately touted the quota issue as the new Republican silver bullet. The Helms victory showed that the issue can indeed move votes, but there are limits to its effectiveness. First, targets of the issue can find "cover": in 1991, supporters of the bill added language that would purportedly ban quotas. Second, the issue can backfire. Although a calm, principled defense of colorblind law would win strong support from most Americans, political campaigns are not calm events. Candidates often get carried away; and on this issue, careless and emotional discussions can invite countercharges that Republicans are "race-baiting." Such attacks could prevent the GOP from increasing its black and Latino vote, which it needs to win seats in the South and Southwest.

Abortion also raises deep feelings, and as mentioned earlier, those feelings are mixed. Pro-life candidates could frame the issue to greater advantage by stressing concerns such as abortion for sex selection; but the public's basic ambivalence about abortion probably rules it out as a path to Republican realignment.

Other social issues appear and disappear. When the Supreme Court invalidated a ban on flag-burning in 1989, Republicans saw yet another silver bullet in a proposed constitutional amendment

---

[45]It is arithmetically impossible to balance the budget by cutting programs earmarked for poor people. Total spending on means-tested entitlements is less than half the size of the deficit. See data in: Congressional Budget Office, *The Economic and Budget Outlook: Fiscal Years 1992–1996* (Washington: Government Printing Office, 1991, 145–155.

to allow such a ban. The year before, the Pledge of Allegiance issue had hurt the Democratic ticket by reminding the public of Dukakis's Harvard Square liberalism. This time the issue fizzled. The Democrats' spokesman on the flag-burning issue was Senator Bob Kerrey of Nebraska. Because he had won the Congressional Medal of Honor and lost a leg in Vietnam combat, no one could question his devotion to the flag. In any event, Democrats found sufficient cover: responding to the decision with a statute rather than a constitutional amendment.

Defense and Foreign Policy

During the 1980s, some Republican activists thought that issues such as Nicaragua and the nuclear freeze would wound the Democrats. But except in times of immediate crisis, interest in foreign affairs is generally confined to specific voter groups with a stake in particular regional issues (e.g., blacks and South Africa, Jewish voters and Israel). Even when international events do move general public opinion, the effect usually wanes. The Iranian hostage crisis pumped up support for defense spending, but by 1982 a plurality of voters had gone back to thinking that we were spending too much.[46] In the 1984 and 1988 elections, less than a quarter of the electorate cited defense or foreign policy issues as the most important in the presidential race.[47] These issues had even less impact at the congressional level.

The wall of public indifference was high but surmountable. Republicans could still have increased the salience of national security by diligently educating the public about their own record and that of the Democrats.[48] Such a project would have required unity and patience, which ran short on the GOP side during the 1980s. In any event, the fall of the Berlin Wall appeared to defuse anticommunism as a potential concern—at least for the time being.

In early 1991, many Republicans thought that the Persian Gulf War would breathe new life into the defense issue. This euphoria faded. Soon after the victory, Americans were turning their attention elsewhere. Said longtime Reagan adviser Lyn Nofziger, "I'll bet not one Democrat loses because of his vote on the war."[49]

---

[46]Stanley and Niemi, *Vital Statistics on American Politics*, 333.

[47]ABC News exit polls, cited in: Carolyn Smith, ed. *The '88 Vote* (New York: Capital Cities/ABC, 1989), 21.

[48]John J. Pitney, Jr., "Lumbering Elephant: Missed Opportunities in the GOP Senate," *Policy Review* 47 (Winter 1989), 62–66.

[49]Donald M. Rothberg, "War's Boon to GOP Seen Fading," Associated Press, June 11, 1991.

Democrats as the Issue

In the early 1980s, House Republicans tried to turn House Speaker Tip O'Neill into a symbol of all that was wrong with Democratic liberalism. They had good reason to resent the Speaker, as he wielded his power in an extremely partisan and aggressive manner. But they could never communicate their anger beyond Independence Avenue, since few Americans worry about the House's officers or procedures. In a Kansas congressional race in 1982, the Republican candidate tried to paint the Democrat as "another Boston liberal." Democrat Jim Slattery effectively dismissed the charge by saying: "This isn't a race between Tip O'Neill and Ronald Reagan. It's between Jim Slattery and Morris Kay."[50]

In 1989, Republicans hoped that Speaker Wright's ethics problems would enable them to frame House elections as referenda on Democratic corruption. For three reasons, this hope crumbled. First, the Wright affair sparked little concern outside official Washington. Second, the HUD and S&L scandals made it hard for Republicans to define corruption as an exclusively Democratic sin. Third, Wright was replaced by Thomas Foley, who symbolized decency as much as Wright had symbolized ethical lapses.

Beyond the Wedge

Wedges account for most of the above-mentioned "silver bullets." Again, wedges such as the quota issue can influence voters and engage genuine political principles, so they have a legitimate place in political campaigns. But a party cannot grow on wedges alone. Rep. Vin Weber describes the House's Young Turks with words that apply more broadly to Republican activists: "Our major mistake has been to focus on *wedge* issues against the Democrats, without also creating *magnet* issues that would attract the public. Both wedge and magnet issues are essential, but because we concentrated on the first while ignoring the second, we acquired a reputation as primarily negative and confrontational."[51]

NEXT STEPS

Echo Chamber, Monologue or Dialogue?

What can the Republicans do? According to Representative Mickey Edwards: "[W]e are talking, not listening. Even though we

---

[50]Cook, "Self-Inflicted Wounds," 609.

[51]Quoted in: Adam Meyerson, "Wedges and Magnets: Vin Weber on Conservative Opportunities," *Policy Review* 52 (Spring 1990), 38–43, at 42.

are the world's leading critics of centralized planning and the Soviet style of top-down control, we continually sit around in small
groups deciding what we are going to put forth as the next big
'wedge' issue. . . . If we were to use our ears instead of our mouths,
we could find out what the concerns of our fellow Americans
are—and respond within our own philosophical framework to
these concerns."[52] Newt Gingrich, who used to clash with Edwards
over party strategy, likewise says that political growth requires "fig-
uring out what's going to work out there."[53]

Republicans have a choice: echo chamber, monologue, or dialogue. If they passively repeat whatever their polls and focus
groups tell them, they will not deserve to win. If they ignore the
voters, they will not be able to win. Rather, as Edwards and
Gingrich suggest, they should apply their own principles to the
voters' concerns and explain them in the voters' language. That
way, they can frame the issues in ways that preserve their integrity
yet gain political advantage.

Take education. If the issue turns on the level of education
funding—or more subtly, "investment in education"—the advantage goes to the party that wants to spend more. In a 1990 poll, 70
percent said that the federal government was spending too little
on education.[54] Republicans will suffer if they disregard this public concern. At the same time, success will also elude Republicans
who indulge in Pavlovian poll reaction and simply call for higher
spending, since they cannot outbid the Democrats anyway. Does
this mean that the issue must hurt the GOP? Not at all. If Republicans listen carefully, they will find that people's real concern is
not with bigger budgets but with better schools. According to a
1990 poll, 62 percent of Americans favor public school choice as a
means to that end.[55] Therefore, if the issue is framed as one of
reducing the bureaucracy and increasing parental choice, then Republicans will do better.

A New Paradigm

School choice is an example of "the New Paradigm" of public
policy. Coined by Bush White House aide James Pinkerton, the
term refers to a new model for defining public issues and

[52]Mickey Edwards, memorandum to House Republican leadership, February
21, 1991.

[53]Donald Lambro, "From Abstract to Specific," Washington Times, March 11,
1991, D3.

[54]NBC News/Wall Street Journal poll, January 13–16, 1990.

[55]Gallup poll reported in: Carol Innerst, "Minorities Overwhelmingly Favor Public School Choice," Washington Times, August 24, 1990, A3.

solutions.[56] Granted, the word *paradigm* will grace no bumper stickers on pickup trucks, but the New Paradigm's importance lies in its content rather than its label. It embraces several common-sensical concepts that could have great popularity, since they emerge from everyday experience and from innovations already underway in the states and localities.

The best way to explain the New Paradigm is to contrast it with the Old Paradigm that has ruled America since the New Deal:

Bureaucracy v. Market Forces. The Old Paradigm sought to bomb public problems with bureaucrats, while the New Paradigm seeks market-oriented and non-bureaucratic solutions. Privatization is an example. A number of cities have contracted services to private companies, thereby saving money, shrinking staff and increasing citizen satisfaction.[57] Unlike public bureaucracies, the private vendors must bid against one another, and so have an incentive to stay lean. Privatization has its problems and limits, but it rings true to anyone who has ever comparison-shopped between the Postal Service and private carriers. Such policies do not constitute an abandonment of public responsibility, as adherents of the Old Paradigm charge. Just the opposite: they represent an effort to provide the people with best possible service in the most efficient way.

Standardization v. Choice. The Old Paradigm implicitly assumed that "one size fits all," whereas the New Paradigm seeks to expand options for individuals and families. As suggested before, education illustrates this contrast. Parents support the education budget with their tax dollars; but until recently, they could benefit from those dollars only if they sent their children to bureaucratic schools of the government's choosing. Under a variety of New Paradigm proposals ranging from public-school choice to full-blown voucher systems, parents would have much more say in how their children are educated. This makes good sense. After all, who has a greater stake in making a wise decision about a child's future: parents or bureaucrats?

The basic principle has other applications. For years, Old Paradigm organizations have cared more for their own convenience than the public's. Many government offices have been open only from nine to five on weekdays—precisely when it is most difficult for working people to reach them. Now, some communities are taking a New Paradigm approach of providing information and

[56]James P. Pinkerton, "The New Paradigm," address to the Reason Foundation, Los Angeles, April 23, 1990.

[57]Michael deCourcy Hinds, "Cash-Strapped Cities Turn to Companies to Do What Government Once Did," *New York Times*, May 14, 1991, A12.

services through "24-Hour City Halls"—user-friendly terminals that resemble automated teller machines.[58] The federal government could follow this example.[59]

Dependency v. Empowerment. Old Paradigm mandarins preferred that people depend upon them. The director of the Detroit Housing Authority displayed this mentality when he said that while tenants might "play a role" in a few aspects of public housing, actual management was best left to "what is already in place: a network of professionals—like myself—men who have made this their life's work."[60] In the New Paradigm, government would help people gain the means for running their own lives: in the early Bush administration, HUD Secretary Jack Kemp fought to give public housing tenants the chance to manage or purchase their own buildings.

Centralization v. Decentralization. During the half-century of the Old Paradigm's dominance, power tended to flow toward Washington, DC. This trend was beneficial, thought the mandarins, since the nation's capital possessed infinitely more enlightenment, expertise, and broad-mindedness than Sacramento or Springfield. The fate of domestic policy in the 1960s and 1970s cast doubt on this assumption. The New Paradigm, by contrast, sees decentralization as a virtue, because it allows for greater innovation and experimentation. States and localities should thus take over programs that have been run by the federal government. This is an old idea given a new life by technology, for even if Washington could once have claimed a monopoly on knowledge, the Information Age has broken it. With a microcomputer and modem, a decisionmaker anywhere can do work that once required a warehouse full of Washingtonians.

Inputs v. Outcomes. The Old Paradigm measured how well government did by how much it spent. At one time, conventional wisdom had it that the "best" educational system was the most expensive. Yet over the past two decades, parents have noticed that test scores have fallen while school budgets have soared.[61] Among the states, moreover, there seems to be little correlation between gold-plating and achievement: in 1988, Mississippi had a better

---

[58]See, for instance, March 1990 bulletin of Public Technology, Inc., Washington, DC.

[59]Newt Gingrich, *Window of Opportunity* (New York: TOR/St. Martin's, 1984), 77.

[60]William Raspberry, "Kemp Believes," *Washington Post,* May 7, 1990, A11.

[61]Between 1960 and 1987, per capita education spending by all levels of government increased more than twenty percent, while combined average SAT scores dropped 4.6 percent. US Census Bureau, *Statistical Abstract of the United States 1990* (Washington: Government Printing Office, 1990), 148, 350.

high-school graduation rate than New York.[62] The New Paradigm would use carefully chosen performance measurements to evaluate and reform government programs.[63]

Reaching the People

When put into concrete local terms, these ideas could appeal to the voters of the 1990s. The specific policy proposals are not carved into granite. Republicans must watch how these innovations work wherever they are tested; and above all, they must listen to how the people react. When facts and public sentiments point to adjustments or further innovations, Republicans should be quick to answer within their philosophical framework.

While held together by core principles, the New Paradigm is broad enough to reach different constituencies. In big cities, candidates could address urban blight through tenant management and enterprise zones. In suburbs, they could stress improved service delivery and policies to foster telecommuting. In rural areas, they could highlight decentralization. This way, they could recapture the spirit of the early Republican Party, which had firm beliefs and could still adapt its campaign messages to the needs of different groups and regions.[64]

Younger voters constitute the New Paradigm's base. Unlike their elders, they do not equate the Old Paradigm with FDR. When they think of the existing order, they think of red tape, poor service, bad schools, bloated budgets, and rotting urban neighborhoods. They want a fresh approach—but the alternative must consist of something more than cutting down the Old Paradigm. Their skepticism about bureaucratic government dwells side-by-side with an idealism about public life: that is why so many young people can revere both Milton Friedman and Martin Luther King, Jr.[65] By offering a positive vision of what an innovative government could do, the New Paradigm could attract these voters to the GOP line in nonpresidential elections[66]—and inspire a new generation of Republicans to seek office. Because many

[62]US Department of Education, "State Education Performance Chart" (Washington: Education Department, 1990).

[63]In some agencies, the task will be more challenging than in others. See: James Q. Wilson, *Bureaucracy* (New York: Basic, 1989), 158–171.

[64]Gienapp, 58–59.

[65]For an extended analysis of such unexpected combinations, see: E.J. Dionne, *Why Americans Hate Politics* (New York: Simon and Schuster, 1991).

[66]Although younger voters tend to identify with the Republican Party, they are not more likely than older voters to vote Republican in House elections. See table of exit polls from 1982 through 1990 in: *New York Times*, November 8, 1990, B7.

New Paradigm ideas apply to towns, cities and counties, it could replenish the party's candidate pool right where the need is greatest: at the local level.

The New Paradigm can help the Republican Party, but it is *not* a silver bullet. Campaign talk about "empowerment" will do little by itself to change voting habits. To have a lasting impact, a campaign message must emerge from policy. Therefore, Republicans must give the New Paradigm a great deal of work: studying problems, crafting bills, and implementing policies wherever possible. This will prove difficult.

STUMBLING BLOCKS

Many New Paradigm innovations have been pioneered by state and local Democratic officials. As Elaine Kamarck says, a number of Democrats are working to identify their party with the New Paradigm at the national level. It may first seem as if Republicans need not worry about the competition. So long as various Old Paradigm lobbies still have clout within the national Democratic Party, the New Paradigm Democrats will face steep odds. But even though Republicans may appear to offer the New Paradigm its natural home, the GOP presents stumbling blocks of its own.

Electoral Engineers and Policy Brahmins
Two kinds of influential Republicans miss the connection between governing and campaign politics. On the one hand are the electoral engineers: political technicians who specialize in soundbites, media buys, and contribution letters. Many of these people neither know nor care about the substance of public policy. Their only concern is with whatever message moves the next tracking poll or fundraising haul; the long-range good of country and party is not their department. They will mock any effort to discuss issues seriously, particularly if the immediate payoff is not obvious.

On the other hand are policy Brahmins, government officials who are so immersed in the fine print of existing policies that they sneer at the first mention of underlying principles or broad visions. The policy Brahmins argue that real change comes slowly and incrementally. This observation often holds true, but it also blinds its holders to those times when a fundamental change is necessary. The Berlin Wall came down all at once, not one brick at a time. And whereas the Salk vaccine was a radical step, the "incremental" remedy for polio would have been a streamlined iron lung.

Faust on the Potomac

Despite its overall problems, the Old Paradigm has brought concentrated benefits to certain groups, some of which have influence within the Republican Party. These groups will fight New Paradigm policies that reduce their benefits for the broader good. Case in point: agriculture subsidies, a classic of Old Paradigm market distortion. In 1990, Congressman Richard Armey (R-Texas) proposed legislation to deny federal crop subsidies to farmers with adjusted gross incomes of more than $100,000 per year. This measure would have saved up to $700 million a year without hurting small farmers, and it would have taken a small step toward the New Paradigm goal of fostering market forces. But under pressure from agribusiness, 62 percent of House Republicans voted against it.[67] (An equal percentage of Democrats also voted no. The AFL-CIO and pro-union Democrats had made a deal: they would oppose the Armey legislation in exchange for farm-state votes for protectionist trade legislation. In this episode, the dead hand of the Old Paradigm had a firm grip on both parties.)

Madisonian Politics

It is perhaps misleading to speak of "the" Republican Party. Under the Madisonian system of federalism, bicameralism, and separated powers, both parties are institutionally fragmented. The House Republicans do not answer to the Senate Republicans, and both groups can act independently of the president. National Republicans cannot dictate to state and local GOP officials, who in turn face institutional divisions within their statehouses and courthouses.

This fragmentation is one stumbling block that should *not* be removed. Decentralization is basic to the New Paradigm, so it would be an utter contradiction in terms to enforce a New Paradigm party discipline from Washington, DC.

The New Paradigm must spread throughout the GOP by persuasion instead of political muscle. And this task requires leadership at the top, because it takes presidents and presidential candidates to identify a political party with a public philosophy. Franklin Roosevelt put the Democratic Party on the side of activist government not just by getting his proposals through Congress, but by preaching his message to the people and setting an example for Democratic policymakers at every level of government.

---

[67]David S. Cloud, "House and Senate Resist Calls to Alter Course on Farm Bill," *Congressional Quarterly Weekly Report*, July 28, 1990, 2393–2396, at 2396. For vote breakdown, see same issue, 2454.

Presidents face conflicting pressures. Short-run demands distract them from long-term goals, and the need for tactical compromise may blur party principles. Most important, the uncertainties of a reelection campaign may lead them to stress self-defense over party building. There is no panacea for these pressures. The president must simply have a personal commitment to the party's highest ideals. Lincoln put it best when he said that government's main object is "to elevate the condition of men—to lift artificial weights from all shoulders—to clear the paths of laudable pursuit for all—to afford all, an unfettered start, and a fair chance, in the race of life."[68]

---

[68]Message to Congress, July 4, 1861. Roy P. Basler, ed., *The Collected Works of Abraham Lincoln*, (New Brunswick, New Jersey: Rutgers University Press, 1953) vol. 4, 438.

THE NEW DEAL, PARTY POLITICS, AND THE ADMINISTRATIVE STATE

Sidney M. Milkis

NEARLY SIXTY YEARS AFTER THE ELECTION OF FRANKLIN D. Roosevelt as president, the New Deal remains central to understanding past and present patterns of American politics. It marked one of the periodic "critical partisan realignments" in American history; one of those rare moments, animated by fundamental and polarizing conflict, that severely test the broad liberal consensus that so many scholars and pundits have portrayed as the essential genius of American politics. These events, which Walter Dean Burnham has characterized as "America's surrogate for revolution," have profoundly affected political parties. They involve dramatic shifts in voter affiliation that transform the basis of party support, major changes in public policy, and the forging of a new public philosophy that reformulates the consensual understanding of the American social contract.[1] In the case of the New Deal, a governing philosophy emerged that made legitimate, for the first time in American history, the expansion of social welfare policies. On the basis of this "programmatic" liberalism, the Democratic party became the majority party, and the Republicans were relegated to minority status after commanding the political system for most of the previous seventy years. There followed a program dedicated to securing the basic security of the American people—to building the welfare state.

Furthermore, the New Deal represented an endeavor to reevaluate the relationship of political parties to constitutional

[1]Walter Dean Burnham, "Party Systems and the Political Process," in *The American Party Systems: Stages of Political Development*, ed. Walter Dean Burnham and William Nisbet Chambers, (New York, London, and Toronto: Oxford University Press, 1975), 289. See also, Walter Dean Burnham, *Critical Elections and the Mainsprings of American Politics* (New York: W. W. Norton, 1970).

principles and institutions. In effect, Roosevelt and his key advisors viewed the American party system as an archaic institution that reinforced what liberal reformers considered outmoded constitutional understandings and mechanisms. In this connection, FDR continued and extended the influence of the progressive tradition in American politics. The American party system was forged on the anvil of Jeffersonian principles, dedicated to establishing a "wall of separation" between the national government and society. As a result, it was, from its inception in the early 1800s, wedded to constitutional arrangements, such as legislative supremacy and states' rights, that were designed to constrain the expansion of national administrative power. Beginning with Woodrow Wilson, therefore, twentieth-century reformers criticized American political parties as an obstacle to the development of a significant progressive program.

In this respect, the New Deal represented the culmination of efforts, which began in the Progressive era, to loosen the grip of partisan politics on the councils of power, with a view to shoring up the administrative capacities and extending the programmatic commitments of the federal government. As such, the New Deal represents a secular change in party politics—one that was deliberately pursued to counteract the traditional pattern of realignment and the habits that sustained it. Simply put, this involved the displacement of party politics by executive administration, whereby political parties were dispossessed of their status as the leading agents of democracy in the United States. Thereafter, the American people looked to a refurbished presidency and newly formed administrative agencies to play that role.

There is a real sense, therefore, in which the New Deal realignment is appropriately viewed as a realignment to make future realignments unnecessary. Previous realignments had strengthened the national resolve and critically changed the American political landscape, but had not altered the principles and institutional arrangements that historically had impeded the development of a "modern" state, that is, a national political power with expansive programmatic obligations. The New Deal realignment, however, was the first to focus national attention on the capacity of the President and administrative agencies to extend the political capability of the American people. Especially during Roosevelt's second term, it emphasized a political program to make party politics less important, and, concomitantly, a "perfected" system of public administration more significant in organizing the work of American constitutional government. To a point, all surrogate revolutions in the United States have touched on constitutional issues that transcend parties; but before the New Deal, none of the reform programs to which the voters subscribed during a realignment created an *institutional* foundation to replace political parties. Thus, although the New Deal strengthened partisanship in the short term, it set the tone for a less partisan future.

In certain respects, the New Deal realignment led to developments that created a more prominent and powerful presidency, which has strengthened the capability of the national government to tackle the pressing domestic and international challenges of the twentieth century. Yet, as this chapter concludes, the emergence of the "modern" presidency has come at the cost of weakening certain valuable institutions such as political parties that traditionally have been critical agents of popular rule. In the end, this has strengthened the national purpose while enervating certain foundational principles and institutions of republican government.

PROGRAMMATIC LIBERALISM AND THE AMERICAN PARTY SYSTEM

In order to understand the New Deal and its effect on the party system, one must begin with the Commonwealth Club address, delivered during the 1932 campaign. This address, properly understood as the New Deal manifesto, spoke of the need to redefine the meaning of liberalism in American politics. This reevaluation led to a "programmatic" form of liberalism as the public philosophy of the New Deal, requiring a fundamental departure from the principles and institutions that had long governed the political system. Hitherto, liberalism, in American politics, was associated with Jeffersonian principles, which followed the natural rights tradition of limited government. According to this tradition, associated with the philosophy expressed in Locke's *Second Treatise* and the Declaration of Independence, government existed to serve certain inalienable individual rights, which presupposed a distinction between state and society. The identification of individual freedom with the obligation to limit the scope of government action in the natural rights tradition gave shape to and guided the development of the American Constitution, a complex system of checks and balances that was intended to stand as a barrier between private and public action. As James Madison put it in *Federalist* No. 48, "It will not be denied that power is of an encroaching nature and ought to be effectively restrained from passing the limits assigned to it."[2]

[2]Alexander Hamilton, James Madison, and John Jay, *The Federalist Papers* (New York: New American Library, 1961), 308.

The theme of the Commonwealth Club address was that the time had come, indeed, it had come three decades earlier, to recognize the "new terms of the old social contract." It was necessary, that is, to rewrite the social contract in order to take account of a development whereby industrial capitalism had wrought a national economy and concentration of economic power, requiring a strong countervailing force—a stronger national state—lest the United States steer, FDR warned, "a steady course toward economic oligarchy." The impetus for the national welfare would thus have to shift from the shoulders of the productive private citizen to the government; the guarantee of equal opportunity now required that individual initiative be restrained and directed by the national state:

> Clearly all this calls for a reappraisal of values. Our task now is not discovery or exploitation of national resources or necessarily producing new goods. It is the soberer, less dramatic business of administering resources and plants already in hand, of seeking to reestablish foreign markets for our surplus production, of meeting the problem of under consumption, of adjusting production to consumption, of distributing wealth and products more equitably, of adapting existing economic organizations to the service of the people. The day of enlightened administration has come.[3]

The creation of a national state with expansive supervisory powers would be a "long, slow task," however. The Commonwealth Address was attentive to the uneasy fit between energetic central government and constitutional principles in the United States. It was imperative, therefore, that the New Deal be informed by a public philosophy in which the new concept of state power would be carefully interwoven with earlier conceptions of American government. The task of modern government, FDR announced, was "to assist in the development of an economic declaration of rights, an economic constitutional order." As such, the traditional emphasis in American politics on individual self-reliance should give way to a new understanding of individualism, by which the government acted as a regulating and unifying agency, guaranteeing individual men and women protection from the uncertainties of the market place. Thus, the most significant aspect of the departure from natural rights to programmatic liberalism was the association of constitutional rights with the extension, rather than the restriction, of the programmatic commitments of the national government.

[3]Franklin D. Roosevelt, *Public Papers and Addresses*, 13 volumes (New York: Random House, 1938–1950), 1:751–752.

The defense of progressive reform in terms of extending the rights of the Constitution was a critical development in the advent of a positive understanding of government responsibility in the United States. Although the progressive tradition anticipated many elements of this understanding of government, FDR was the first advocate of an active federal government to "appropriate" the term liberalism and make it part of the common political vocabulary.[4] Before the New Deal, American liberalism was associated with its Jeffersonian origins, which identified positive government with conservative efforts, beginning with Hamilton's economic policy, to advantage unjustly business enterprise. Even Woodrow Wilson's program of extending the role of the national government remained in its essentials committed to decentralization of power. Herbert Croly and Theodore Roosevelt expressed an alternative progressive understanding, one that envisioned a "new nationalism" as "the steward of the public welfare."[5] As Croly wrote in *The Promise of American Life,* the aim of progressive reform was "to give democratic meaning and purpose to the Hamiltonian tradition and method."[6] Yet it was Wilson's progressive vision, one more closely tied to "Jeffersonianism," that triumphed in the election of 1912. The victory of Wilson over Theodore Roosevelt in that campaign, in which the latter as the standard bearer of the Progressive Party was the only candidate to advocate "the substitution of frank social policy for the individualism of the past," ensured the triumph, Croly lamented, of "a higher conservatism over progressive democracy."[7]

The more decisive break with the American tradition of limited government anticipated by the Progressive Party campaign of 1912 came at the hands of Franklin Roosevelt during the 1930s. Roosevelt's triumph was greatly aided, of course, by the economic exigencies created by the Great Depression. Yet the advent of the New Deal would not have been possible without FDR's deft

[4]Ronald D. Rotunda, "The Liberal Label: Roosevelt's Capture of A Symbol," in *Public Policy,* ed. John D. Montgomery and Albert O. Hirschman (Cambridge: Harvard University Press), vol. 17 (1968), 399; Samuel Beer, "In Search of A New Public Philosophy," in *The New American Political System* ed. Anthony King (Washington, D.C.: American Enterprise Institute, 1979); and James Ceaser, "The Theory of Governance of the Reagan Administration," in *The Reagan Presidency and the Governing of America,* ed. Lester M. Salamon and Michael S. Lund (Washington, D.C.: Urban Institute, 1981).

[5]Theodore Roosevelt made the first of a number of speeches on the New Nationalism at Osawatomie, Kansas, in August, 1910, printed in Theodore Roosevelt, *Works of Theodore Roosevelt* (New York: Da Capo Press, 1923–1926), 9:10–30.

[6]Herbert Croly, *The Promise of American Life* (New York: E. P. Dutton, 1963), 169.

[7]Herbert Croly, *Progressive Democracy* (New York: MacMillan, 1914), 15.

reinterpretation of the liberal tradition. The distinction between progressives and conservatives, as most boldly pronounced by Croly, all too visibly placed reforms in opposition to constitutional government and the self-interested basis of American politics. The use of the term liberalism by Roosevelt gave legitimacy to progressive principles by embedding them in the parlance of constitutionalism and interpreting them as the expansion, rather than the transcendence, of the natural rights tradition.

The need to establish an economic constitutional order, first declared in the Commonwealth Club address, was a consistent theme of Roosevelt's long presidency. Significantly, it was the principal message of Roosevelt's first re-election bid in 1936, a decisive triumph which first established the Democrats as the dominant party in American politics. The Democratic party's platform for that campaign, drafted by Roosevelt, was written as a pastiche of the Declaration of Independence, thus emphasizing the need for a fundamental reconsideration of rights. As the platform claimed with respect to the 1935 Social Security Act:

We hold this truth to be self-evident—that the test of representative government is its ability to promote the safety and happiness of the people. . . . We have built foundations for the security of those who are faced with the hazards of unemployment and old age; for the orphaned, the crippled, and the blind. On the foundation of the Social Security Act we are determined to erect a structure of economic security for all our people, making sure that this benefit shall keep step with the ever-increasing capacity of America to provide a high standard of living for all its citizens.[8]

The creation of a structure of economic security, as FDR would later detail in his 1944 State of the Union Address, required that the inalienable rights provided by the Constitution—free speech, free press, trial by jury, freedom from unreasonable searches and seizures—needed to be supplemented, so to speak, by a second bill of rights, "under which a new basis of security and property can be established for all—regardless of station, race, or creed." Among the second bill of rights were the right to a useful and remunerative job, the right to own enough to provide ade-

---

[8]"Democratic Platform of 1936," in *National Party Platforms*, ed. Donald Bruce Johnson (Urbana: University of Illinois Press, 1978), 360. Evidence of FDR's dominant role in drafting the platform can be found in the President's Secretary File 143, Folder: "Democratic Platform," *Franklin D. Roosevelt Papers*, Hyde Park, New York. Upon reading FDR's draft, his aide Stanley High wrote enthusiastically, "Apropos of the platform memorandum which you showed me yesterday afternoon, . . . I think the use of the phrase 'We hold this truth to be self-evident' is great." High, Memorandum for the President, June 18, 1936, ibid.

quate food and clothing and recreation, the right to adequate medical care, the right to a decent home, the right to adequate protection from the economic fears of old age, sickness, accident, and unemployment, and the right to a good education.[9]

These rights, of course, were never formally ratified as amendments to the Constitution; nor were they fully codified in statutes and policies.[10] But they became the foundation of political dialogue in the United States, thus redefining the role of the national government. The new social contract heralded by Roosevelt marks the beginning of what has been called the "rights revolution"—a transformation in the governing philosophy of the United States that has brought about major changes in American political institutions.[11]

Roosevelt's reappraisal of values is important in understanding the New Deal, but it is likewise important in understanding FDR's impact on party politics. The new understanding of the Declaration required an assault on the established party system, which had long been a steadfast ally of constitutional forms that favored a decentralization of power. This effort to weaken traditional partisan organizations and loyalties began during the Progressive

[9]Roosevelt, *Public Papers and Addresses*, 13:40.

[10]In truth, the New Dealers were somewhat ambivalent about whether the economic bill of rights should be treated as a formal constitutional program. This was less important, in the final analysis, than the redefinition of the fundamental political law, which organized the powers and distributed the functions of government, in a way that secured the longevity of New Deal programs. Such a concern was voiced by Chester Bowles, head of the Office of Price Administration, who urged FDR to make the Second Bill of Rights the centerpiece of his 1944 State of the Union message. The President's message should "outline a *Second* Bill of Rights for all Americans," he wrote in a memo of December 23, 1943. These rights should "not *necessarily*...be adopted into the Constitution, although the idea should be studied." The most important objective, Bowles concluded, "was to articulate "a program which everyone can understand, and which will bring to all men in our armed forces and to millions of men, women and children here at home, new hope for the future which lies ahead." Chester Bowles to Samuel Rosenman, and attached "Outline of A Suggested Home Front Speech," Box 1, Folder: Bowles, Chester, Samuel Rosenman Papers, Franklin D. Roosevelt Library (emphasis in original). See also, John W. Jeffries, "The 'New' New Deal: FDR and American Liberalism, 1937–1945," *Political Science Quarterly*, vol. 105 (Fall, 1990), 415–416.

[11]As R. Shep Melnick has observed: "The 'rights revolution' refers to the tendency to define nearly every public issue in terms of legally protected rights of individuals. Rights of the handicapped, rights of workers, rights of students, rights of racial minorites, linguistic, and religious minorities, rights of women, rights of consumers, the right to a hearing, the right to know—the have become the stock and trade of political discourse." See his "The Courts, Congress, and Programmatic Rights," in *Remaking American Politics*, ed. Richard A. Harris and Sidney M. Milkis (Boulder, Colorado: Westview Press, 1989), 188.

period; but it fell to FDR and the architects of the New Deal to make progressivism an enduring part of American politics.

The progressive animus against parties is often misconstrued as an expression of intractable hostility to party politics within a regime that is exceptionally dedicated to individualism. In fact, a party system was formed during the first half-century of the Constitution's existence that was compatible with the celebration of the personal independence of the democratic individual in America. James Madison, in fact, the architect of what Richard Hofstadter calls a "Constitution-Against-Parties," played a key part in giving rise to this party politics.[12]

Political parties are usually understood to link government and society, a view which is based on the development of parties in Europe at the end of the nineteenth century. But whereas parties such as the German Social Democratic party and the British Labour party were organized by and represented private and the British Labour party were organized by and represented private interests in order to advance the cause of national reform, American party politics long impeded, rather than abetted, the development of a national state with expansive responsibilities to direct social and economic developments. In fact, although Alexis de Tocqueville believed that equality generally required centralization of authority, American democracy and party politics remained allied to decentralization until the New Deal. This alliance, as Tocqueville observed, owed much to the extraordinary commitment in the United States to "provincial liberties." Certain "peculiar and accidental causes" in the American case, especially the lack of a feudal tradition, "diverted" the United States from centralized government. "The American destiny is unusual," Tocqueville wrote. "[T]hey have taken from the English aristocracy the idea of individual rights and a taste for local freedom, and they have been able to keep both these things because they have no aristocracy to fight."[13]

The American commitment to local freedoms was supported by the understanding of ardent defenders of popular rule, such as Jefferson, that decentralization of powers was necessary to make government understandable and accessible to the people and, thereby, to nurture an active and competent citizenry. Significantly, national party politics in the United States originated in an

[12]Richard Hofstadter, *The Idea of A Party System: The Rise of Legitimate Opposition in the United States, 1789–1840* (Berkeley: University of California Press, 1969), 40–73.
[13]Alexis de Tocqueville, *Democracy in America*, J. P. Mayer, ed. (New York: Doubleday, 1969), 676.

endeavor by Jefferson and his political allies, the most important being James Madison, to protect local freedom from the challenge to it they perceived in Hamilton's project to strengthen the national government. As Secretary of the Treasury in the Washington administration, Hamilton had proposed a program of economic nationalism, based on a national bank and a system of tariffs. Jefferson and Madison opposed this plan, claiming that this program would unfairly benefit commercial interests. Yet the attack on Hamilton's policies, on his plan to construct a strong central government was not undertaken merely to get government off the people's backs. Rather, the assault on Hamiltonian nationalism, which led to the founding of the Democratic-Republican party, was based on a political doctrine dedicated to strengthening the democratic character of the Constitution. The "consolidation" of responsibilities in the national government that would follow from Hamilton's commercial and international objectives presupposed dominant executive leadership in formulating and carrying out public policy. The power of the more decentralizing institutions—Congress and state governments—would necessarily be undermined in this enterprise. In order to keep power close enough to the people for republican government to prevail, Jefferson and Madison formulated a public philosophy to support a strict interpretation of the national government's powers. This also became a party doctrine, and the principal task of the triumphant Democratic-Republicans after the critical election of 1800—or, as Jefferson called it, the "revolution of 1800"—was to dismantle Hamilton's program for a strong executive. The purpose of presidential leadership in the Jeffersonian mold was to capture the executive office in order to contain and minimize its potential. As James Piereson has written:

Out of this original clash there developed in America the tension between party politics, on the one hand, and governmental centralization and bureaucracy, on the other.... The leaders of the original [Democratic]-Republican party attacked Hamilton's program, and the politics on which it rested, by organizing voters, and by appealing to them on the basis of Republican principles, which were inherently decentralizing and hostile to administration, as was the very process of party politics.[14]

American political parties, then, were formed to restrain the role of the executive, especially with respect to expanding the scope of national administrative power. These political associations

[14]James Piereson, "Party Government," *The Political Science Reviewer,* 12 (Fall, 1982), 51–52.

were popular organizations, but they were formed at a time when popular rule meant limiting government power. Apparently, the founding of the Democratic-Republican party did not mean that Madison and Jefferson had fundamentally changed their views, expressed during the founding of the Constitution, that a strong majority party—and raw and disruptive partisan conflict—posed a threat to individual liberty. They did not expect a formal two party system to become a permanent part of the American polit-ical system, but to wither away after Hamilton and his allies in the Federalist party were defeated. During the Jacksonian era, how-ever, Martin Van Buren, supported by a forceful and popular pres-ident, defended the party as a legitimate constitutional institution, one that would take its shape from Jeffersonian principles. Con-sequently, before the New Deal, presidents who sought to exercise executive power expansively, or perceived a need for the expan-sion of the national government's powers, were thwarted, as Stephen Skowronek has written, "by the tenacity of this highly mo-bilized, highly competitive, and locally oriented democracy."[15]

The origins and organizing principles of the American party system established it as a force against the creation of a "modern" state. The New Deal commitment to building such a state—a na-tional political power with expansive programmatic responsibili-ties—meant that the party system either had to be weakened or reconstituted. Paradoxically, FDR's leadership both weakened and reconstituted parties. Under the leadership of Roosevelt, the Dem-ocratic party became the instrument of greater national purpose. Ultimately, this purpose was dedicated to the creation of an ad-ministrative state that would displace partisan politics with "en-lightened administration."[16] This attempt to *transcend*, rather the

[15]Stephen Skowronek, *Building A New American State: The Expansion of National Administrative Capacities, 1877–1920* (Cambridge: Cambridge University Press, 1982), 40.
[16]It is worth noting that the draft of the Commonwealth Club address, which Ad-olf Berle wrote, declared that "The day of the manager has come." The final ver-sion of the speech, fashioned by Raymond Moley and Roosevelt, himself, proclaimed the "day of enlightened administration" instead, thus pushing home more clearly than the draft language the extent to which the reform of American democracy seemed to bring with it administrative aggrandizement. The task was not merely to accentuate the role of expertise within public councils, but, to elevate administrative officials and agencies to a central position in the realization of a pro-gressive democratic policy. Berle's final draft was the last of three he wrote, a pro-cess that involved continual interplay between him and Roosevelt. The first two drafts can be found in The Adolf Berle Papers, Roosevelt Library, Box 17, Folder: "Speech Draft: Individualism." Berle's final draft is also in his papers, Box 18,

reform, the American party system bespeaks the limited prospects for establishing party government in the United States.

For New Dealers, the idea of the welfare state was not a partisan issue. The enactment of New Deal programs, considered tantamount to rights, was defined as a "constitutional" matter which required eliminating partisanship about the national government's obligation to provide security for the American people. Nevertheless, the displacement of partisan politics required a major partisan effort in the short-run in order to generate popular support for the economic constitutional order. To a point, this made partisanship an integral part of New Deal politics. It was necessary, therefore, to remake the Democratic party as an instrument to free the councils of government, particularly the president and bureaucracy, from the restraints of traditional party politics and the constitutional understanding it reflected.

NEW DEAL PARTY RESPONSIBILITY

In the introduction to the 1938 volume of his presidential papers and addresses, written in 1941, Roosevelt explained that his efforts to modify the Democratic party were undertaken to strengthen party responsibility to the electorate and to commit his party more fully to progressive reform:

I believe it is my sworn duty, as President, to take all steps necessary to insure the continuance of liberalism in our government. I believe, at the same time, that it is my duty as the head of the Democratic party to see to it that my party remains the truly liberal party in the political life of Americans.

There have been many periods in American history, unfortunately, when one major political party was no different than the other major party—except only in name. In a system of party government such as ours, however, elections become meaningless when the two major parties have no differences other than their labels. For such elections do not give the people of the United States an opportunity to decide upon the type of government they prefer for the next two or the next four years as the case may be. . . .

Generally speaking, in a representative form of government there are generally two schools of political belief—liberal and conservative.

Folder: "Commonwealth Club." I am grateful to Robert Eden, who generously shared materials with me that he discovered in his own research on the Commonwealth Club address.

The system of party responsibility in American politics requires that one of its parties be the liberal party and the other be the conservative party.[17]

Roosevelt's party politics, then, were based on constitutional and policy concerns. FDR believed that democratic government required a more meaningful link between the councils of government ment and the electorate. Furthermore, he reasoned that the clarification of political choice and centralization of authority would establish more advantageous conditions to bring about meaningful policy reform in the political system. In pursuance of these objectives, Roosevelt undertook an assault on the party system to make it more national and principled in character. He wanted to overcome the state and local orientation of the party system, which was suited to Congressional primacy and poorly organized for progressive action by the national government, and to establish a national, executive-oriented party, which would be more suitably organized for the expression of national purposes.

Roosevelt was no doubt influenced in this understanding by the thought of Woodrow Wilson. The reform of parties, Wilson believed, depended upon extending the influence of the presidency. The limits on partisanship inherent in American constitutional government notwithstanding, the president represented his party's "vital link of connection" with the nation: "He can dominate his party by being spokesman for the real sentiment and purpose of the country, by giving the country at once the information and statements of policy which will enable it to form its judgment alike of parties and men."[18]

Nevertheless, Wilson found it very difficult to reconcile progressivism with the demands of party leader. To be sure, Wilson established himself as the leader of public opinion in a way that contributed significantly to the transformation of the presidency; and his ability to bring the pressure of public opinion upon Congress and assert dominance over the House and Senate party caucuses established Wilson as the principal spokesman for the Democratic party. But he was persuaded by his Postmaster General Albert Burleson, who was appointed to the President's cabinet largely because of his thorough knowledge of affairs on the Hill, to accept traditional partisan practices concerning legislative deliberations and appointments. Wilson's decision to work through reg-

---

[17]Roosevelt, *Public Papers and Addresses*, 7:xxviii–xxix.
[18]Woodrow Wilson, *Constitutional Government in the United States* (New York: Columbia University Press, 1908), 68–69.

ular partisan channels was a major factor in his nearly absolute mastery over the Democratic party and the Democratic members in Congress. At the same time, this political method failed to strengthen the Democratic party's organization or its fundamental commitment to progressive principles.[19]

Roosevelt, however, was less committed to working through existing partisan channels; and, more importantly, the New Deal represented a more fundamental departure than did Wilsonian progressivism from traditional Democratic policies of individual autonomy, limited government, and states' rights.

As President-elect, Roosevelt began preparations to modify the partisan practices of previous administrations. For example, feeling that Wilson's adherence to traditional partisan practices in staffing the federal government was unfortunate, Roosevelt expressed to Attorney General Homer S. Cummings his desire to proceed along somewhat different lines, with a view, according to the latter's diary, "to building up a national organization rather than allowing patronage to be used merely to build Senatorial and Congressional machines."[20] Roosevelt followed traditional patronage practices during his first term, allowing Democratic chairman James Farley to coordinate appointments in response to local organizations and Democratic Senators, but the recommendations of organization people were not followed as closely after his reelection. Beginning in 1938 especially, as Ed Flynn, who became Democratic chairman in 1940, indicated in his memoirs, "the President turned more and more frequently to the so-called New Dealers," so that "many of the appointments in Washington went to men who were supporters of the President and believed in what he was trying to do, but who were not Democrats in many instances, and in all instances were not organization Democrats."[21]

---

[19]Arthur S. Link, "Woodrow Wilson and the Democratic Party," *Review of Politics* 18 (April, 1956): 146–156. On the contribution of Woodrow Wilson to the development of modern executive leadership, see Jeffrey Tulis, *The Rhetorical Presidency* (Princeton, New Jersey: Princeton University Press, 1987), Chap. 5. Tulis's very important discussion of Wilson's contribution to presidential leadership of public opinion—the "rhetorical presidency"—is insufficiently attentive to the important role that party organization played in Wilson's administration. As Link has observed, Wilson disappointed many progressives by his willingness to subordinate leadership of public opinion to the task of forming strong bonds with his party and its congressional leadership.

[20]Personal and Political Diary of Homer Cummings, January 5, 1933, box 234, No. 2, 90, Homer Cummings Papers (no. 9973), Manuscripts Department, University of Virginia Library, Charlottesville, Virginia.

[21]Edward J. Flynn, *You're the Boss* (New York: Viking, 1947), 153.

From a political point of view, this departure from conventional patronage practices resulted, as Paul Van Riper has noted, "in the development of another kind of patronage, a sort of intellectual and ideological patronage rather than the more traditional partisan type."[22] The administration's circumvention of state and party leaders and the national committee in selecting personnel, a practice especially common in staffing new programs, was, in a sense, politically nonpartisan; however, careful attention was given to the political commitments and associations of job candidates, thus resulting in a loosely knit, albeit well-defined, group of individuals whose loyalties rested with the New Deal rather than the Democratic party.

The New Dealers' attempt to make the party into a more national organization focused not only on the national committee, which represented the concerns of state and local party leaders in the distribution of patronage, but also in Congress, which registered state and local policy interests at the national level. Whereas Wilson took care to consult with legislative party leaders in the development of his policy program, Roosevelt relegated his party in Congress to a decidedly subordinate status. He offended legislators by his use of press conferences to announce important decisions and, again unlike Wilson, eschewed the use of the party caucus in Congress. Roosevelt rejected as impractical, for example, the suggestion of Representative Alfred Phillips, Jr., "that those sharing the burden of responsibility of party government should regularly and often be called into caucus and that such caucuses should involve party policies and choice of party leaders."[23]

Roosevelt's refusal to confine his consultation to the party leaders, relying instead upon New Deal loyalists, many of whom had little connection to the regular Democratic organization, marked an unprecedented challenge to party responsibility as traditionally understood in American politics. "If Democrats on Capitol Hill have any pride in the New Deal," the former White House advisor Stanley High wrote in 1937, "it is certainly not the pride of authorship. Its authorship goes back to the President himself, and to the assortment of political hybrids with which he was surrounded."[24]

[22]Paul Van Riper, *History of the United States Civil Service* (Evanston, Illinois: Row, Peterson, 1958), 327.

[23]Phillips to FDR, June 9, 1937; and FDR to Phillips, June 16, 1937; President's Personal File 2666, Roosevelt Papers.

[24]Stanley High, "Whose Party Is It?" *Saturday Evening Post*, February 6, 1937, 34.

The most dramatic moment in Roosevelt's challenge to traditional party practices was the "purge" campaign of 1938. This campaign involved FDR's direct intervention in one gubernatorial and several congressional primary campaigns in a bold effort to replace conservative Democrats with candidates who were "100 percent New Dealers." Such intervention was not unprecedented. William Howard Taft and Wilson had made limited efforts to remove recalcitrants from their parties. But Roosevelt's campaign took place on an unprecedentedly large scale and, unlike previous efforts, made no attempt to work through the regular party organization. The degree to which such action was viewed as a shocking departure from the norm is indicated by the press's labeling of it as the "purge," a term associated with Adolf Hitler's attempt to weed out dissension in Germany's National Socialist party and Joseph Stalin's elimination of "disloyal" party members from the Soviet Communist party.

The special concern of New Dealers in this campaign was the south, a Democratic stronghold since the Civil War, but, given the commitment to states' rights in that region, also the greatest obstacle to the transformation of the Democratic party into a purposeful liberal organization. Southern Democrats played a leading role in forming a bipartisan conservative coalition in the 75th Congress (1937–1939) that scuttled many key New Deal initiatives. As Thomas Stokes wrote after analyzing the important part southern legislators played in impeding and compromising the wages and hours bill: "Southern Democracy was the ball and chain which hobbled the party's forward march."[25] For this reason, Roosevelt selected most of the individual targets of the purge campaign from conservative southern and border states. If the Democratic party was eventually to become a national liberal party, Southern Democracy would have to be defeated.

Roosevelt undertook the purge not only to overcome the obstacle posed by conservative Democrats to the completion of the New Deal, but also to alter the structure of the party. The President realized that there would be an uncertain place for programmatic liberals in future Democratic administrations, unless Chief Executives were somehow made less dependent on the convention system and the regular party apparatus, which was dominated by Congress and state party leaders. The development of a more national and programmatic party politics required a revamped party structure, within which the President, as the only true national

[25]Thomas Stokes, *Chip Off My Shoulder* (Princeton, New Jersey: Princeton University Press, 1940), 503.

representative would become, as Woodrow Wilson put it, "the vital link of connection between party and nation."

The Roosevelt administration had won an important victory in this campaign for a more national and programmatic party at the 1936 Democratic convention, where it led a movement to abolish the two-thirds rule. This rule for Democratic national conventions required backing from two-thirds of the delegates for the nomination of President and Vice-President. Support for the two-thirds rule originated in the South during the 1830s, and that section had long regarded it as a vital protection against the nomination of candidates unsympathetic to its problems. Although assailed by certain quarters in the party as violating the democratic principle of majority rule, allowing as it did one third of the delegates to prevent a decision, it was defended and maintained on the philosophical ground that democracy owes protection to the minority. The two-thirds rule was also justified, its adherents argued, because it guarded the firmest Democratic section since the Civil War, the South, against the imposition of an unwanted nominee by the less habitually loyal North, East, and West.[26] Elimination of this rule, therefore, both weakened the influence of Southern Democracy and facilitated the adoption of a national reform program. More significantly, it removed an important obstacle to the transformation of a decentralized party, responsible only to a local electorate, into an organization more responsive to the will of a national party leader—the President—and the interests of a national electorate.

Nevertheless, Roosevelt's command of the party, as events during the 75th Congress were to reveal, had not overcome factionalism within the party; instead, New Deal programs and organizational reforms such as the abolition of the two-thirds rule altered the structure within the party. Hitherto a multi-factional party dominated by sectional interests, the Democrats became, after 1936, a bifactional party, with durable ideological and policy divisions.[27] Roosevelt's disregard for conventional partisan practices during his first term opened its ranks to an array of liberal groups and movements, thus making possible the reestablishment of the party's majority for the first time since the Civil War. But the

[26]A lengthy primary account of the debate over the two-thirds rule as it took shape during the 1930s is provided by Frank Clarkin, "Two-Thirds Rule Facing Abolition," *New York Times*, January 5, 1936, Section 4, 10.

[27]Ralph M. Goldman, *Search for Consensus: The Story of the Democratic Party* (Philadelphia: Temple University Press, 1979), 326.

aspirations of the new liberal claimants—notably, labor, Blacks, and women—clashed with most southern Democrats, who still maintained a strong presence in the party councils.[28] Southern Democrats played the leading role in weakening the wages and hours bill, and in defeating the controversial institutional reforms that dominated Roosevelt's second term, namely, the Court reform bill and the executive reorganization proposal. As Homer Cummings wrote in his diary on August 1, 1937, "[I]t is generally felt that back of all these various fights, including the Supreme Court fight, there lies the question of the nomination of 1940, and the incidental control of party destinies."

An "elimination committee" was formed a few months later in anticipation of taking this struggle for the soul of the Democratic party to the American people during the 1938 primary campaigns. It was headed by two intimate White House advisors—Harry Hopkins, who assumed a general supervisory role, and Thomas Corcoran, who became the day to day head of operations. Roosevelt formally launched the purge campaign with his fireside chat to the nation on June 24, 1938. The speech was prepared by Corcoran and another member of the elimination committee, Ben Cohen; but Roosevelt himself dictated the most vital passage of the message—that drawing a distinction between liberals and conservatives and proclaiming his intention to liberalize the Democratic party. Liberals, the President told the nation, insisted that "new remedies could be adopted and successfully maintained in this country under the present form of government if we use government as an instrument of cooperation to provide these remedies." This was a process, FDR continued, that was far from complete. True liberals were opposed, therefore, "to the kind of moratorium on reform which, in effect, is reaction itself." In contrast to the liberal pursuit of circumspect, but intrepid progress, conservatives rejected change willy-nilly. "The ... conservative school of thought ... does not recognize the need for government itself to step in and take action to meet these problems," FDR argued. "It believes individual initiative and private philanthropy will solve them—that we ought to repeal many of the things we have

---

[28]The "solid South" enabled Democrats from below the Mason-Dixon line to benefit disproportionately from the seniority rule—many Southerners, as a result, held key committee positions. Moreover, the South was important to party finances; owing to the effectiveness of Farley's organization there, more than 37% of all Democratic contributions of $100 or more in 1936 came from the South. See Louise Overacker, "Campaign Funds in the Presidential Election of 1936," *American Political Science Review*, vol. 31 (1937), 496.

done and go back . . . to the kind of government we had in the twenties."[29]

The critical question in the coming primaries, Roosevelt concluded, was to which of these general schools of thought do the candidates belong. As head of the Democratic party, he argued, he was charged with the responsibility of carrying out liberal principles as set forth in the 1936 platform. He had every right, therefore, to speak "in those few instances where there may be a clear issue between Democratic candidates for a Democratic nomination." Leaving little doubt as to where those critical contests would take place, FDR characterized his political opponents as Copperheads, an allusion to the bitter sectional conflict of the Civil War period. "Never before have we had so many Copperheads," he said of those who counseled an end to reform, "and you will remember that it was the Copperheads who, in the days of the war between the states, tried their best to make Lincoln and his Congress give up the fight, let the nation remain split in two and return to peace—peace at any price."[30] Roosevelt's reference to the events of the Civil War and the fact that he most actively sought to unseat incumbent Democrats in the South, conjured up images in Southerners of a renewed Northern assault that, as the conservative Virginia Senator Carter Glass wrote a friend, "will soon precipitate another reconstruction era for us."[31]

A New Deal reconstruction of southern politics portended more than a cyclical realignment of parties. It suggested the possibility of a party transformation that would end in an alignment of liberals and conservatives that many progressive reformers, beginning with Woodrow Wilson, had long hoped for.[32] As Roosevelt observed a few years later in defending his attack on conservative Democrats who were reluctant to go along with the New Deal program:

> My participation in these primary campaigns was slurringly referred to, by those who were opposed to liberalism, as a "purge." The word became a slogan for those who tried to misrepresent my conduct to make it appear to be an effort to defeat certain Senators and Representatives who had voted against one measure or another recommended by me. . . . Nothing could be further from the truth. I was not interested in personality. Nor was I interested in particular measures. . . . I was, however, primarily interested in seeing to it that the

[29]Roosevelt, *Public Papers and Addresses*, 7:398–399.
[30]Ibid., 395.
[31]Glass to Jack Dionne, October 17, 1938, Carter Glass Papers, Accession Number 2913, Box 383, University of Virginia Library.

Democratic party and the Republican party should not be merely
Tweedledum and Tweedledee to each other. I was chiefly interested in
continuing the Democratic party as the liberal, forward looking party
in the United States.[33]

ADMINISTRATIVE REFORM AND THE NECESSITY OF PARTY DECLINE

After the 1938 purge campaign, the columnist Raymond Clapper observed that "no president has ever gone as far as Mr.
Roosevelt in striving to stamp his policies upon his party."[34] This
extraordinary partisan effort began a process whereby the party
system was eventually transformed from local to national and programmatic party organizations. At the same time, the New Deal
made partisanship, at least as it affected the beliefs and habits of
the electorate, less important. Roosevelt's partisan leadership, although it did effect important changes in the Democratic party,
and eventually the Republican party as well, ultimately envisioned
a personal link with the public that would better enable him to
make use of his position as leader of the nation, not just the leader
of the party governing the nation.[35]

The members of the elimination committee, like most of the
so-called New Dealers, were executives and lawyers who were essentially without organizational or popular support. "The New
Dealers without Roosevelt were a sect, not a majority," the historian Joseph Lash has written of the purge committee. "Roosevelt's
majority in the absence of party control was impotent."[36] In the
face of this difficulty, the task as defined by FDR was not to systematically overhaul the party organization—the purge team by
temperament and background was ill-suited to such a project.
Rather, Roosevelt sought to put his stamp upon the Democratic
party by transmuting collective into executive responsibility.

[33]Roosevelt, *Public Papers and Addresses*, 7:xxxi–xxxii.
[34]Raymond Clapper, "Roosevelt Tries the Primaries," *Current History*, 49 (October, 1938), 16.
[35]Morton J. Frisch, *Franklin D. Roosevelt: The Contribution of the New Deal to American Political Thought and Practice* (Boston: St. Wayne, 1975), 79.
[36]Joseph Lash, *The Dealers and the Dreamers: A New Look at the New Deal* (New
York: Doubleday, 1988), 353. Former NRA director General Hugh Johnson
dubbed the members of the purge committee "White House Janizaries." Janizaries
were soldiers (at first, mostly castrated personal slaves, later conscripts and sons of
subject Christians) who served Turkish Sultans from the 14th to the 19th centuries; the Janizaries became so potent that, when they revolted in 1826, thousands
of them had to be killed, the rest dispersed, their organization abolished. By his
appellation, Johnson meant to imply, not without cause, that the purge committee
was comprised of an inner-circle of political isolates who were vainly seeking to remake the Democratic party. *Time*, September 12, 1938, 22.

In all but one of the 1938 primary campaigns in which he participated, Roosevelt chose to make a direct appeal to public opinion rather than attempt to work through or reform the regular party apparatus. This undertaking of a large-scale appeal to the nation was encouraged by Progressive reforms, especially the direct primary, which had begun to weaken the grip of party organization on the voters. For example, William H. Meier, Democratic County Chairman from Nebraska, wrote Farley in 1938 that his state's direct primary law had "created a situation which has made candidates too independent of the party."[37] The loosening of candidates and voters from party organizations was a development FDR supported and hoped to advance further. Like Wilson, as he made clear in his fireside chat initiating the purge, Roosevelt endorsed a selection process that "abolished the convention system and gave party voters themselves the chance to pick their candidates."[38]

The spread of the direct primary gave the President the opportunity to make a direct appeal to the people over the heads of congressional candidates and local party leaders. Thereby, it provided an attractive vehicle for Roosevelt to put his own stamp upon the party. Radio broadcasting had made the opportunity to appeal directly to large audiences even more enticing. Of course, this was bound to be especially tempting to an extremely popular President with as fine a radio presence as Roosevelt.

After the defeat of the court-"packing" plan, FDR's close associate Felix Frankfurter wrote the President a long handwritten letter, urging him to allay the bewilderment then reigning in the country over the President's struggles with the Supreme Court and Congress. "The public is . . . greatly confused," Frankfurter wrote on August 9, 1937, "and you alone can dissipate this confusion and renew . . . their dependence on you by a clear, detailed simple explanation as only you are capable of conveying." The total effect of such a message, the Harvard law professor continued, would be magnified by FDR's extraordinary skill in using the airwaves. "The contagiousness of your personality over the radio, the warmth of your voice and your being," would reawaken the "past accumulation of your meaning in their feelings," he assured Roosevelt. "You are absolutely right about the radio," FDR responded a few days later. Perhaps in anticipation of the purge

[37]William H. Meier to James Farley, December 23, 19, Official File 300 (democratic National Committee), Roosevelt Papers.

[38]Roosevelt, *Public Papers and Addresses*, 7:397–398.

campaign, he wrote, "I feel like saying to the country—'You will here from me soon and often. This is not a threat but a promise.' "[39]

In the final analysis, the "benign dictatorship" Roosevelt sought to impose on the Democratic party was more conducive to corroding the American party system than to reforming it. Wilson's prescription for party reform—extraordinary presidential leadership—posed a serious, if not intractable dilemma: on the one hand the decentralized character of politics in the United States can be modified only by vigorous presidential leadership; on the other hand, a President determined to fundamentally alter the connection between the executive and his party eventually will shatter party unity. In this light, Herbert Croly criticized Wilson's concept of presidential party leadership:

At the final test the responsibility is his rather than that of his party. The party which submits to such a dictatorship, however benevolent, cannot play its own proper part in a system of partisan government. It will either cease to have any independent life or its independence will eventually assume the form of a revolt.[40]

Roosevelt was well aware of the limited extent to which his purposes could be achieved by party government in the American context. In fact, it is useful to consider further Croly's criticism of Wilson's concept of party leadership, because as FDR was sensitive to this criticism, it sheds light on the long-term objectives and consequences of New Deal reform.[41]

[39]Frankfurter to FDR, August 9, 1937, Thomas Corcoran Papers, Box 210, Folder: Franklin D. Roosevelt, 1937; and FDR to Frankfurter, August 12, 1937, Felix Frankfurter Papers, Microfilm Reel 60; both collections in Library of Congress, Manuscript Division, Washington, D.C.

[40]Croly, *Progressive Democracy,* 346.

[41]Croly's critique of Wilson was apparently on the mind of the celebrated journalist W. A. White in October, 1937. Writing to Frankfurter, he expressed, in words that were strikingly similar to Croly's, that if FDR "expected to maintain a monolith party in a democracy, he should have reinforced it with steel rods of counsel! Otherwise a monolith party either crumbles or, if maintained, is not a democratic institution." Two months later, White's message reached the White House through Farley, who received, and, in turn, showed the President, an almost identical letter as the one previously sent to Frankfurter. An additional thought was expressed in the letter to Farley, however. In reference to the great differences dividing the "blocks" that added up to Roosevelt's 1936 landslide, White suggested a separate presidential New Deal coalition might emerge from the inevitable demise of the Democratic organization. "If our beloved leader cannot find the common multiple between John Lewis and Carter Glass," White wrote on December 28, "he will have

In Croly's understanding of progressive democracy, Wilson was correct in viewing nineteenth century constitutional mechanisms and party politics as impediments to programmatic reform. He was wrong, however, in not facing up to the fact that true reform presupposed not the reform of the party system but its demise. The popularity of measures such as direct democracy in the United States revealed how centralized and disciplined parties went against the looser genius of American politics. To the extent that the government became committed to a democratic program that was essentially social in character, the American people would find intolerable a two-party system that stood between popular will and governmental machinery.[42]

At the same time, Wilson's false hope for partisanship caused him to underestimate the degree to which progressive democracy required administrative aggrandizement, that is, the development of administrative agencies as the principal instruments of democratic life. For Croly, progressive democracy's commitment to expanding the programmatic responsibilities of the national government "particularly need[ed] an increase of administrative authority and efficiency." In addition, the growing dependence of elected officials upon public opinion would yield a more flexible and fluid method of representation, thus necessarily imposing an increased burden on the administrative department of government. The American party system, however, was established as an institution to control administrative authority—it "bestowed upon the divided Federal government a certain unity of control, while at the same time it prevented the increased efficiency of the Federal system from being obnoxious to local interests." Consequently, the weakening of administrative authority, although rooted in the "pioneer" conditions of the nineteenth century, was an essential and incorrigible aspect of the two party system in the United States. "Under American conditions," therefore, "a strong responsible and efficient administration of the law and public business would be fatal to partisan responsibility."[43]

---

to take a mantel and crack the monolith, forget that he had a party, and build his policy with the pieces which fall under his hammer." In a sense, this is what FDR attempted in undertaking the purge campaign the following summer. White to Frankfurter, October 11, 1937, Microfilm Reel 60, Frankfurter Papers; and White to Farley, December 28, 1937, Box 35, Folder: Roosevelt, Franklin D., 1938—January-April, James Farley Papers; both collections housed in the Library of Congress, Manuscripts Department.

[42]*Progressive Democracy*, 345–348.

[43]Ibid., 346–347.

Wilson did, in fact, find it necessary as President to sacrifice administrative reform on the altar of party unity. At the time of his election to the Presidency, Wilson was one of the Vice-Presidents of the Civil Service League; and he had declared his support on numerous occasions for the merit system. But especially during his first term, there was a reaction against the substantial expansion of civil service protections carried out by his two Republican predecessors, Theodore Roosevelt and William Taft. Moreover, as noted, to the dismay of the President's progressive supporters, traditional patronage practices dominated his appointments to executive departments and agencies.

In Croly's view, the triumph of progressive democracy necessarily required, as Theodore Roosevelt's bolt from the Republican ranks in 1912 foreshadowed, the destruction of the American party system. Indeed, the Progressive party's support for a more "direct government," organized by measures such as the direct primary, as well as the initiative, referendum, and recall, reflected its commitment to dispense with the two party system. As the historian Barry Karl has written of the Progressive party's 1912 campaign, it "was as much an attack on the whole concept of political parties as it was an effort to create a single party whose doctrinal clarity and moral purity would represent the true interest of the nation as a whole."[44]

The debate within the progressive tradition concerning the appropriate role of party is a critical precursor to New Deal partisanship. Unlike Croly, Roosevelt was not willing to abandon the two party system. He believed party leadership within the traditional party framework, at least for the time being, was necessary to organize public opinion into a governing coalition.[45] FDR was

[44]Barry Karl, *The Uneasy State: The United States from 1915 to 1945* (Chicago: University of Chicago Press, 1983), 234–235.

[45]In 1929, John Dewey and other progressives organized the League for Independent Political Action, which called for the formation of a third party that might serve as a vehicle for meaningful reform. "Quite apart from a deliberate and sinister connection with malefactors of great wealth, the parties are out of touch with present needs and realities," Dewey wrote in an essay for the *New Republic*. "They perpetuate and cling to ideas and ideals of a past that has forever departed. . . . They mouth the watchwords of bygone generations, they appeal to Jefferson and Lincoln, because they are themselves anachronisms." "The Present Crisis," first published as part of a four part series in the *New Republic*, March 18, 1931, 115–117, printed in *The Works of John Dewey*, ed. Jo Anne Boydston (Carbondale and Edwardsville: Southern Illinois University Press, 1985), 6:159. In this position, Dewey had the strong support of Paul Douglas, a fellow member of the League for Independent Political Action, whose 1932 volume *The Coming of A New Party*, was brought to the attention of FDR by a charter member of the Brains Trust, Rexford

persuaded, however, that the tradition of party politics dictated that strengthening the state required the decline, if not the demise, of partisan politics. He shared the view of New Nationalists that the traditional party apparatus was for the most part beyond repair, so wedded was it to the fragmented institutions of American politics. For example, when Ray Stennard Baker, Wilson's close associate and biographer, wrote FDR in September, 1936, complaining of the Democratic machine in Massachusetts, which was dominated by the notorious local boss, James Curley, Roosevelt's response was one of sympathetic resignation. "There is, I fear, much too much in what you say," the President answered, "but what is a poor fellow to do about it: I wish I knew."[46]

Even if the intransigent localism of the party system could be eliminated, and a more national party system formed, there would still be the Constitution's division and separation of powers to overcome. These institutional arrangements, even if nationalized, would still encourage the free play of rival interests and factions, thus making ongoing cooperation between the President and Congress unlikely. This skepticism about party government—about the possibility of parties providing a political basis for cooperation between the President and Congress within the Constitution— helps to explain why the purge campaign was limited to a few Senate and House contests, for the most part in the South, rather than planned as a more systematic nationwide attempt to elect New Dealers. Many members of the elimination committee wanted to make, with just a few exceptions, 100 percent "followship" of presidential measures the criterion, with support of the court bill the

---

Tugwell. Roosevelt, then fighting for the Democratic nomination, dismissed the proposal for a third party. According to Tugwell's account, FDR said of Douglas and Dewey: "[S]uppose someone with similar ideas, but with more political forsight, . . . got a major party's nomination and was elected; wasn't that better? In a practical sense—that is, in the sense of making headway toward such objectives— was there any other way in a democracy?. . . . The Democratic offering would be less than the radicals would like, but it would be something voters would accept." R. G. Tugwell, *The Brains Trust* (New York: The Viking Press, 1968), 161. FDR understood that the incorrigible character of the party system did not simply reflect its decrepitude. In fact, its institutional fragmentation and ideological promiscuity were symptomatic of obstacles to party government deeply ingrained in the U.S. Constitution. Just as New Dealers chose to circumvent or reappraise fundamental constitutional principles and mechanisms rather than assault them directly, so the Roosevelt administration's party politics avoided a full-scale challenge to the traditional patterns of partisan practices.

[46]Baker to FDR, September 26, 1936; FDR to Baker, September 30, 1936; both in President's Personal File 2332, Roosevelt Papers.

acid test. Enthusiastic backers of the purge who participated in the counsels of the committee, including Harry Hopkins and Thomas Corcoran, were not discouraged by the fact that such a standard would mark one-half of the Democratic senators seeking renomination and fully a majority of the members of the House. This would be a "straightforward way to go about the realignment of liberals and conservatives as recommended by FDR in his fireside chat," the more militant members of the purge committee believed. But Roosevelt's finer political instincts dictated a less inclusive list. "He sought to make a few examples," Raymond Clapper wrote in 1938, "hoping thereby to cow other Senators and Representatives into more submissive behavior and to keep his fight and his program a live crusading, dynamic thing in the public mind."[47]

The immense failure of the purge to imprint the New Deal indelibly upon his party majority only reinforced FDR's disinclination to seek a fundamental restructuring of the party system. In the dozen states where the President acted against entrenched incumbents, he was successful in only two—Oregon and New York. Moreover, the purge campaign galvanized opposition throughout the nation, apparently contributing to the heavy losses the Democrats sustained in the 1938 general elections. E. E. Schattschneider calls the purge campaign "one of the greatest experimental tests of the nature of the American party system ever made."[48] Yet this experiment seemed to indicate the recalcitrance of traditional party politics. Former Wisconsin Governor, Philip La Follette, one of several progressives who went down to crushing defeat in the wake of FDR's attempt to strengthen discipline within the party councils, wrote in *Nation* soon thereafter: "The results of the so-called purge campaign by President Roosevelt showed that the fight to make the Democratic party liberal is a hopeless one." Yet the problem went beyond the Democratic party. Another defeated progressive Governor, Frank Murphy of Michigan, lamented the "combination of habit and tradition . . . that brought reactionary victories in many states." Roosevelt's defeat in 1938, therefore, reflected aspects of American politics that were "deep-rooted,"

[47]Clapper, "Roosevelt Tries the Primaries," 18. See also, Turner Catledge, "The New Deal Councils Split Over Choice of Foes For Purge," *New York Times,* June 29, 1938, 1, 6.

[48]E. E. Schattschneider, *Party Government* (New York: Farrar and Rinehart, 1942), 163.

Murphy observed, "and can be permanently overcome only by the slow process of education."[49]

Schattschneider, chairman of the American Political Science Association Committee on Political Parties, drew a different conclusion. FDR's party leadership anticipated and influenced the report of the APSA Committee, published in 1950, which called for a party system comprised of national policy-oriented organizations capable of carrying out platforms or proposals presented to the people during the course of an election.[50] In one of a series of lectures that would serve as the substantial core around which the Committee would construct its final handiwork, Schattschneider asserted that the failed purge campaign did not render the struggle for party government a moot point. "The outcome of the purge of 1938," he argued, "does not prove that a more serious attempt supported by the whole body of national party leaders could not bring overwhelming pressure to bear on the local party leaders who control congressional nominations."[51] But neither FDR nor any President since has risked a similar effort, let alone a more expansive one, to hold their fellow partisans to a national party program. Indeed, the purge campaign and its aftermath suggest how resistance to party government under presidential leadership is not merely built into the Constitution and laws. It is deeply rooted in a regime that gives preference to a different way of governing.[52]

The Roosevelt administration's rejection of party government thus developed for reasons both practical and principled, for constitutional considerations that are at once excruciatingly American and a severe challenge to the traditional concept of government responsibility in the United States. The "economic constitutional order" conceived of New Deal programs, like social security, as rights. In principle, therefore, these programs should be set up as permanent entitlements, like speech and assembly, beyond the vagaries of public opinion, elections, and party politics. Once established, as a member of the Roosevelt administration's Committee

---

[49]Philip LaFollette, Elmer Bensen, and Frank Murphy, "Why We Lost," *The Nation*, December 3, 1938, 587, 590. In the general election, the Democrats lost eighty seats in the House and eight in the Senate, as well as thirteen governorships.

[50]American Political Science Association Committee on Political Parties, *Toward A More Responsible Two-Party System* (New York: Rinehart, 1950).

[51]E. E. Schattschneider, "The Struggle For Party Government," originally published in 1948, printed in *The Party Battle* (New York: Arno Press, 1974), 40.

[52]For a good historical treatment of the limits of party government in the United States, see James Sterling Young and Russell L. Riley, "Party Government and Political Culture," Paper presented at the American Political Science Association Annual Meeting, San Francisco, September, 1990.

on Presidential Management (the so-called Brownlow Committee) put it:

We may assume the nature of the problems of American life are such as not to permit any political party for any length of time to abandon most of the collectivist functions which are now being exercised. This is true even though the details of policy programs may differ and even though the old slogans of opposition to governmental activity will survive long after their meaning has been sucked out.[53]

Thus, the most significant institutional reforms of the New Deal did not promote party government, but fostered instead a program that would help the President govern in the *absence* of party government. This program, as embodied in the 1937 executive reorganization bill, was based on the Brownlow Committee report. It proposed measures that would significantly expand the staff support of the executive office and greatly extend presidential authority over the executive department, including the independent regulatory commissions. The strengthened executive that would emerge from this reform would also be delegated authority to govern, so that as Luther Gulick, a member of the Brownlow Committee, anticipated, laws would be little more than "a declaration of war, so that the essence of the program is in the gradual unfolding of the plan in actual administration."[54]

Party politics, therefore, would be displaced by executive administration, by an executive-centered administrative politics generated by the activities of a dominant and dominating Presidency. Whereas a reconstituted party system would have established stronger linkages between the executive and legislature, the administrative program of the New Deal would combine executive

---

[53]Joseph Harris, "Outline for a New York Conference," April 8, 1936, *Papers of the President's Committee on Administrative Management*, Roosevelt Library. The President's Committee on Administrative Management, headed by Louis Brownlow, played a central role in the planning and politics of institutional reform from 1936–1940. It's 1937 report, according to Theodore Lowi, represents the most important "contribution by academics to public discourse on the fundamentals of American democracy." Lowi, *The Personal President: Power Invested, Promise Unfulfilled* (Ithaca: Cornell University Press, 1985), 68. Lowi rates the aforementioned report of the APSA Committee on Political Parties, *Toward A More Responsible Two-Party System*, second only to the Brownlow Committee report in its contribution to public discussion about the genius of American democracy. Interestingly, these two contributions offer alternative paths to a more progressive democracy, reflecting a disagreement that touches on important constitutional issues.

[54]Luther Gulick, "Politics, Administration, and the New Deal," *The Annals*, vol. 169 (September, 1933), 64.

action and public policy, so that the President and administrative
agencies would be delegated authority to govern, thus making unnecessary the constant cooperation of party members in Congress
and the States. Louis Brownlow, in a 1943 memorandum, reflected
on this objective of executive reorganization: "We must reconsider
critically the scholarly assumption, which has almost become a
popular assumption, that the way to produce unity between legislature and executive is to take steps towards merging the two."
Thus, commenting specifically on a proposal that the United
States abandon its presidential system in favor of a parliamentary
system, Brownlow adds:

In view of the extreme improbability that such a measure would receive
organized support, it is worth mentioning only because it carries to a
logical conclusion the common proposals (1) to have Congress establish
by statute a cabinet or administrative council for the president; (2) to
give department heads or "Cabinet" members seats in Congress, the
right to take part in Congressional discussions, or the duty to defend
their administration before Congress; (3) to set up a joint legislative-
executive committee, or committees, to plan policy and supervise administration; and (4) to create a committee of congressional leaders to
advise the President. . . . *In direct opposition to this assumption and these proposals, it may be suggested that the objective to be sought is not to unify executive
and legislature, but to unify governmental policy and administration.*[55]

Thus, Roosevelt and the members of the administrative management committee rejected the curiously persistent idea, first advocated by Wilson, that it was possible to strengthen the party
system by remodeling the Presidency somewhat after the pattern
of the British Prime Minister. They looked instead to presidential
government to achieve an activist state on American soil.

This did not mean, however, that political parties were irrelevant to the task of strengthening national administrative power. In
fact, the administrative reform program became, at FDR's urging,
a *party* program; as a result, ironically, a policy directed to making
party politics less important became a major focus of party respon-

---

[55]Louis Brownlow, "Perfect Union," January 27, 1943, Appendix to Official Files
101 and 101b, 38–39, Roosevelt Papers. Significantly, the President's Committee on
Administrative Management rejected a paper it had commissioned from William Y.
Elliot, professor of government at Harvard, which recommended the creation of an
American variant of Cabinet government. Considering party government neither
practical nor desirable, the Committee did not have Elliot's paper published among
its supporting documents in 1937. Don K. Price, *America's Unwritten Constitution:
Science, Religion, and Political Responsibility* (Cambridge: Harvard University Press,
1985), 121.

sibility. So strongly did Roosevelt favor this legislation that House majority leader Sam Rayburn appealed for party unity before the critical vote on the executive reorganization bill, arguing that the defeat of this legislation would amount to a "vote of no confidence" in the President.[56]

FDR lost this vote of confidence on administrative reform in April, 1938, as the House of Representatives, with massive Democratic defections, voted down the legislation. It was a devastating defeat for Roosevelt, and, as noted, it had an important influence on his decision to undertake the purge campaign a few months later. The defeat of the administrative reform proposal, coming on the heels of the defeat of the court-"packing" plan, which, itself, was closely linked to the task of strengthening national administrative power, left Roosevelt little recourse but to go to the country.[57] The purge failed at the polls, but it scared recalcitrant Democrats who became more conciliatory toward their President on a few matters after the 1938 election. Administrative reform was one of these and in 1939, a compromise but nonetheless significant reorganization bill passed the Congress.

Although considerably weaker than FDR's original proposal, the 1939 Executive reorganization Act provided authority for the creation of the White House Office and the Executive Office of the President; and it enhanced the Chief Executive's control over administrative agencies. As such, the 1939 administrative reform legislation represents the genesis of the institutional presidency, which was better equipped to govern independently of the constraints imposed by the division and separation of powers. It set off a new dynamic whereby executive administration, coupled with the greater personal responsibility of the President enhanced by FDR's political leadership and the emergence of the mass media, displaced in important ways collective responsibility.

---

[56]*Congressional Record*, 75th Congress, 3rd Session, April 8, 1938, 5121.

[57]Significantly, the two Supreme Court cases that triggered the dispute between Roosevelt and the judiciary were *Humphrey's Executor* v. *U.S.* (295 U.S. 602, 1935) and *A.L.A. Schecter Poultry Corp. et al.* v. *United States* (295 U.S. 553, 1935), both of which imposed constraints on the administrative authority of the president. William Leuchtenburg notes that FDR's angry reaction to the *Humphry* decision, which denied Roosevelt's right to remove a commissioner from an independent regulatory agency, is misunderstood as an arbitrary act of retaliation in the face of a personal blow from the Supreme Court. In fact, it was "a rational attempt to enable the presidency to emerge as the central institution to cope with the problems of the twentieth century world." Leuchtenburg, "The Case of the Contentious Commissioner: Humphry's Executor vs. U.S.," in *Freedom and Reform*, Harold M. Hyman and Leonard W. Levy, eds. (New York: Harper and Row, 1967), 312.

The battle for the destiny of the Democratic party during FDR's second term, therefore, was directly tied to strengthening the presidency and the executive department as the vital center of government action, of "enlightened administration." In this way, the Democratic party was transformed into a party of administration, dedicated to enacting an institutional program that would make parties less important. It became a party to end party politics. Theodore Roosevelt and Herbert Croly had conceived of the Progressive Party campaign as an assault on party politics. Unlike his cousin, however, Franklin Roosevelt presided over a full-scale partisan realignment, the first in American history that placed executive leadership at the heart of its long-term approach to politics and government. The traditional party system had provided Presidents with a stable basis of popular support and, episodically, during critical partisan realignments, with the opportunity to achieve national reform. What was once episodic, liberal reformers insisted, must now become routine. As the Brownlow Committee Report put it, "Our national will must be expressed not merely in a brief, exultant moment of electoral decision, but in persistent, determined, competent day-by-day administration of what the nation had decided to do."[58]

Thus, the New Deal realignment prepared the ground for the decline of party, a development that FDR explicitly anticipated and supported. Interestingly, Roosevelt chose the 1940 Jackson day dinner, a party event, to herald a less partisan future. To establish the right mood, FDR went so far as to invite the Republican leaders to the Democratic celebration, an invitation they politely declined. In his address, Roosevelt observed that the independent vote was on the increase, that party loyalties were becoming less significant, and that, as he put it, "the future lies with those wise political leaders who realize the great public is interested more in government than in politics."[59] The resurgence of party politics in the 1930s, then, disguised how the New Deal continued the progressive project to dismantle the party system—how programmatic liberalism required the emergence of a policy-making state, in which party politics and debate were subordinated to a "second bill of rights" and the delivery of services associated with those rights.

For a time, the modern presidency was at the center of this new political universe. With the strengthening of executive administration, the presidency became disassociated from party politics,

[58]*Report of the President's Committee on Administrative Management* (Washington D.C.: Government Printing Office, 1937), 53.
[59]Roosevelt, *Public Papers and Addresses*, 9:28.

undermining the latter's importance. As the presidency gradually evolved into a ubiquitous institution, it preempted party leaders in many of their most important tasks: linking the President to interest groups, staffing the executive department, policy development, and, most important, campaign support. No longer were Presidents clearly elected and governing as head of a party, but instead were elected and governed as the head of a personal organization they created in their own image.[60]

The purpose of New Deal reform, however was not to strengthen presidential government in the United States *per se*. Rather, the Presidency was strengthened under the assumption that, as the national office, it would be an ally of progressive reform. Consequently, executive power was refurbished in a way that was compatible with the objectives of programmatic liberalism. In fact, a major purpose of the administrative reform program was to insulate reformers and reforms from the presidential election cycle. By executive orders, issued with authority granted by the 1939 Executive Reorganization Act, most of the emergency programs of the New Deal were established as permanent institutions. Moreover, the Roosevelt administration obtained legislative authority in the 1940 Ramspeck Act to extend Civil Service protection over most of the New Deal loyalists who were brought to Washington to staff the newly created welfare state.[61] New Deal civil service reform, therefore, did not replace politics with civil service procedures dedicated to "neutral competence." Rather, it transformed the political character of administration.

Previously, the choice was posed as one between politics and spoils on the one hand, and nonpartisan, nonpolitical administration on the other. The New Deal celebrated an administrative politics that denied nourishment to the regular party apparatus, but

---

[60]Although the literature on party development has generally neglected the importance of presidential leadership and the evolution of the presidency as an institution, there are a few exceptions. See, especially, Harold Bass, "The President and National Party Organization," in *Presidents and Their Parties: Leadership or Neglect?*, ed. Robert Harmel, (New York: Praeger, 1984); Theodore Lowi, *The Personal President: Power Invested, Promise Unfulfilled* (Ithaca: Cornell University Press, 1985), especially Chapters 3 and 4; and Lester G. Seligman and Carey R. Covington, *The Coalitional Presidency* (Chicago: The Dorsey Press, 1989).

[61]The Ramspeck Act authorized the extension by the President of the merit system rules to nearly 200,000 positions previously exempted by law. Roosevelt took early advantage of this authorization in 1941 and by executive order extended the coverage of civil service protection to the point where about 95 percent of the permanent service was included. Leonard D. White, "Franklin Roosevelt and the Public Service," *Public Personnel Review*, 6 (July, 1945), 142.

fed instead an executive department oriented toward expanding liberal programs.

The new merger of politics and administration that developed during the New Deal took an interesting course with the passage of the Hatch Act in 1939. Until the passage of this bill, which barred most federal employees from participating in campaigns, the Roosevelt administration had used the growing army of federal workers in state and local political activity, including some of the purge campaigns. The Hatch Act demolished any prospects for building a national Roosevelt political machine that was distinct from the regular party organization. Many New Dealers urged the President to veto this legislation, fearing that it would undo what they viewed as a felicitous union of politics and administration. Charles M. Shreve, Executive Director of the Young Democrats of America, argued as much in a letter sent to Roosevelt while the President was considering whether to sign the Hatch bill. "Democracy racy will receive a great setback and the calibre of our public servants will drop drastically, if it becomes law," Shreve wrote. "There is no justification for making eunuchs of the future statesmen and leaders of our Democracy."[62]

Congress's enactment of the Hatch bill, however, was not so clearly a political defeat for Roosevelt, for FDR never wanted to create a "modern Tammany." He was more interested in orienting the executive branch for the formation of liberal public policy than in developing a national political machine, and the insulation of federal officials from party politics was not incompatible with such a task. The purge campaign revealed how the involvement of New Dealers such as Harry Hopkins and Thomas Corcoran in partisan politics could possibly undermine their usefulness in developing and carrying out welfare policy. The task of "circumspect but intrepid social enterprise," as Croly put it, required custodians of social welfare policy who were more than experts; however, government service imposed limits on the lengths to which policy activists could be promoters and propogandists. "If men like the New Dealers are to become permanently useful public servants, political eunuchs is precisely what they must be," the journalists Joseph Alsop and Robert Kintner wrote in 1939.[63]

In the final analysis, programmatic liberalism did not require an elaborate party apparatus for its success because the state cre-

---

[62]Charles H. Shreve to Thomas Corcoran, and attached letter to FDR, July 24, 1939, Box 253, Corcoran Papers.

[63]Herbert Croly, *Progressive Democracy*, 361, 368–369; Joseph Alsop and Robert Kintner, *Men Around the President* (New York: Doubleday, Moran, 1939), 196.

ated by the New Deal Democratic party would organize its supporters through the disbursement of welfare benefits. This
explains why Roosevelt, although he fought passage of this legislation, decided to sign the Hatch bill. Not only would such a veto
have split his supporters irretrievably, but it also would have
worked against the achievement of Roosevelt's reform program.[64]

The second Hatch Act, passed in 1940, extended restrictions
on party politics to state and local workers whose principal employment was in connection with any activity that was financed in
whole or in part by the federal government. Roosevelt called for
such an extension upon signing the 1939 bill, lest the restriction
on federal workers rebound to the benefit of state and local machines and further subordinate matters of broad national concern
to private and provincial interests. This concluded a compromise
with Congress that went a long way toward strengthening the non-
partisan character of the New Deal. The complex web of American constitutional government shaped progressive reform in the
1930s so that Roosevelt's extraordinary party leadership was, for a
time, to render party politics remarkably obsolete.[65]

[64]The Roosevelt administration did seriously consider vetoing the Hatch Act.
Thomas Corcoran and Ben Cohen, with the assistance of the Justice Department,
sought to obviate the debate between traditional partisans and nonpartisan reformers by calling for an alternative bill that would restructure rather than transcend
parties. This message criticized the Hatch bill for not covering state and local officials, an oversight that would subject national politics "more than ever . . . to the
influence and control of state and local machines." In addition to recommending
the extension of the Hatch Act to states and localities, the veto message proposed
that campaign finance be revamped. It called for Congress "to recognize the fact of
the party system in American politics by prohibiting all private campaign contributions and appropriating public funds for the use of political parties. Such a measure, the draft veto message averred, might free political associations from "the
dominance or influence of sinister elements and yield unexpected returns in the
elevation of the whole tone of political life." In the end, however, Roosevelt chose
to sign the Hatch bill on the last day this measure would become law without the
President's signature. Although Roosevelt asked the Congress to extend the act to
state and local officials in the future, he made no mention of restructuring the
party system. Corcoran to FDR, July 30, 1939, and attached "Draft Speech on Returning the Hatch Bill," dated July 29, 1939; both located in President's Secretary
File 152, Roosevelt Papers.

[65]The Hatch Act is newly relevant. In May, 1990 the Congress passed a bill that
would have substantially modified the 1939 statute. Under the bill, Federal workers covered by the Hatch Act would have continued to be barred from many partisan activities, such as seeking public office and engaging in political activities
while on the job. But for the first time in half a century, they would have been allowed to hold office in political groups, to endorse candidates publicly, to organize
fund-raising events and political meetings, and to distribute campaign literature.
Charging that the bill "incorrectly politicized the Civil Service," President Bush ve-

CONCLUSION—THE NEW DEAL INHERITANCE AND
PARTY GOVERNMENT

Towards the end of the 1970s, political analysts kept a death watch over the American party system. Reforms and the mass media had deprived political parties of their limited but significant place in American politics, scholars lamented, and there was little prospect of recovery. The decline of party was taken by advocates of party government as cause to press their case anew, with greater urgency. Indeed, many political scientists questioned whether the decline of party was a symptom of fundamental flaws in the American constitution and the philosophy that informed its creation. According to Walter Dean Burnham, the forlorn state of parties pointed overwhelmingly to the conclusion that the American polity had entered the most profound turning point in its history. The task confronting it now was no less than the "construction of instrumentalities of domestic sovereignty to limit individual freedom in the name of collective necessity." This would require "an entirely new structure of parties and of mass behavior, one in which political parties would be instrumentalities of democratic collective purpose." But, Burnham argued, "this in turn seems inconceivable without a preexisting revolution in social values."[66]

The decline of parties in the twentieth century, however, is not the result of ineluctable constitutional forces. It is rather a partisan project, one sponsored by the Democratic party that was built on the foundation of the New Deal realignment. As James Piereson had observed, nearly every reform of the past half century that has weakened the existing parties in the electoral process—more primaries, public financing of campaigns, quotas for constituent groups in the national conventions, and the elimination of patron-

---

toed the legislation, and in a vote that was largely along party lines the Congress upheld the President's vote, albeit by only a two vote margin in the Senate. This was the closest Congress had come to substantially amending the Hatch Act since its enactment in 1939. The partisan vote reflected the consensus view that the legislation would prove a windfall for the Democrats who are generally favored by unions of Federal employees. See Richard L. Berke, "Senate Upholds Veto of Bill on U.S. Workers in Politics," *New York Times,* June 22, 1990, A15. The fight over this effort to amend the Hatch Act was one of several partisan battles for control of administration that broke out during the 1980s and 1990s. These battles, reflecting the renewal of party politics within a framework structured by the administrative state, are discussed briefly in the conclusion. For a more detailed treatment, see Sidney M. Milkis, *The New Deal, the Modern Presidency, and the Transformation of the American Party System* (New York: Oxford University Press, forthcoming), Chapter 9.

[66]Walter Dean Burnham, *Critical Elections and the Mainsprings of American Politics* (New York: W. W. Norton, 1970), 188–189.

age—had been sponsored by the Democratic party, and within that party by its most liberal wing.[67] Furthermore, reforms that weakened the influence of party organizations in the electoral process were concomitant with the reform and expansion of executive administration, a result of the same doctrinal change reflected in the shift from classical to programmatic liberalism. Reforms directly attacking the electoral role of party organizations certainly reduced the partisan character of campaigns; but the development of administrative politics further contributed to the decline of parties by making collective partisan appeals less meaningful in the eyes of the voters in the first place. This is particularly likely to happen when programs or benefits are viewed as "rights." Because it conceives of specific programs as entitlements, programmatic liberalism gave rise to a veritable "administrative constitution," in which policies are deemed worthy of protection from the vagaries of party competition and the electoral process.[68]

The most ardent and effective aspirations for reform since the New Deal have been expressed in demands for new rights, thus continually reducing the political space that allows for party deliberation and choice. It might be said, therefore, that the New Deal reform program preempted the constitutional transformation anticipated by the advocates of "responsible" party government. It did so by sponsoring institutional changes that chartered an alternative path to a more national and programmatic government. This path, the New Dealers believed, was more compatible with the principles and history of American constitutional government. One of the principal architects of this program, Charles Merriam, had observed in 1931 that he did not expect to see the development of a British-style party government in the United States. "There is little probability of a modification of the Constitution either by amendment or custom in such a fashion as to permit the adoption of a parliamentary system," he surmises, "in view of the fact that the trend is strongly in the directions of

[67]Piereson, "Party Government," 46.
[68]E. Donald Elliot has suggested that the expansion of administrative power over the past century has created a "Constitution of the Administrative State," but that this expansion has not been accompanied by formally amending the Constitution. This "quasi-constitutional evolution," as Elliot notes, "is not a mere additive change to the structure of government. Inevitably it has transformed the nature and functions of existing institutions as well." See his "INS v. Chadha: The Administrative Constitution, the Constitution, and the Legislative Veto," *Supreme Court Review* (1983), 167.

Presidential government, with constant strengthening of executive power."[69]

Merriam's commentary was not simply prescient. As a member of the Brownlow Committee, he would play an important part in consolidating the trends he observed. That contribution, however, was made possible by a dramatic, though short-lived, commitment to party responsibility. Roosevelt imposed the task defined by the Brownlow Committee on the Democratic party. By doing so, he strengthened partisanship in the short term and carried out a great experiment on the character of the American party system. But this test of responsible party government transformed the Democratic party into a way station on the road to administrative government—that is, to a centralized and bureaucratic form of democracy that focused on the president and executive agencies for the formulation and execution of public policy. Concomitantly, this development diminished the role of traditional party politics, Congress, and the state legislatures.

As a party of administration, the Democrats established the conditions for the end of parties unless, or until, a party sprang up that was anti-administration. No such party has arisen in American politics, although the Republican party has slouched toward that role. As programmatic liberalism began to lose support, the Republican party under Richard Nixon and especially Ronald Reagan embraced programs such as New Federalism and Regulatory Relief that challenged the institutional legacy of the New Deal. This bolder conservative posture coincided with the construction of a formidable national organization, with strength at the national level that is unprecedented in American politics. From the perspective of the 1980s, some observers have suggested that the New Deal did not lead to the decline of party but to the development of a more national and issue-oriented one.[70]

Nevertheless, the importance of presidential politics and unilateral executive action suggest that Nixon and Reagan essentially continued the institutional legacy of the New Deal. Thus, Repub-

[69]Charles Edward Merriam, "The Written Constitution and Unwritten Attitude," in *The Party Battle*, 85.

[70]For examples, see A. James Reichley, "The Rise of National Parties," in *The New Direction in American Politics*, ed. John E. Chubb and Paul E. Peterson (Washington, D.C.: Brookings Institution, 1985); Cornelius Cotter and John F. Bibby, "Institutionalization of Parties and the Thesis of Party Decline," *Political Science Quarterly*, 95 (Spring, 1980): 1–27; Joseph A. Schlesinger, "The New American Party System," *American Political Science Review*, 79 (December, 1985): 1152–1169; and Paul S. Herrnson, *Party Campaigns in the 1980s* (Cambridge: Harvard University Press, 1988).

lican Presidents, intent upon transforming the liberal political order, have conceived of the presidency as a two-edged sword which could cut in a conservative as well as a liberal direction. The pursuit of conservative policy objectives through administrative action has continued with the accession of George Bush to the White House.[71] Indeed, given that the New Deal was based on a party strategy to replace traditional party politics with administration, it is not surprising that the challenge to liberal policies has produced a conservative "administrative presidency," which has also retarded the revival of partisan politics.[72]

The administrative ambition of Republican Presidents is supported by a modern conservative movement whose advocates prefer not so much to limit the state as to put it to new uses. Thus, the Reagan administration, while promising to bring about "new federalism" and "regulatory relief," was stalled in these tasks by the conviction that a strong national state is necessary to foster economic growth, oppose communism, and nurture "traditional" values.

That the challenge to welfare state politics has focused on the presidency reinforces the need to strengthen executive power as a means to conservative ends. Ironically, the attempt to bring about changes in public policy with administrative tools that were created, for the most part, during Democratic administrations has been thought useful by Republican Presidents facing a hostile Congress and bureaucracy intent upon preserving the programs of those administrations. Conservative presidencies have thus deepened the commitment in the political system to executive administration, by demonstrating (or attempting to demonstrate) that centralized power can serve the purposes of those who oppose the welfare state.

The conservative administrative presidency, of course, has not gone unchallenged. As a program of the Democratic party, the modern presidency depended upon a broad agreement among the Congress, the bureaucracy, and eventually, the courts, to expand programmatic rights. Energetic administration, therefore,

[71]For example, as was the case in the Reagan era, the Bush administration's efforts to weaken environmental, consumer, civil rights, and health regulations have come not through legislative change but through administrative action, delay, and repeal. See Robert Pear, "U.S. Laws Delayed by Complex Rules and Partisanship," *New York Times*, March 31, 1991, 1, 18.

[72]The term *administrative presidency* comes from Richard Nathan's seminal work on the employment of executive action by modern presidents to pursue policy objectives. See Nathan, *The Administrative Presidency* (New York: John Wiley, 1983), which focuses on the Nixon and Reagan programs of administrative management.

depended upon a consensus that powers should be delegated to the executive. By the time Lyndon Johnson left the White House, support for unilateral executive action had begun to erode, occasioned by the controversial use of presidential power in prosecuting the Vietnam War. It virtually disappeared under the strain of divided government that has prevailed virtually without interruption since 1968.

The modern presidency was conceived as an ally of programmatic reform. When this supposition was seemingly violated by Vietnam and subsequent developments, reformers set out to protect liberal programs from unfriendly executives. The result was a "reformation" of New Deal administrative politics, which brought Congress and the courts into the details of administration. The judiciary became an unexpected and especially important source of political energy in the new administrative politics. Indeed, the conception of liberal programs as rights and the evolution of a liberal judiciary combined by the 1970s to establish the courts as the guardians of the liberal order.[73]

Party organization and conflict are certainly not absent from the administrative politics spawned by the New Deal and the opposition it aroused. In fact, the New Deal—and the erosion of traditional decentralized parties—had made possible a new blending of partisanship and administration, one in which administration has become a vehicle for partisan objectives. Parties have shifted much of their effort from the building of constituencies to the administration of public policy; as such, party politics have come to focus on the management of the economy and which party can best cope with problems in the political economy. Moreover, the concept of rights has become increasingly associated with the expansion of national administrative power—even conservatives in the abortion dispute talk of the rights of the unborn.[74] The expansion of rights has further shifted partisan politics away from parties as associations that organize political sentiments into an electoral majority. When rights dominate policy discourse, majority sentiments are commonly viewed as the problem and not the solution. Consequently, as the ongoing dispute between Democratic legislators and the Republican White House over judicial appointments and rulings demonstrates, the Supreme Court has

---

[73]Richard B. Stewart, "The Reformation of Administrative Law,' *Harvard Law Review*, vol. 88 (June, 1975): 1669–1813; Melnick, "The Courts, Congress, and Programmatic Rights."

[74]Harvey C. Mansfield, Jr., "The 1984 Election: Entitlements Versus Opportunity," *Government and Opposition*, vol. 20 (Winter, 1985), 17.

displaced elections as the primary institutional focus of partisan politics. Because administration is so central to current political debates and conflicts, both parties are *above all* parties of administration. The Republicans are the party of administration through the executive branch, while the Democrats are the party of administration through the Congress.[75]

The American people, one suspects, are somewhat mystified by all this, and comforted only in part by the way divided government moderates the ideological polarization and administrative aggrandizement that characterizes modern party politics in the United States. The decentralized parties that once organized political life in the United States were wedded to a commitment to limited government and thus tended to confine our political battles to "safe" issues. The emergence of activist government since the New Deal, however, has attenuated the "constitutional" boundaries that once contained political conflict; and the Reagan "revolution" has further eroded the wall that separates politics and society. The checks that divided government imposes on the extreme tendencies of Democrats and Republicans provide some protection against the abuses of centralized administration; but this security does not come without its costs. The dark side of divided government is that it tends to obscure political responsibility and to mire the government in petty clashes that undermine respect for American political institutions. The 1988 election, in fact, signaled a new low point in the deterioration of our representative institutions that is now more than two decades old. Less than one-half of the eligible electorate bothered to vote in 1988, the lowest turnout in a presidential contest since 1924.

Progressive reformers understood that the development of a more purposeful national government meant loosening the hold of traditional parties on the loyalties and voting habits of citizens. But they failed to appreciate the purpose these parties served as effective channels of democratic participation. American parties, which traced their origins to Jefferson, were critical agents in counteracting the tendency of citizens in the United States to shut themselves up in a limited circle of domestic concerns that were out of reach of broader public causes. By enticing individuals into neighborhood organizations and patronage practices that expanded their tiny private orbits, traditional party organizations

---

[75]Robert Eden, "Partisanship and Constitutional Revolution: The Founders' View Is Newly Problematic," in *Constitutionalism in Perspective: The United States Constitution in Twentieth Century Politics*, ed. Sarah Baumgartner Thurow (Lanham, New York, and London: University Press of America, 1988).

were the primary schools of democracy in which Americans learned the art of association, of citizenship, and formed attachments to government associations.[76]

With the decline of the traditional party system, there has arisen a politics of entitlements that belittles efforts by Democrats and Republicans alike to define a collective purpose with a past and a future—and yields instead a partisanship joined to a form of administrative politics that relegates electoral conflict to the intractable demands of policy advocates. Indeed, a partisanship that emphasizes national administration in support of programmatic rights has little chance to reach beyond the Washington beltway and influence the perceptions and habits of the American people. In V. O. Key's terms, the emergence of parties of administration has strengthened the national organization and the party-in-government, but at the cost of enervating the party-in-the-electorate.[77] This development does not mean, necessarily, that the Democrats and Republicans consider elections unimportant and have despaired of extending their influence through them. It does suggest that, as parties of administration, the Democrats and Republicans are hobbled in their efforts to form vital links with the public.

The political legacy of the New Deal seems to be a more active and better equipped national state, but one without adequate means of common deliberation and judgment. This is the novel and pressing challenge for those who would take the idea of party renewal seriously as the American polity approaches the twenty-first century.

---

[76]Even when political parties were relatively indifferent to broad moral questions and dedicated to the personal ambitions of their members, Tocqueville found them to be valuable political associations in which individuals learned the art of cooperation and became citizens. Tocqueville, *Democracy in America*, 189–195, 509–513, 520–524. See also Wilson Carey McWilliams, "Parties As Civic Associations," in *Party Renewal in America*, Gerald M. Pomper, ed. (New York: Praeger, 1980).

[77]V. O. Key, Jr., *Politics, Parties and Pressure Groups*, 5th edition (New York: Thomas V. Crowell, 1964). For a discussion of the electorate during the 1980s and the prospect for party renewal, see Walter Dean Burnham, "Elections As Democratic Institutions," in *Elections in America*, Kay Lehman Schlozman, ed. (Boston: Allen and Unwin, 1987), 58–60; Martin P. Wattenberg, *The Decline of Political Parties, 1952–1984* (Cambridge: Harvard University Press, 1986); and Benjamin Ginsberg and Martin Shefter, *Politics By Other Means: The Declining Importance of Elections in America* (New York: Basic Books, 1990).

THE NEW DEAL
REVALUATION OF
PARTISANSHIP

Robert Eden

IN THE UNITED STATES, WE TEND TO OVERLOOK THE ROLE OF INTER-
pretation in shaping partisanship because received political traditions and institutions shape our partisans so steadily and unobtru-
sively. They do so in part by upholding a definite notion of the
limits of acceptable, respectable partisanship.[1] Yet while such an interpretation is at work, restraining, directing, and moderating partisan self-assertion, it is chiefly apparent in forbearance, or in the
absence of the behavior it discourages.[2] The interpretations of partisanship that both major political parties embody are normally
unnoticed. They are not the subject of party competition. They are
not disputed in electoral campaigns. They are so widely shared and
seldom contested that almost all Americans take them for granted.[3]

I am grateful to Robert K. Faulkner, Sidney M. Milkis, and Mickey Craig for
thoughtful criticism on an earlier draft of this chapter.

[1] As regards FDR's sensitivity to such interpretations, consider this remark on the
British: "I think they're much more sensible about politics than we as. . . . Clear
down the line, there's a respectability attached to politics in Great Britain that isn't
found here." Diary Notations, Stanley High Papers, October 28, 1936 FDR Library.
Quoted in Milkis, *The Modern Presidency and the Transformation of the American Party
System* (book in manuscript, Oxford University Press).

[2] Forbearance might be said to be the main theme of Martin Van Buren's interpretation of partisanship, on which the American party system was based. See
James W. Ceaser, *Presidential Selection: Theory and Development* (Princeton, NJ:
Princeton University Press, 1979), 123–169; Robert Eden, "Curing the Mischiefs of
Ambition: Party and Constitution in Martin Van Buren's Inaugural Address of
1837." (Paper presented to the Conference on "The Constitution: The Founding
and the Present." The University of Dallas October 16–17, 1987.)

[3] In one respect, the notion that interpretations of party play an important role
in political life is widely accepted: American political scientists have taught for
many years that the Framers adopted a short-sighted, anti-party interpretation of

Only during periods of crisis, like the New Deal, are these long-standing interpretations openly challenged within one or both of the major parties. Only then does the nature and direction of partisan politics become, for a time, a controversial public affair, about which we may deliberate politically and choose.[4] Yet, during such crises we seldom have the leisure (and few have the detachment) to wonder much about the nature of partisanship.[5] The rarity of great political upheavals in American political life; the success of our parties in confirming widely-shared beliefs about the limits of partisanship; and the failure of our political science to cultivate the capacity for wonder—commonly all these combine to make American partisanship appear stable, predictable, routine, and dull. Although many observers have learned from Tocqueville that to domesticate partisanship in this way is a major accomplishment, even those who appreciate the achievement seldom reflect on how it is done.[6]

The New Deal changed our assessment of partisanship, reorienting ambition toward new political objects, directing political passion into new channels, and reshaping the economic rights on

---

partisanship; that the Constitution itself exercised a depressing influence on American political life when the constitutional system was at its height in the 1890s. They understand their scholarship as a corrective to an influential interpretation. In particular, the doctrine of responsible party government was conceived as an alternative to the interpretation of partisanship that informed the Constitution and that could ultimately be traced to the Framers. See James Piereson, "Party Government," *The Political Science Reviewer* 12 (1982:2–53).

[4]Harry V. Jaffa, *Crisis of the House Divided: An Interpretation of the Lincoln-Douglas Debates* (Seattle: University of Washington Press, 1973); William E. Gienapp, *The Origins of the Republican Party, 1852–1856* (New York: Oxford University Press, 1987).

[5]For activists, the advent of crisis may mean "opportunity at last"—the time has come to act, the time for thought is past. This was the response of many Progressives who devoted considerable thought to partisanship during the decades before the New Deal. Compare note 28, on Charles Beard, below; and see John Dewey, "Individualism, Old and New," in *The Later Works, 1925–1953*, ed. Jo Ann Boydston, *Volume 5: 1929–1930*, 91–2; "John Dewey Assails the Major Parties," 442, and his calls for a new party, 444–449; *Volume 5: 1931–1932*, 149–152, 156–189.

[6]Wilson C. McWilliams, Jr. "Tocqueville and Responsible Parties: Individualism, Partisanship and Citizenship in America," in *Challenges to Party Government*, ed. James Mileur and John Kenneth White (Edwardsville, IL: Southern Illinois University Press, 1992). The initial focus of scholarship and commentary was on how parties made the constitutional system work. See James Bryce, *The American Commonwealth* (New York: Commonwealth, 1908), 2:1–3; Roy F. Nichols, *The Invention of the American Political Parties; A Study of Political Improvisation* (New York: The Free Press, 1967): xi–xii; Tocqueville's concern, by contrast, was with the excesses of partisanship—too much in revolutionary France, but also (as he feared would be the case in the United States) too little; great parties and great revolutions in opinion might become impossible due to the political apathy and individualism of a commercial people. See Robert Eden, "Tocqueville on Political Realignment and Constitutional Forms," *The Review of Politics* 48, No. 3 (Summer 1986): 348–372.

which political parties depend. Although many details were improvised, on the whole this transformation was intentional: The New Dealers, and especially Franklin D. Roosevelt, meant to change our political habits in accordance with a new, more "liberal" or Progressive conception of the common good.[7] It is generally acknowledged, of course, that the New Deal set in motion a great transformation in public life by initiating the American welfare state. But the meaning of this change, as it bears upon political parties and habits of partisanship, has been a topic of much controversy.[8] This chapter is an attempt to broaden the perspective in which the New Deal reshaping of American politics is considered. My purpose is not to gauge precisely what the New Dealers accomplished through their reinterpretation of partisanship; that task should engage historians more knowledgeable than I. My concern will rather be to indicate the criteria by which this New Deal accomplishment is to be measured. I shall indicate that primarily by comparing the New Deal revaluation with the Founders' critique of partisanship.

THE FRAMER'S CRITIQUE

To be a partisan is to take a part, to become a partner, in an ongoing political endeavor. In assuming some measure of responsibility for such an endeavor, the partisan lets a harness of mutual obligations prompt his own conduct or rein it in. He allows himself to be tugged by the threads of the moral life that connect the members of the partnership together, and he pulls them in turn. From those threads much of the fabric of his political life will eventually be woven. The web of partisan engagements shapes him morally by drawing him closer to his political friends.[9]

Thus, parties are made up of citizens whose engagement in politics leads them to associate and, in so doing, to distinguish themselves from other citizens—to identify themselves as standing with one side against another in a public contest or dispute.

---

[7]Donald R. Brand, *Corporatism and the Rule of Law: The National Recovery Administration* (Ithaca, NY: Cornell University Press, 1988), 53–80; Robert Eden, "Dealing Democratic Honor Out: Reform and the Decline of Consensus Politics" in ed. Richard A. Harris and Sidney M. Milkis, *Remaking American Politics* (Boulder, CO: Westview Press, 1988), 52–85.

[8]On the study of the impact of the New Deal on political parties, see *The New Deal and its Legacy: Critique and Reappraisal*, ed. Robert Eden (New York: Greenwood Press, 1989), 9–10; 124–133; and Milkis, *The Modern Presidency*, Chs. 1–5.

[9]Among the best accounts are Baker's discussions of "partisan roots" and "a sense of party"; see Jean H. Baker, *Affairs of Party: The Political Culture of Northern Democrats in the Mid-Nineteenth Century* (Ithaca: Cornell University Press, 1983), 27–70, 108–140.

Political parties are composed of citizens who are able and willing to stand *with* their political friends, *against* other citizens. Such opposition gives rise to an obvious, and serious, moral problem: in separating the partisan from other citizens, a political division may lead him to sever the threads that would otherwise bind him to them. As a consequence, his moral development as a citizen may be stunted or seriously warped.[10] The partisan is one who sees the authoritative association of the polity, and its civil traditions, through the lenses of a lesser association, composed of his political friends and colleagues. A party is a whole made up of partisans, but a partial whole, whose effect on citizens can be to shield them from the moral influence of the wider political community and its best traditions.[11]

Since in the United States those traditions are centered upon the Constitution, a certain moral tension between citizenship and partisanship, between political parties and the Constitution, is always latently on our public agenda. From the standpoint of engaged partisans, the Constitution is necessarily suspect because it may impartially require them to offend against the moral code of friendship between political associates. Their watchword is always the same: "What's the Constitution between friends?" Conversely, from the standpoint of constitutional citizenship, the partisans are always on probation because they offend against a parallel code of mutual obligations among political associates that embraces the whole citizenry or "the public."

Moreover, the establishment of the Constitution was accompanied by a memorable effort to keep partisans on constant probation by articulating a kind of honor code governing political

[10]One purpose of Van Buren's autobiographical writing was to indicate how he had avoided the stunting and warping effects of partisanship. Kleppner and others who admire the "party period" in American politics do not, I think, take this problem nearly as seriously as Van Buren did. See Paul Kleppner, "Partisanship and Ethnoreligious Conflict: The Third Electoral System, 1853–1892," in Paul Kleppner, ed., *The Third Electoral System, 1853–1892: Parties, Voters, and Political Cultures* (Chapel Hill, NC: University of North Carolina Press, 1979), 113–146. That Van Buren manages to persuade the skeptical reader of his completeness—both as a citizen and as a man—is one measure of his considerable literary and political skill. Van Buren saw clearly that one key to establishing a two-party system would be whether friendship, respect, and civility could be cultivated across partisan lines. Hence his solicitude, throughout his public life, to maintain good personal relations with leading men in the Whig party. See *The Autobiography of Martin Van Buren* (New York: Chelsea House, 1983). As Jean Baker notes, Van Buren was singularly responsible for the ethos of "interparty comity" which came to characterize American political parties. Baker, *Affairs of Party*, 129.

[11]See Edward J. Erler, *The American Polity: Essays on the Theory and Practice of Constitutional Government* (New York: Crane Russak, 1991), x–xi.

friendship between citizens.[12] This was one great accomplishment of *The Federalist;* and it has been an irritant, a stumbling block, and a challenge to American partisans ever since. They could never safely ignore *The Federalist* because it was so universally useful. It provided an arsenal of arguments that partisans could deploy against their political opponents. It also supplied effective means of defense against such attacks. *The Federalist* thereby pointed the way toward defensible parties, without sanctioning them. It articulated a multitude of political tasks and constitutionalist causes which political parties could honorably pursue. It furnished partisans a candid view of estimable goals for political ambition, and offered respectable pretexts for concerted political effort.[13]

Yet all this was done with no concession on the crucial point. Instead of harmonizing the moral tension between partisanship and citizenship, *The Federalist* accentuated that tension and made its causes so perspicuous that on this point public skepticism became a pronounced and permanent feature of American public opinion: henceforth, no informed citizen expected the tension to be resolved.[14] As I have explained, the cause of this embarrassment to partisans was no mere figment of the Framers' imaginations. American partisans need a favorable interpretation of partisanship, in the first instance, because parties divide the

[12] As George Carey observes, "*The Federalist*...provides us with what can appropriately be termed a 'constitutional morality'.... That is, comcommitant with its effort to render the proposed Constitution a coherent whole, it urges upon the rulers and ruled alike standards of behavior conducive to maintaining and perpetuating this coherence...." George W. Carey, *The Federalist: Design for a Constitutional Republic* (Chicago: University of Illinois Press, 1989), xii.

[13] This may be said not only of *The Federalist* but of many early state papers of the early Republic. It holds as well for Washington's Farewell Address, on which more below. Compare Eden, "Partisanship and the Constitutional Revolution: The Founders' View is Newly Problematic," in *Constitutionalism in Perspective: The Constitution in Twentieth Century Politics,* ed. Sarah Baumgartner Thurow (Lanham, MD: University Press of America, 1988), 51–65.

[14] This skepticism is viewed with disfavor by American political scientists because it contradicts a dearly held doctrine of responsible party government. That doctrine locates them squarely in the Progressive tradition. Many American students of British politics in the late 19th century—above all, Woodrow Wilson—were deeply influenced by the British practice of party government, and by Edmund Burke's rationale for it. As a result they came to equate two rather different tasks and to assume that establishing standards of performance for parties requires agreement on an argument for party government. The American experience contradicts this assumption: with regard to partisanship, establishing standards of performance does not always entail an argument for party government, or even for a party system to regulate nominations and the conduct of electoral campaigns. The Framers instituted a standard of judgment by which the performance of partisans was to be judged; but they did so without giving sanction to any particular mode of party conduct.

citizenry against itself; what the parties divide, the Constitution must unite. That is a moral tension inherent in the republican form of political life. The Founders merely made it difficult for Americans to forget this constant tension. To remove it from public view, one would not only have to silence *The Federalist* and uproot the political tradition it consolidated; one would ultimately have to dismantle the Constitution as well.[15]

Since the New Deal, we have increasingly taken it for granted, both in scholarship and in public discourse, that neither the Constitution nor *The Federalist's* defense of it were designed to shape citizenship. As a result, we assume that neither was designed to shape partisanship. In recent scholarship, virtually every document in the historical record that testifies to the Founders' effort to shape partisanship by this critical standard is deployed to prove that they were dogmatically "anti-party," and consequently, could not possibly have engaged in a serious effort to shape partisanship.[16] Accordingly, we have ceased to look to the Founding for useful instruction about the shaping of partisanship.

To correct this distortion in practice would require a revolution in American politics, a restructuring of what Walter Dean Burnham called "the American political universe."[17] Nothing of the sort seems to be on the horizon for the immediate future. A very different interpretation of partisanship is now deeply embedded in long-standing practices, entrenched interests, and habits; perhaps one cannot expect these to change quickly. But to correct the distortion at the level of scholarship and theory is not so laborious; for as Hobbes said, "Thought is quick." It is sufficient to place the Founders' critique of partisanship back into the context of the political experiment of instituting the first successful republic. That experiment was undertaken against a background of discouraging precedent. All previous republican governments had failed; all previous republican peoples had shortly proven themselves incapable of self-government. The Founding, from the American Revolution through the adoption of the Constitution and well beyond, was therefore an experiment. The Americans were already a republican people; but they had been so only briefly. It was not yet clear that a republican people could prove

---

[15]See Mahoney, "A Newer Science of Politics: *The Federalist* and American Political Science in the Progressive Era," *Saving the Revolution: The Federalist Papers and the American Founding*, Charles R. Kesler, ed., (New York: The Free Press, 1987), 250.

[16]Baker, *Affairs of Party*, 115–118. Richard Hofstadter, *The Idea of a Party System: The Rise of Legitimate Opposition in the United States, 1780–1840* (Berkeley, CA: University of California Press, 1970), 40–73.

[17]Walter Dean Burnham, "The Changing Shape of the American Political Universe," *American Political Science Review* 59 (1965), 12–23.

themselves demonstrably capable of self-government over the long pull. If they could remain one under a sound constitution, they might "by their conduct and example. . . . decide the important question, whether societies of men are really capable or not of establishing good government from reflection and choice, or whether they are forever destined to depend for their political institutions on accident and force."[18] Seen from this angle, the Constitution itself was only one of several distinctive contributions that the Founding generation made to "a fair and full experiment."[19] By *their* "conduct and example," they sought to establish lasting standards. They understood that it was necessary to engage the heart and imagination of a republican people, as well as their reason and judgment, in the success of the experiment. And it is above all in the context of the Founders' effort to consolidate the sound political habits and sentiments of a republican people that we must place their critique of partisanship and political parties. The choice their critique posed was between attachment to a republican form of government, articulated in the Constitution, and partisan attachment—between love of a party and love of country—between partisanship and republican patriotism.[20]

To understand the full implications of this choice, we must be clear that republican patriotism was undeniably understood by the Framers to be an elevated or noble kind of partisanship.[21] The former colonies were not the whole of mankind; they were not even the whole of the English Protestant part of mankind to which the colonies had been most directly attached. The Framers were enlightened and cosmopolitan enough to show "a decent respect

[18]Alexander Hamilton, James Madison, and John Jay, *The Federalist*, ed. Benjamin F. Wright (Cambridge: Harvard University Press, 1966), No. 1, 89. If American self-government depended on circumstances denied to the rest of mankind, their success would be dependent upon accident rather than upon reflection and choice. Hence to the degree that America is a geographic exception uniquely favored by special circumstances, this republican argument for the peculiar significance (for mankind and for political science) of America's republican experiment, would be vitiated.

[19]George Washington, "Farewell Address," in *George Washington: A Collection*, compiled and edited by William B. Allen (Indianapolis: Liberty Classics, 1988), 517.

[20]"The Framers intended the regime they were creating to be . . . a political regime in the fullest sense. Partisanship in support of constitutional government was to be the necessary and ordinary spring to politics. Citizens of the new democratic republic would ordinarily be partisans of constitutional government because they were partisans of liberty." Erler, *The American Polity*, 61.

[21]"[*The Federalist*] is surely a partisan document, but it is partisan for a Constitution, not merely for a transient issue of the day. There is a higher and a lower sense of 'partisan'—the responsible partisan versus the one who seeks his own advantage." Harvey C. Mansfield, Jr., *Taming the Prince: The Ambivalence of Modern Executive Power* (New York: Free Press, 1989), 249.

to the opinions of mankind" in the Declaration of Independence; and Publius speaks of "republican jealousy" as an obstacle in *Federalist* No. 1.[22] Patriotism as a matter of partial attachment, hence as partisan, and potentially inimical to Union, was an immediate concern because American patriotism was initially centered on the States. The friends of Union feared that lesser patriotisms—"local discriminations"—might weaken the bonds of reason and sentiment tying citizens to the Constitution and the Republic.[23] One purpose of keeping partisanship on probation was to center political passion on the Union. "Citizens by birth or choice, of a common country, that country has a right to concentrate your affections."[24] The original critique of partisanship was instrumental to an effort to elevate, intensify, and perfect the political attachments between republican citizens.

One of the expedients of Party to acquire influence, within particular districts, is to misrepresent the opinions and aims of other districts. You cannot shield yourselves too much against the jealousies and heart burnings which spring from these misrepresentations. They tend to render Alien to each other those who ought to be bound together by fraternal affection.[25]

This was a critique of partisanship intended to temper, refine, and in a manner heighten partisanship, by giving it a more sublime and more worthy object, making "the continuance of Union . . . a primary object of Patriotic desire."[26] The constitutionalist critique of faction on which Federalists and Anti-Federalists came to agree was emphatically a republican, political critique of partisanship. It was instrumental to their shared purpose of forming a republican people capable of good government. The great party division that emerged shortly after Ratification, and came to a head in the election of 1800, was a division over how that purpose could best be realized.[27]

[22]See ibid., 250–257; Patrick C. Garrity, "Foreign Policy and *The Federalist*," in *Saving the Revolution*, 88.
[23]Washington, "Farewell Address," in *George Washington*, 515; *The Federalist* No. 46, 330.
[24]Ibid., 515.
[25]Ibid., 517.
[26]Ibid., 517.
[27]"In America the two parties agreed on the most essential points. Neither of the two had, to succeed, to destroy an ancient order or to overthrow the whole of a social structure." Alexis de Tocqueville, *Democracy in America*, trans. by George Lawrence, ed. J. P. Mayer (Garden City, NY: Doubleday, 1966), 1:175. See Charles R. Kesler, "*Federalist* 10 and American Republicanism," in Kesler, ed., *Saving the*

Until the New Deal, these distinctions were exhibited, in the traditions of both major parties, in a universally accepted ranking of the Founders as exemplars of patriotism and republican citizenship.[28]

We have difficulty taking this ranking seriously. It would strike us as antique if a candidate today used the classic phrases and gestures in which that ranking was articulated on public occasions. We can hardly recall a time when such speeches—consider John Quincy Adams's great eulogies on Washington, Madison, and Monroe—were approved by majority opinion and thus reinforced from every direction.[29] It is not thought odd if a gifted young man models his aspirations on Roosevelt, Kennedy, or Reagan; but on Madison, Washington, or Hamilton would seem bizarre indeed. This reorientation should not be attributed to "the media." For the media follow; they do not lead.[30]

THE NEW DEAL CRITIQUE: CONSTITUTIONAL TRADITIONALISM

FDR did lead. As a result of the New Deal revaluation, to be a partisan for the American Founding in this traditional sense came

---

Revolution, 11–39. Murray Dry, "The Debate Over Ratification of the Constitution," in *The Blackwell Encyclopedia of the American Revolution,* ed. Jack P. Greene and J.R. Pole (Cambridge, MA: Blackwell, 1991); Forrest McDonald, *Alexander Hamilton: A Biography* (New York: W.W. Norton, 1979): 237–353; Roy F. Nichols, *The Invention the American Political Parties: A Study of Political Improvisation* (New York: The Free Press, 1967), 183–230.

[28]An anecdote from the career of Charles A. Beard may illustrate the force of this active regard for the Founders. "Beard was also an important early reformer in public administration. The New York Bureau was a mecca and a model for governmental reform for the entire country, especially at state and local levels. Beard was named the bureau's director in 1915, and in this position he continued and broadened the bureau's reform mongering. . . . Despite Beard's aggressive leadership at the New York Bureau, he was forced to resign in 1920 because of his growing reputation as a wild-eyed and even unpatriotic iconoclast, an image that can be traced to his critique of the Founders in 1913. When writing his famous book Beard had been affiliated with the bureau, and increasingly his presence at its helm was a fund-raising liability among businessmen in the New York area." Charles T. Goodsell, "Charles A. Beard, Prophet for Public Administration," Public Administration Review (March/April 1986): 106. Goodsell is referring to Beard's *An Economic Interpretation of the Constitution of the United States* (New York: MacMillan, 1913, 1935, 1961). In his new Preface to the 1935 edition of *An Economic Interpretation of the Constitution,* Beard seized the opportunity that the advent of the New Deal provided, to consolidate a new public view of the meaning of impartial government and of parti pris.

[29]See *The Selected Writings of John and John Quincy Adams,* ed. Adrienne Koch and William Peden (Westport, CT: Greenwood Press, 1981), 373–379, 384–388.

[30]Harvey C. Mansfield, Jr., "The Media World and Democratic Representation," *Government and Opposition* 16 (Summer 1982): 318–334.

to seem less legitimate and less respectable than what FDR called "enlightened administration." Indeed, in certain respects it came to be regarded with opprobrium, as a perversely partisan approach to the common good.[31] During the New Deal, this original or Constitutionalist critique of parties was ushered out and ceased to set the standard of respectability for partisanship in American public life. Although in key respects the New Deal was a revival of Hamiltonian nationalism, the Federalist (or Hamiltonian) formulation of this critique was repudiated by the New Deal.[32] And, while FDR likened his work as a party leader to Jefferson, he rejected the critique of partisanship that Madison and Jefferson developed as their rationale or pretext for creating the Republican party in the 1790s.[33]

While the New Deal abandoned the more strident and confrontational posture toward the Constitution that some Progressives had advocated, FDR and the New Dealers succeeded in discrediting constitutionalism by identifying concern for formalities and traditional constitutional forms with reactionary conservatism on the pressing socio-economic demands of the day.[34] The starting point of FDR's critique was the Progressive conviction that the Framers' Constitution had become a tool of financial and in-

---

[31]Consider Charles Beard's argument in *An Economic Interpretation of the Constitution of the United States.*

[32]Following the formulation of Herbert Croly, some scholars have suggested that the New Deal adopted Hamiltonian means to a Jeffersonian or populistic end. On Hamilton's formulation, however, there are no distinctively "Hamiltonian" means, for the reason given by John Marshall: "Let the end be legitimate, let it be within the scope of the constitution, and all means which are appropriate, which are plainly adapted to that end, which are not prohibited, but consist with the letter and spirit of the constitution, are constitutional." McCulloch v Maryland, 17 U.S.(4 Wheat.) 315, 316 (1819). What "Hamiltonianism" meant during the New Deal is evident in the identification of laissez-faire policies with abdication of rationality. "The year 1933 must remain memorable for the part played by conscious and deliberate action." Frederic C. Mills, "Economic Recovery," in *Social Change and the New Deal (Social Changes in 1933)*, ed. William F. Ogburn, (Chicago: University of Chicago Press, 1934), 10. Hamilton would never have made the ideological assumption that entrepreneurial capitalism was not "conscious and deliberate action." On New Deal criticism of Progressive anti-constitutional doctrines of public administration, see John A. Rohr, *To Run a Constitution: The Legitimacy of the Administrative State* (Lawrence, KS: The University of Kansas Press, 1986).

[33]Sidney M. Milkis, "Party Politics, Administrative Power, and Representation in American Politics—The Roots of New Deal Reform," in Milkis, *Modern Presidency and the Transformation of the American Party System* (New York: Oxford Univ. Press) forthcoming. Also his chapter, "New Deal Party Politics, Administrative Reform, and the Transformation of the American Constitution," in *The New Deal and its Legacy*, 123–154.

[34]Brand, *Corporatism*, 33–52.

dustrial magnates. According to the Progressives, constitutional formalities that dated from before the industrial age had become playthings in the hands of those who could wield economic power in the private sector. Those who governed in the economy were effectually beyond the control of officials elected by the people, and ruled the people through the formalities of constitutional arrangements. "They created a new despotism and wrapped it in the robes of legal sanction. In its service new mercenaries sought to regiment the people, their labor, and their property."[35] "Private government" was the most pressing problem, and was chiefly a problem of real, informal power.[36] Concentration of effective political power, growing out of concentrated financial and managerial power in the economy, was evident at the level of the working constitution; it became invisible when one focused upon the formal constitution.[37] The New Deal sought to combat this invisibility by focusing upon informal power; those who tried to keep public attention on formal arrangements were accused of "blinding" the public to the true problems. "In their blindness they forget what the Flag and the Constitution stand for."[38] Strict constitutional construction was an obstacle to the clear delineation of these new working power relationships.[39] The Court-packing plan of 1937 dramatized it as a legal obstruction centered in the courts. But FDR's attempt in 1938 to purge southern conservatives from the Democratic Party for opposing key New Deal measures, signalled his conviction that strict constitutionalism was equally

[35]*The Public Papers and Addresses of Franklin D. Roosevelt*, ed. Samuel I. Rosenman (New York: Random House, 1938), Vol. 5, 1936, 232.

[36]I take the convenient term "private government" from Grant McConnell, *Private Power and American Democracy* (New York: Vintage Books, 1966); see also Brand, *Corporatism*, 53–80. After describing private government, FDR remarked "that the responsible heads of finance and industry instead of acting each for himself, must work together to achieve the common end. They must, where necessary, sacrifice this or that private advantage; and in reciprocal self-denial must seek a general advantage. *It is here that formal Government—political Government, if you choose—comes in.*" (Emphasis added). Roosevelt, "Campaign Address on Progressive Government," *The Public Papers and Addresses of Franklin D. Roosevelt*, 754–755. See also ibid., 749, 750 (economic oligarchy), 751.

[37]Hence Beard's insistence upon knowledge of the economic interests at work in modern politics; without such information, citizens were bound to become, in Beard's view, "victims of history—clay in the hands of its makers." The great accusation against formal, institutional political science was its failure to disclose "determinism, necessity, in the world of political affairs." Charles A. Beard, 1935 Preface to *An Economic Interpretation*, xvi.

[38]*The Public Papers*, 5:234.

[39]*The Public Papers*, Vol. 6, March 4, 1937, 113–121. See note 28 above.

objectionable in construing the task of political parties.[40] Consequently, in the new party system that the New Deal brought into being, neither party placed the task of guarding the Constitution at the center of its program or made that task the standard of patriotic devotion to the common good.[41]

In American public life today one is advised to give the Founders "a low profile." One may do lip service to their achievements, but one should not activate their example of patriotism and republican citizenship. We find it hard to imagine how such traditional rhetoric could be connected to a serious legislative or executive program addressed to the demands of the day. Yet such programs could rather easily be couched in constitutionalist terms, if we thought the effort would be productive. The New Dealers were persuaded that it would be counter-productive, and we remain under the sway of their assessment.[42]

To appreciate the magnitude of this reorientation, one must recognize why it was necessary: the New Dealers thought the old critique of partisanship was an encumbrance precisely because it was not idle rhetoric or mere "expressive behavior." It produced habits and opinions that powerfully shaped the milieu of political life. This was not accidental. The Framers' critique was an attempt

[40]Sidney M. Milkis, "Presidents and Party Purges: with Special Emphasis on the Lessons of 1938," in Robert Harmel, editor, *Presidents and their Parties: Leadership or Neglect?* (New York: Praeger, 1984), 151–175.

[41]"The Roosevelt tradition demands inquiring minds, not minds that blindly accept or blindly oppose every new proposal. We believe in a two-party system and if that system is to function properly, the opposition party ought not to be either a me-too or a view-with-alarm party. It should seek out the vulnerable points in the position of the majority. Its concrete and intelligent criticism should keep the majority party alive and alert and on its toes. . . . But unfortunately we do not get that sort of constructive opposition from a party that couches its criticism in fatuous words breathing sound and fury and signifying nothing. The absence of an opposition party willing to face up to the facts of American life and destiny in the twentieth-century world threatens the effective functioning of the two-party system." Address of Benjamin V. Cohen at the Second Annual Roosevelt Day Dinner of Americans for Democratic Action, Chicago, Illinois, January 27, 1950. Franklin Delano Roosevelt Library, Joseph Lash Papers, "Ben Cohen Speeches and Articles." See also Robert Eden, "Partisanship and the Constitutional Revolution: The Founders' View is Newly Problematic," in *Constitutionalism in Perspective: The Constitution in Twentieth Century Politics*, ed. Sarah Baumgartner Thurow (Lanham, MD: University Press of America, 1988), 51–65.

[42]See the comparison developed by Herman Belz, "The Realist Critique of Constitutionalism in the Era of Reform," *The American Journal of Legal History* 15 (1971): 288–306, and "Changing Conceptions of Constitutionalism in the Era of World War Two and the Cold War," *Journal of American History* 59 (December 1972): 640–669.

to *rule* the partisanship of a republican citizenry, to establish a standard of political rule in the habits of a republican people.

Of all the objections which have been framed against the federal Constitution, this is perhaps the most extraordinary. Whilst the objection itself is levelled against a pretended oligarchy, the principle of it strikes at the very root of republican government. The aim of every political constitution is, or ought to be, first to obtain for rulers men who possess most wisdom to discern, and most virtue to pursue, the common good of the society; and in the next place, to take the most effectual precautions for keeping them virtuous whilst they continue to hold their public trust.[43]

The ruling embodied in the Framers' critique of partisanship was direct rule, suasion in person, an on-the-job effort to establish a kind of ranking in the souls of citizens. The Framers' distinction between respectable politics and partisanship, or between good citizenship and bad partisanship, was one of the "ways and means" available to republican statesmen who sought to form the characters and mould the political sentiments of their fellow citizens.[44] This was explicit in Washington's most influential anti-party statement, his Farewell Address. There, a critique of "the spirit of party" was advanced as a salutary means of directing "the force of public opinion."

[I]n Governments purely elective, it is a spirit not to be encouraged. From their natural tendency, it is certain that there will always be enough of that spirit for every salutary purpose. And there being constant danger of excess, the effort ought to be, by force of public opinion, to mitigate and assuage it. A fire not to be quenched; it demands a uniform vigilance to prevent its bursting into flame, lest instead of warming it should consume.[45]

As the New Dealers conceived the original constitutional tradition, it was primarily an answer to tyrannical, unaccountable power; hence, one test of fidelity to the tradition was posed by new

---

[43]*The Federalist* No. 57, 383.

[44]Can this dimension of the Founders' work be reconciled with their debt to Locke? That is a proper subject for further inquiry. See Thomas L. Pangle, *The Spirit of Modern Republicanism: The Moral Vision of the American Founders and the Philosophy of Locke* (Chicago: University of Chicago Press, 1988), 124–127; Charles R. Kesler, "The Founders and the Classics," *The American Founding: Essays on the Formation of the Constitution*, ed. J. Jackson Barlow, Leonard W. Levy and Ken Masugi, (Westport, CT: Greenwood Press, 1988), 57–90.

[45]Washington, "Farewell Address," 520.

forms of power. The purpose of constitutional arrangements was to counter pride, ambition, and recklessness in the use of power. Significant new manifestations of such pride or recklessness should call forth resistance and counter-action. The New Dealers argued that strict constructionism violated the spirit of the American tradition: instead of calling forth organized resistance and counter-action to concentrated economic power, generating new constitutional responses to ambition and recklessness, "the old leadership" attempted to confine Americans to "horse and buggy constitutionalism." New Deal political strategy and rhetoric was a campaign to discredit that leadership. FDR succeeded in doing so by demonstrating—at least to the satisfaction of his main constituencies—that the old partisanship had become a crippling form of traditionalism. One might say that he discredited strict constructionism on its own terms by returning to its first principles.[46]

The strict constructionists, according to FDR, had lost touch with Jefferson and had forgotten why the rights of property and personal competency that the Constitution was to secure had been given priority in the first place.[47]

Nothing differentiates the New Deal from Progressivism, Franklin Roosevelt from Woodrow Wilson, so sharply as Roosevelt's peculiar mimicry of Jefferson. That mimicry—his sustained "homage to the sage of Monticello"[48]—was made evident in his conception of party leadership and in his repeated claim that the New Deal realignment was a reenactment of the Jeffersonian triumph of 1800. It was also exhibited in many turns of phrase, introducing the Democratic Platform with the sentence, "we hold this truth to be self-evident," alluding in other ways to the Declaration of Independence, and characterizing his goal as "an economic Bill of Rights."[49]

To say that FDR broke with Wilsonian idealism in returning to these Jeffersonian phrases is not to say that he was less radical than Wilson as an opponent of Jeffersonianism. It is to keep us close to the impression we all have of the New Deal as thoroughly contaminated by utilitarianism, aiming at achievements that were both

[46]Charles R. Kesler, "The Reagan Revolution and the Legacy of the New Deal: Obstacles to Party Realignment," in The 1984 Election and the Future of American Politics, ed. Peter W. Schramm and Dennis J. Mahoney (Durham: Carolina Academic Press, 1987), 245–264; Kesler, "The Political Philosophy of the New Freedom and the New Deal," in The New Deal and its Legacy, 155–166.

[47]The Public Papers, 1:745–746, 754.

[48]Ibid., 5:240.

[49]Sidney M. Milkis, "Party Politics," see note 33.

lower than those of Wilsonian idealism, and more solid.[50] The achievements of the New Deal remind us more of self-preservation and of classical natural rights than of ideal rights to self-expression and the development of "individuality."[51] FDR could liken his program to the creation of an economic Bill of Rights because it would establish the fundamental principle of consent in the domain of private government which the original Bill of Rights had established in the domain of public government. The rights alluded to in The Declaration of Independence were privileged above all others because the most fundamental right is the individual right to consent to the power to make law, to consent to government, a consent without which no other rights could be protected.[52] The New Deal succeeded in persuading an American majority that this most fundamental of rights, the right without which no other rights could be protected, was primarily endangered by concentrated financial and managerial control over economic life. The claim was that a new power to make law and to govern had arisen as a result of the American industrial revolution. Left to its old devices, the old leadership meant to carry on the old constitutional tradition but to ignore the new powers generated by economic development.[53]

The charge of "economic royalism" was designed to bring to light the effects of private government and to disclose a wide domain of social life in which government was prevented from securing the rights of individuals against arbitrary and capricious rule.[54] The New Dealers sought to constitutionalize a battlefield of economic and social conflict that had long since become politicized, and to establish norms of partisan conduct in this field.[55] They sought to transpose many earlier established habits from the political arena and electoral competition into the arena of industrial conflict resolution, habits of civility in the conduct of serious disputes. They encouraged collective organization and legitimated

[50]Edgar Kemler, *The Deflation of American Ideals* (Washington, DC: 1941). Charles R. Kesler, "The Political Philosophy of the New Freedom and the New Deal," in *The New Deal and its Legacy*, 155–166.

[51]On Wilsonian idealism and individuality, see Robert Eden, *Political Leadership and Nihilism: A Study of Weber and Nietzsche* (Gainesville: University Presses of Florida, 1984), 10–11, 32–33.

[52]*The Public Papers and Addresses of Franklin D. Roosevelt*, 5:231–233.

[53]Ibid., 1:745, 752, 755; 5:232–234.

[54]Ibid., 5:232–234, 568.

[55]Ibid, 5:569–570.

conflict between great interests; simultaneously, they attempted to regularize conflict and to formalize it.[56]

This emphasis helps to explain why FDR's electoral victories resulted in the demoralization and political marginalization of the old leadership. For elections can be expressions of principled consent, ratifying and consenting to a broad direction of policy. They may tell us what the voters understand consent to be. Hence elections can be managed to create the impression (illusory or justified) that their outcome is a demonstration not merely of consent to a candidate and his program, but of consent to an interpretation of consent itself—an interpretation of the rights that are most critically connected to the consent of the governed.

In certain respects, FDR's constitutionalist rhetoric was deceptively conservative because it concealed a decisive choice. FDR formulated his program moderately in the 1932 campaign as an *augmentation* of the Framers' effort to constitutionalize political power.[57] This brilliantly understated the terms of conflict, placing the onus for partisanship on the traditionalists. FDR portrayed the spirit of the New Deal as the spirit of American constitutionalism, addressing new forms of tyrannical power by constitutionalizing newly concentrated economic power.[58] As FDR posed the issues, the old Constitution with all its mechanisms for preventing the concentration of political power would remain intact, yet ineffectual, if the strict constructionists had their way, for the grave contemporary danger to the original principle of consent would be ignored. The New Deal would keep it intact but reinvigorate it and make it effectual.[59]

CARING AND GUARDING

This was a considerable understatement of the decision that FDR was attempting to precipitate. For the difference between "the old leadership" and the new, or between the old and new standards of partisanship, was not essentially between two styles of defending liberty or of guarding constitutional forms. The New Dealers were constitutionalists insofar as they advocated a new constitutional rule of law and promoted partisanship on behalf of

---

[56]John A. Wettergreen, "The Regulatory Policy of the New Deal," in *The New Deal and its Legacy,* 199–213.

[57]*The Public Papers,* 1:744–745.

[58]Ibid., 1:746–752; 5:231–234.

[59]Ibid.

the rule of law. At the same time, they were quite self-conscious about the broad difference that set them apart from the old approach to law and constitutional forms. They were convinced that their conception of law provided a better foundation for government in the age of concentrated economic power.[60]

In the Framers' assessment of partisanship, good citizenship was defined as the perpetuation of our political institutions, that is, as guarding constitutional norms, practices and institutions against encroachment.[61] Each party accused the other of encroachment, holding up its own program and agenda of guardianship. In principle, this elevation of guarding required a certain detachment from normal caring. Friendship and affection between partisans, or even between citizens, was politically suspect; it had to be justified by the higher standard set by the task of guardianship. Constitutional politics requires not only that partisanship be limited, but that it be limited by the partisans themselves. The Founders did not expect these bonds of affection to be negligible. Nepotism, local ties, kinship, and political friendship were great forces to be conjured with. They were among the great engines of partisan passion. The distinction between good citizenship and bad partisanship, as the Founders formulated it, was between the guarding of constitutional forms through reason, public spirit, and law on the one hand, and the rule of sentiment, passion, and affection, on the other. Guarding was placed in the ascendancy above caring.[62]

[60]See the analysis of Jacobus Ten Broek's critical jurisprudence in Danny M. Adkison, "The Federalist and Original Intent," *The Political Science Reviewer* 17 (1987), 219–240; Brand, *Corporatism*, 33–52; Thomas G. West, "The Rule of Law in *The Federalist*," in Kesler, ed., *Saving the Revolution*, 150–167. Jeremy Rabkin, "Bureaucratic Idealism and Executive Power: A Perspective on *The Federalist*'s View of Public Administration," ibid., 185–202.

[61]Martin Van Buren chose the phrase "the perpetuation of our political institutions "as the theme of his Inaugural Address in 1837; as Major Wilson points out, Lincoln's famous speech on the same theme was a Whig reply to Van Buren. See Major L. Wilson, "Another Look at the Lyceum Address," *Civil War History* 29 No. 3 (1983), 197–211.

[62]The spirit of the older constitutional guarding is clear in its deliberate use of the verb for caring. Official care should not be for persons or parties but for impersonal law and the common good, as when the Constitution charges the President to avow that he will "take care that the laws be faithfully executed." See *Federalist* No. 66: "[T]he security to the society must depend on the care which is taken to confide the trust to proper hands, to make it their interest to execute it with fidelity, and to make it as difficult as possible for them to combine in any interest opposite to that of the public good." On this view of partisanship, caring is exhibited almost exclusively in guarding, in "care to preserve," Nos. 31, 39; "care of the safety of the nation" Nos. 23, 25.

Citizenship was identified with guarding, mere partisanship with passion or affection.[63]

Franklin Roosevelt's "reappraisal of values" was an attack upon this hierarchic ranking of guarding and caring.[64] From what has been said so far, FDR might seem merely to deny that the old leadership had done a good job by the old standard—had failed as guardians. But as FDR explained it to the American people, the root cause of this failure was their conception of the task of leadership and government as a task of guarding. "Rather the occasional faults of a Government that lives in a spirit of Charity than the consistent omissions of a Government frozen in the ice of its own indifference."[65] FDR's "new leadership" was distinguished by its elevation of caring above constitutional guarding, a ranking that was essential to what FDR meant by "enlightened administration." He even appealed beyond the Constitution to a higher standard to justify this new ranking. As he put it in his Philadelphia acceptance speech in 1936, "[T]he immortal Dante tells us that divine justice weighs the sins of the cold-blooded and the sins of the warm-hearted on a different scale."[66]

The New Deal was intended as a comprehensive effort to deal a new hand to people who would administer governing authority and wield private economic power in a qualitatively different spirit. "We seek not merely to make Government a mechanical implement, but to give it the vibrant personal character that is the very embodiment of human charity."[67] FDR denounced "economic royalists" to dramatize the principle that no citizen should enjoy the prerogatives of a king in governing his employees, his business associates, investors or shareholders. "The royalists of the

---

[63]The exception to this pattern of usage appears, as one would expect, in passages on local government, and here the authors of *The Federalist* may be seen attempting to turn republican suspicion, regarding the corrupt merging of personal care and political duty, toward the states:

Many considerations . . . seem to place it beyond doubt that the first and most natural attachment of the people will be to the governments of their respective states. Into the administration of these a greater number of individuals will expect to rise. From the gift of these a greater number of offices and emoluments will flow. By the superintending care of these, all the more domestic and personal interests of the people will be regulated and provided for. With the affairs of these, the people will be more familiarly and minutely conversant. And with the members of these, will a greater proportion of the people have the ties of personal acquaintance and friendship, and of family and party attachments; on the side of these, therefore, the popular bias may well be expected to incline. (No. 46, 330.)

[64]See *The New Deal and its Legacy*, ix.
[65]*Public Papers*, 5:235.
[66]Ibid.
[67]Ibid.

economic order have conceded that political freedom was the business of the Government, but they have maintained that economic slavery was nobody's business. . . . These economic royalists complain that we seek to overthrow the institutions of America. What they really complain of is that we seek to take away their power. Our allegiance to American institutions requires the overthrow of this kind of power."[68] The deeper point was that no citizen should tolerate such prerogatives in the economic realm; that businessmen themselves should first be liberal democrats (Jefferson would of course have said "republicans"), and construe their responsibilities in that light. The point of driving the difference home was not to pillory individuals but to establish a new spirit of responsibility. The older partisanship—"the old leadership"—had not steadily restrained human pride, ambition, and recklessness in financial and industrial circles. It had failed to instill, or to activate and enliven, the norms of responsibility appropriate wherever power is wielded in a democratic society. According to FDR, therefore, it was not an accident that the Depression had come. It came as the climax of decades of private government characterized by caprice and irresponsibility.[69]

The New Deal interpretation of partisanship was not only intended to release the restraints imposed by strict constitutional construction upon the potential collective power by which consumers, small investors, and workers could assert and protect their rights. It was not just a way of promoting new cadres of leadership and new modes of organization. The New Deal critique of partisanship was intended to make Americans ashamed of the old notion of responsibility and hence to exercise a new kind of prior restraint on self-assertion or on "the old individualism." What FDR chiefly had in mind when he employed the rhetoric of a "Bill of Rights" was that these newly discovered economic rights would soon become invested with the same customary, unquestionable sense of obligation that adhered to the rights addressed in the first ten amendments, " . . . as ingrained in our American natures as the free elective choice of our representatives itself."[70] In addition to using the coercive power of legislation and regulation, his intention was to establish customary or unwritten limits on the power by which Americans could assert and protect other rights, especially the rights of property.[71]

[68]Ibid., 233–234.
[69]Ibid., 568; 2:10–12.
[70]Ibid., 8:142.
[71]Ibid., 1:771–780.

The New Deal reassessment shifted the principal focus of politics by elevating "the caring issues" over what I have described as "the guarding issues."[72] This revaluation made the pre-political conditions of politics the principal focus of political activity. This change came about not as a by-product of the main tasks the New Deal set itself, but rather because changing the focus of partisanship was a major objective of the New Deal.[73]

On the old doctrine, the Constitution provided a standard superior to the parties by which the common good could be discerned and upheld against merely partisan or factional assertions. As the embodiment of the requirements of the safety and security of the people, the Constitution could provide a standard for judging parties. While the parties might aspire to bear the mantle of guardians of the Constitution, they could never permanently bridge the distance and achieve constitutional sanction.[74]

After the New Deal reappraisal, socio-economic needs gradually became identified in the public mind with "the safety of the people" and supplanted the Constitution as the impartial standard by which political parties and partisanship were to be judged. What is administered through enlightened administration is an enlightened understanding of the socio-economic demands of the day, or of the sub-political necessities to which all citizens are subject. As the authoritative interpreters of the socio-economic demands of the day, social scientists and public administrators trained in social scientific thinking articulated the new impartial standard. They became the ultimate arbiters of the programs of American political parties. Over the long pull, therefore, enlightened administration informed by social science would take the place of the republican tradition of guarding constitutional forms.[75] In the short run, however, these old habits of guarding and of standing up for one's rights would, in a manner, take on

[72]Irving Bernstein, *A Caring Society: The New Deal, the Worker, and the Great Depression, 1933–1941* (Boston: Houghton Mifflin, 1985), 44: "With the New Deal, the Wisconsin Idea went national." See Peter J. Coleman, "The World of Interventionism, 1880–1940," in *The New Deal and its Legacy*, 49–75, and his *Progressivism and the World of Reform: New Zealand and the Origins of the American Welfare State* (Lawrence, KS: University Press of Kansas, 1987).

[73]Milkis, *The Modern Presidency*, Ch.5.

[74]Charles R. Kesler, "Natural Law and the Constitution: *The Federalist's* View," in *Constitutionalism in Perspective*, 155–181.

[75]This direct rule should be distinguished from the indirect modes of ruling to which modern intellectuals are attracted, and which was so striking to a young New Dealer like Corcoran in its classic formulation by Oliver Wendell Holmes Jr.:

new life by coming to the defense of new institutions, such as unions, consumer associations, and public interest lobbies. Thus FDR could sound the tocsin of 1776: "[T]he average man once more confronts the problem that faced the Minute Man."[76] To redeploy old habits in this way, however, Roosevelt had to be confident that they were on the way to extinction. Republican guarding could then become an instrument of enlightened administration. The guarding gestures would be guided by a different ethos, which I have summed up in the familiar phrase "the caring issues."

Like patriotic citizenship in the Founders' constitutionalist assessment, enlightened administration was a severe standard of public discipline. The New Dealers identified it with the rule of law and scientific reason over partisan passions.[77] Like constitutionalist citizenship, which it displaced, enlightened administration was also a higher form of partisanship, a way of serving one's country and one's fellow citizens. The New Dealers argued that the guarding issues were historically retrogressive; if we did not displace them we would "revert to those systems of self-perpetuating power."[78] Placing the caring issues above the guarding issues was of the essence of public service. The traditional tasks of guarding were antithetical to enlightened administration as provision for major social needs. When the "caring issues" are elevated as a standard by which to judge partisans, and by which to distinguish public-spirited liberals from mean-spirited bigots—it means that caring has become an impersonal public and professional

---

No man has earned the right to intellectual ambition until he has learned to lay his course by a star which he has never seen. . . . Thus, only you can gain the secret isolated joy of the thinker, who knows that, a hundred years after he is dead and forgotten, men who never heard of him will be moving to the measure of his thought.

Tommy Corcoran took this passage (from Holmes's 1886 lecture on "The Profession of Law") as the text for a 90th birthday celebration, just after Hoover had passed up the opportunity to make Holmes Chief Justice of the Supreme Court. See Joseph P. Lash, *Dealers and Dreamers: A New Look at the New Deal* (New York: Doubleday, 1988), 67. He later applied it to the quietest mover and shaker of the New Deal, Ben Cohen. "Ben is entitled to what Holmes described," he declared, and quoted this passage. Speech by Thomas G. Corcoran introducing Benjamin Cohen as chief speaker at 44th Annual Reunion of the New Deal Dinner at Mayflower Hotel, 4 March 1977; Franklin Delano Roosevelt Library, Joseph Lash Papers, "Ben Cohen Speeches and Articles."

[76]*Public Papers* 5:232.
[77]On the emergence of the rational, disciplined caring professions see John F. McClymer, *War and Welfare, Social Engineering in America, 1890–1925* (Westport, CT: Greenwood, 1980).
[78]*Public Papers*, March 4, 1939, 8:151.

responsibility that can be discharged, and indeed must be discharged, by duly constituted (and credentialled) authorities.[79] Not caring as such, but caring as a public matter, was the principle of the New Deal ranking of public issues.[80]

In this reassessment, the traditional tension between law and reason on the one hand, and partisan affection or passion on the other, was replaced by the distinction between "enlightened administration" on the one hand, and unenlightened or traditionalist caring on the other. As we have seen, enlightened administration meant an educated, professionally trained provision for needs. Insofar as "caring" meant what it had always been thought to mean—affectionate solicitude for family, friends, kin, neighbors and colleagues—it might well be uninstructed, irrational, and inimical to the long-range plans of the New Deal.[81] The New Dealers accordingly rediscovered the animus of the older constitutional tradition against partiality and partisan attachment to one's locality or kin. The New Dealers denigrated that partiality as "the old individualism"—withdrawing from society at large in favor of one's local circle.[82] They likewise decried candidate—rather than issue—oriented politics. This dimension of the New Deal critique of partisanship was given classic articulation in V.O. Key's great study, *Southern Politics.*[83]

RESHAPING PRIVATE GOVERNMENT

The caring issues were to be elevated to the top of the public agenda in order to transform the economic activities through

[79]See John Ehrenreich, *The Altruistic Imagination: A History of Social Work in the United States* (Ithaca, NY: Cornell University Press, 1985), 106–107: Social work had changed almost overnight from a "Cinderella that must be satisfied with the leavings" into one of the "primary functions of government," wrote former Association of American Social Workers president Frank Bruno. See also William Hodson, "The Social Worker in the New Deal," *Proceedings of the National Conference of Social Work, 1934,* 3–12.

[80]"Without bloodshed the New Deal defanged our most dangerous internal crisis since the crisis of 1861. This it accomplished by institutionalizing compassion and recognizing the political indispensability for a democracy of hope in all its people." Speech by Thomas G. Corcoran introducing Benjamin Cohen as chief speaker at 44th Annual Reunion of the New Deal Dinner at Mayflower Hotel, 4 March 1977; Franklin Delano Roosevelt Library, Joseph Lash Papers, "Ben Cohen Speeches and Articles."

[81]Compare with Dewey, "Individualism Old and New," 83, 85–86.

[82]The Commonwealth Club Address ("On Progressive Government") was originally entitled "Individualism Old and New." Beatrice Bishop Berle and Travis Beal Jacobs, eds., *Navigating the Rapids 1918–1970: From the Papers of Adolf A. Berle* (New York: Harcourt, Brace, Jovanovich, 1973): 57, 62.

[83]V.O. Key, Jr., *Southern Politics in State and Nation* (New York: Knopff, 1949).

which Americans provided for their material needs. And one purpose of the new ranking was to shift public attention away from
productivity. The new focus was not the amount or quality of the
goods generated, but rather the damaging effects—upon workers,
small investors, and consumers—of given modes of production
and distribution.[84]

The older partisanship pitted political ambition against political ambition, party against party, especially in electoral contests
and within formal governing bodies. The new partisanship, focused on the caring issues and provision for sub-political needs,
was bound to pit political ambition against very different kinds of
ambition. Most obviously, during the New Deal, public servants
pitted their efforts against business elites in a struggle to determine the ethos of the American regime.[85]

Because businessmen had recently enjoyed unprecedented
prestige, they were most immediately affected, and offended, by
the New Deal regime of "enlightened administration." But equally
bitter and difficult struggles were to follow in the unions. Once
one grasps the principle of the New Deal understanding of partisanship, and the import of "enlightened administration" as a
higher, more rational and professional approach to the caring issues, one can see that the potential range of struggle extends to all
organized social life. The New Dealers' initial concern was to establish new modes of interaction between government and business; these modes were only paradigms for a more comprehensive
transformation.[86]

Both in the early "corporatist" National Recovery Administration and in later institutional experiments, the New Deal
agencies were attempts to generate a symbiotic, quasi-political
leadership within every sector of the economy.[87] One important

[84]See Roosevelt, *Public Papers* 1:751–755.

[85]On the new ethos, see Robert Eden, "Dealing Democratic Honor Out: Reform and
the Decline of Consensus Politics" in Harris, ed., *Remaking American Politics*, 52–85.

[86]The most contentious and bitter issue here has been racial discrimination by
unions. "In the legal framework of collective bargaining established by the National
Labor Relations Act of 1935, employers accepted racial segregation and discrimination as a basic demand of organized labor. In effect, the NLRA legalized and
made the federal government a party to the discrimination practiced by the union
movement. By giving organized labor formal recognition in national law, the act
also made it possible to apply anti-discrimination pressure on the unions when job
bias became an issue of civil rights concern in the 1940s." Herman Belz, *Equality
Transformed: A Quarter-Century of Affirmative Action* (New Brunswick, NJ: Transac-
tion Press, 1990), 13.

[87]See Thomas K. McCraw, *Prophets of Regulation* (Cambridge, MA: Harvard University Press, 1984) on James M. Landis's successful strategy for regulating the

function of the farm programs, for example, was to cultivate national and regional political leaders from within the agricultural sector who would collaborate in the work of "enlightened administration."[88]

Because moral standards and redistributionist concerns stood very high on the New Deal agenda, such representatives were to take the lead in transforming the private sector, to foster cooperation with enlightened administration and to promote voluntary compliance with New Deal legislation. The aim was to reorient leadership within the private sector away from the primacy of productivity and the generation of wealth. Professionalizing "the caring issues" meant reordering productive activities and the world of economic exchange from within, as well as by governmental and political pressure from without.[89]

Because production and exchange had to be rethought in terms of the caring issues, "enlightened administration" implied a new order of social and moral supervision. The New Dealers improvised with many different methods to promote this supervi-

---

Securities industry; Roosevelt, *Public Papers* 1:754–755. One study insightfully treats the collaboration between bureaucracy and the "welfare capitalists" as a chapter in business history parallel to the emergence of "the visible hand" described by Alfred D. Chandler, Jr. See Edward D. Berkowitz and Kim McQuaid, *Creating the Welfare State: The Political Economy of Twentieth-Century Reform* (New York: Praeger, 1980), x.

[88]The careful phasing of early New Deal legislation, traced by Romasco, can be understood in this light: the most represented and politically effective groups were arguably most critical to the success of FDR's policy of creating a new leadership in the private sphere. See Albert U. Romasco, *The Politics of Recovery: Roosevelt's New Deal* (New York: Oxford University Press, 1983). Consider also Tugwell's observation that "FDR . . . also knew about the farmers. . . . They were also diehard individualists, the thorniest of all citizens for bureaucrats to organize. . . . " Rexford G. Tugwell, "On the Verge of the Presidency," *In Search of Roosevelt* (Cambridge, MA: Harvard University Press, 1972), 228. Compare Ellis W. Hawley, "The New Deal State and the Anti-Bureaucratic Tradition," in *The New Deal and its Legacy,* 77–92. McConnell, "Private Power," see note 36. See also Brand's effective critique of Theodore J. Lowi, *The End of Liberalism: The Second Republic of the United States* (New York: Norton, 1979), in Brand, *Corporatism.*

[89]"In an interdependent society, organized power is necessary to conserve as well as to promote human welfare. Not only big government, but big business and big labor seek, and within bounds yet to be determined, may justify their existence by their contributions to human welfare. But vast concentrations of power do involve threats and dangers to individual liberty which cannot be ignored. . . . What do we really know about the forces and restraints which influence and determine the decisions of the custodians of organized power, public or private?" Remarks of Benjamin V. Cohen at Conference on Freedom and Law, University of Chicago Law School, 7 May 1953. Franklin Delano Roosevelt Library, Joseph Lash Papers, "Ben Cohen Post-WWII Writings." See also, Roosevelt, *Public Papers,* 1:754–755

sion. They sought a novel kind of partisanship that would divide each profession or productive activity within itself, forging an alliance with those leaders in, say, medicine or business administration who understood the progressive role that government intervention could play in providing for the just distribution of the profession's services, or for the regulatory framework which best satisfied society's needs.[90] The purpose of much of the special-interest corporatism with which FDR experimented was not primarily to find a way out of the Depression, but rather to generate the new arrangements and the new collectively-minded leadership he thought would be required for the long future.

For a very long time before the New Deal, political parties had been closely intertwined with corporate industrial and financial management. The New Deal accepted the Progressive critique of these arrangements, but although FDR revived the memory of Jacksonian parties by adopting Jeffersonian gestures and rhetoric, and did shake up the alignments within and between the existing parties, on the whole the New Deal accepted the basic arrangement as a given. FDR made no attempt to revive Jeffersonian republicanism as the heart of the Democratic Party, nor did his remarkable institutional experimentation include a search for participatory equivalents to the earlier arrangements of the Van Burenite parties. Instead, the New Deal sought to forge parallel arrangements linking political parties to the corporate world, but also to other concentrations of managerial and professional leadership. The symbiosis between New Deal parties and these leaderships was founded upon a different ethos and a different ranking of issues; it represented a new interpretation of partisanship. But in comparison to the Van Burenite model, the New Deal was far closer to the system of governance that immediately preceded it, in which a managerial and entrepreneurial elite collaborated closely with the political parties. The Van Burenite parties had been animated by a spirit and purpose, and attuned to methods, inimical to the alliances between business leadership and

[90]Readers today may see a contradiction between their dominant impression of the New Deal as an attempt to get the economy going again, and my account of its character as a revolution in the American regime. But the New Dealers would have seen no contradiction here. As Tommy the Cork Corcoran observed, "What made the New Deal's miracle of the spirit work was the interaction between the imagination and devotion of those who came here wanting to make the world over and those who only hoped they could make it work." Speech by Thomas G. Corcoran introducing Benjamin Cohen as chief speaker at 44th Annual Reunion of the New Deal Dinner at Mayflower Hotel, 4 March 1977; Franklin Delano Roosevelt Library, Joseph Lash Papers, "Ben Cohen Speeches and Articles."

parties that prevailed in the decades just prior to the New Deal. FDR sought to reshape these alliances on New Deal terms to insure that they would serve programmatic liberalism and foster enlightened administration.

The class rhetoric that FDR exploited in his Philadelphia Acceptance Speech in 1936 was both more deeply formative of partisan habits and more profoundly misleading about the actual divisions promoted by the New Deal than one might have thought at first glance. The discrepancy reflected the disparity between electoral and administrative politics in FDR's long term strategy. Although political parties and electoral coalition-building were vital during the formative period of the New Deal, FDR foresaw from the outset that his new liberal partisanship would be hampered if a party oligarchy held the balance of authority in the national councils of power. He therefore sought to disconnect the office of the President from his own party, and to fashion a new kind of political apparatus, composed very largely of partisans holding administrative positions—partisans of the new administrative programs, insulated from electoral accountability. Class hatreds could be sported within electoral politics precisely because electoral politics would no longer determine the course of programs and policies. FDR could exploit the imagery of class warfare in full confidence that such simplistic appeals would not be translated into legislation or administrative programs. They would first have to pass muster as enlightened administration. To insure this, the executive office had to be reorganized and the major New Deal programs had to be fortified against electoral setbacks. The true cleavages that the New Deal promoted were therefore not the class divisions that FDR dramatized in Philadelphia, but rather the cleavages produced by the partisan pressure exerted over a much longer term by "enlightened administration." In this respect, one may take the demagogic veneer of FDR's electoral rhetoric as a feint that confused both the opposition and the electorate as a whole. This misdirection drew attention away from the divisions that New Deal partisanship institutionalized and promoted. The real divisions did not pit wealth against poverty or business against labor. Corporate business and labor were to prosper mightily as allies of enlightened administration. "Farming the government," as wealthy farmers soon learned, was a well-paved path to further enrichment; and the New Deal programs outside of agriculture opened similar avenues to enthusiastic unions and corporations eager for self-aggrandizement. The New Deal promoted cleavages that ran across rather than along class lines. The fault-line was determined by the New Deal program, shaped and channelled by the institutions of enlightened administration, and guided by liberal initiatives. The principal cleavage privileged those in every sector of the economy who were willing to collaborate in building a new regime of enlightened administration, and set them against those in every sector who were opposed or uncooperative. The assumption was that "history," meaning the main path of development in industrial societies, was moving away from class divisions. Hence the rhetoric of class conflict could be made a plaything of respectable candidates, with FDR leading the way. In the New Deal perspective, that rhetoric corresponded to nothing real. It had almost become a matter of taste or mere style. Despite the angry denunciations of businessmen, FDR was confident that in the long run the main players would come around: there was plenty of room for modern corporations and corporation men in the New Deal regime.

Thus, FDR offered a comprehensive interpretation of partisanship. The New Deal reassessment justified a new partisan division within American society, not merely in public life and electoral politics, but in every major sector of the economy. It made enlightened administration, as a higher kind of partisanship, newly respectable in American public life. But it also sought to precipitate or sharpen a moral division in the internal governance of the private sector, fostering a new definition of social responsibility that was inseparable from partisan confrontation in the public arena.

Parties "in the American mould" were originally loose local associations of political friends in a common alliance. When such an alliance was formed around constitutional guarding, it confronted politically organized and capable enemies, the members of the opposed party. But a party today, operating on New Deal suppositions, is not respectable if it aims its artillery primarily, or exclusively, at the other party. To earn its keep, it must seek partisan adherents who will help transform society in accordance with a vision of social justice and a programmatic understanding of enlightened administration. This description of partisanship applies with equal validity to the Republicans' present conception of their task, for theirs too has become a party of administration—though with recognizably different content.

Like the contest between Republicans and Federalists, which came to a head in 1800, and like the Civil War, the New Deal was a political struggle that shaped the historical imagination and partisan habits of Americans for generations. Eventually, such partisan habits are bound to become almost universally suspect and obnoxious. We cease to be moved by the passions that originally animated those habits. We grow tired of being manipulated through them. The electorate becomes ornery, unpredictable, and remote; eventually, no one jumps when the old buttons are pushed. An electoral day of reckoning finally arrives: a candidate with confidence in his own political judgment decides that established habits have lost their hold, that the moment has come to break them forever, to sweep the old away and assert a new standard of partisanship. The serious citizen must then resort to criteria not bound to the discredited political custom. Perhaps, therefore, it is appropriate to leave the reader with a question. When it is time to pass judgment on the partisanship of enlightened administration, by what criteria will you judge?

POLITICAL PARTIES AND THE NEW DEAL

Donald R. Brand

BY THE 1970S AMERICAN POLITICAL PARTIES WERE IN SUCH A SERI-
ous state of decay that many wondered whether they would ever
recover. Candidates were creating their own organizations in running for office and they were gaining access to voters through the
media rather than through party precinct workers. Party nominees were being selected by primaries rather than by the party
leadership and the party had little control over the nominees who
won elections. Party voting in Congress declined as representatives
asserted their independence. Voters were identifying with candidates rather than with parties. They were also increasingly likely to
vote a split ticket, a sign of weak party identification. Voter turnout was steadily declining and parties were therefore failing to accomplish one of their most important tasks—to mobilize voters
and get them to the polls. Every indicator pointed to the weakness
of our parties.

Political scientists studying these phenomena understandably
focused their attention on the role which the increasing use of primary elections have played in undermining parties. Between 1960
and 1980 the number of presidential primaries increased from 17
to 37 and the percentage of delegates to national conventions selected by primaries increased from 38 to 75 percent. These were
also the decades during which the decline of political parties became manifest to all politically aware citizens. It is virtually a matter of definition that a heavy reliance on primaries will weaken
political parties. Political parties are institutions which mediate the
relationship between elected officials and the electorate; primaries
establish a direct linkage between elected officials and the electorate and thereby circumvent party as a mediating institution.

If one focuses on the role which primaries have played in undermining parties it is natural to lay a great deal of blame for the
decline of parties on the 1970 McGovern-Fraser Commission. This

commission called for extensive democratizing reforms in the Democratic Party to avoid a repetition of the 1968 Democratic convention in Chicago. In that convention, Hubert Humphrey had been selected as the Democratic Party standard-bearer despite his unpopularity with grass roots activists who held him partially responsible for our deepening involvement in the Vietnam War. The reforms which were adopted provided for a more open caucus system as well as for the use of presidential primaries, but a presidential primary appeared to be the most democratic option available and democratization was the imperative of the day. Most states instituted primaries through reform laws which applied to the Republican as well as the Democratic Party.

In retrospect these reforms were clearly misguided. In the name of democracy they weakened political parties even though parties would appear to be indispensable in the governance of liberal democracies. Nevertheless, the McGovern-Fraser reforms were just as clearly weakening an institution which was already in trouble. Voter turnout had been declining throughout the 1960s. The percentage of the electorate which considered themselves independent, rather than identified with a major party, increased from 23 to 31 percent during the same period. Split-ticket voting for President/Senate elections increased from 11 to 28 percent between 1960 and 1972, and from 14 to 30 percent for President/Representative elections.[1] Dwight Eisenhower and Adlai Stevenson dominated the presidential politics of the 1950s and both were admired and respected because they were not career politicians or party men. Their public personae seemed to rise above politics. John Kennedy demonstrated the possibility of building a coalition based on individual charisma rather than partisan loyalty as early as 1960. The crisis of our parties antedated the McGovern-Fraser reforms.

Paradoxically, the source of the contemporary crisis in political parties may lie as far back as the New Deal. This is paradoxical because the immediate impact of the New Deal was to strengthen parties. Franklin Roosevelt was one of those leaders who either elicited love or hate. His New Deal polarized the political system into supporters and detractors and the coalitions which resulted endured until at least the late 1960s. When parties offer voters a clear choice between distinct political agendas and voters come down clearly and decisively on the side of one of the parties, political scientists have described such elections as realigning. The

---

[1] Warren E. Miller, Arthur H. Miller, and Edward J. Schneider, *American National Elections Studies Data Sourcebook,* 1952–1978 (Cambridge: Harvard University Press, 1980), 81,385,387.

elections cited as realigning are among the most famous in American political history: 1800 and the victory of the Jeffersonians over the Federalists; 1828 and the rise of Jacksonian Democracy; 1860 when Lincoln and the Republican party came to power; and 1896 when the Republicans defeated William Jennings Bryan. Most political scientists believe that the New Deal was the occasion of such an electoral realignment, although they are more likely to identify the 1936 Presidential election, rather than the 1932 election, as the critical election. In 1932 people were rejecting Hoover, whereas in 1936 they were embracing Roosevelt and his New Deal. Realigning elections have historically invigorated political parties, and if the 1936 election was a true realigning election it should have had this effect as well. While the New Deal did decisively shape the American party system for many years to come, its invigoration of political parties proved amazingly short-lived.[2]

One possible explanation for the ambiguous legacy of the 1936 election is that it differed in a fundamental way from the 19th century realigning elections with which it is usually linked. Each of the 19th century realigning elections could be described at least in part as a contest over ideas or moral principles. The programs of each of the competing parties was associated with a particular conception of justice, and the realignment marked the clear victory of one of these conceptions of justice. While the New Deal has often been described in similar terms, such a description is misleading. The New Deal was in fact unique because it represented not the triumph of a particular conception of justice but rather the triumph of an economic perspective over any conception of justice.[3] This may well be the case in the final analysis, but politically speaking even the appearance of abstraction from moral concerns may have significant consequences. Or perhaps it would be more accurate to say that while concerns of justice did not altogether disappear during the New Deal, its democratic and equalitarian claims were filtered through an economic lens which tended to obscure their moral status.

The New Deal's attempt to replace moral reasoning by economic reasoning was not unprecedented. Liberalism as a political philosophy has been associated with an expansion of the economic

---

[2]Walter Dean Burnham, "The End of American Party Politics," *Society* 7:2 (December 1969).

[3]Philosophers may object that the science of economics and/or decisions about the scope of its application may rest upon moral premises, and that the triumph of the economic perspective during the New Deal therefore represents the triumph of a particular moral perspective which would include a specific conception of justice.

realm and a contraction of the political realm, although some liberals have embraced this project more enthusiastically and without reservation than others. The intellectuals and philosophers who fashioned liberalism in the 17th and 18th centuries were appalled by the consequences of religiously inspired conflict, and they recognized that the prevailing moral codes and their associated conceptions of justice were grounded in religious beliefs. To defuse these conflicts, liberals developed a scientific psychology which debunked the pretensions of the morally self-righteous by unmasking the true motives hiding behind seemingly high-minded actions. Justice was a front for pride, the love of domination, and even tyranny.

Liberals dismissed a politics based on pride as focusing on symbolic issues, as if such issues were epiphenomenal and would be unimportant to an enlightened man. A lasting peace could only be achieved if man renounced the quest for justice and thereby prideful self-assertion, recognized the equality of all men, and turned from a politics based on pride to a politics based on the satisfaction of bodily needs and desires. A politics based on self-interested economic claims was supposed to have the virtue that such claims were easily moderated and therefore provided a foundation for compromises. In its most radical form a politics based on bodily needs and desires is not a politics at all but rather is more properly described as an administration of the economic realm. The New Deal is an example of a radical form of this project.

If competing conceptions of justice invigorate party systems, then it would be easy to understand why the New Deal did not invigorate the American party system for very long. The triumph of economics, a perspective which demands systematic abstraction from moral concerns, would probably have the same consequences for partisanship as the emergence of widespread cynicism concerning either the possibility of achieving justice or the possibility of knowing the just. Detachment from the quest for justice is enervating. Before we can examine the consequences of the New Deal for political parties, however, we must first demonstrate that the New Deal was a radical attempt to displace politics by economics. This characteristic of the New Deal is most visible in the early New Deal.

THE EARLY NEW DEAL AND THE NRA

Most historians divide the New Deal into two periods, each of which was initiated by a flurry of legislative activity lasting approximately one hundred days. The early New Deal extended from 1933 to 1935 and was launched during the first one hundred days when such landmark legislation as the Securities Act, the Agricultural Adjustment Act of 1933, the Tennessee Valley Authority Act, and the Glass-Steagall Banking Act were rushed through Congress. As important as the reforms introduced by these pieces of legislation were, they are dwarfed by comparison with the most important single act of the early New Deal, the National Industrial Recovery Act (NIRA). The NIRA and the National Recovery Administration (NRA) which it established were the keystone of Roosevelt's early New Deal. They were intended to simultaneously promote economic recovery and fundamentally alter the character of our economic and political system. Under the NRA an economy based upon competition was to be replaced by an economy based upon cooperation.

Virtually everyone who examines the NRA describes it as a corporatist program, indeed the most expansive peacetime experiment with corporatism in American history. There are unresolved debates concerning the appropriate definition of corporatism, but most scholars would at least agree that non-authoritarian corporatism is an attempt to institutionalize bargaining among economic interests for the sake of achieving consensus and cooperation among these interests on matters of economic policy. The division between capitalists and workers has been the source of some of the most bitter conflicts among economic interests, and the paradigm cases of corporatism, countries like Sweden and Austria, encourage bargaining between peak associations of labor and capital to achieve consensus. Sectoral conflicts, particularly conflicts between the agricultural and industrial sectors, are another important source of conflict in modern economies which corporatist institutions have attempted to mediate. Government may be a party to the negotiations which occur in a corporatist context, but it is supposed to act as a neutral umpire facilitating voluntary solutions rather than as a heavy handed arbitrator imposing solutions from without.

Intellectuals have inspired and supported corporatist experimentation in Western Europe and the United States by arguing that corporatism provides the most durable and appropriate institutional foundation for liberal democracy. This argument was developed most extensively by neo-Hegelians during the latter part of the nineteenth and the early part of the twentieth century. These thinkers sought to reestablish a basis for community in the modern state by refurbishing interest groups or economic classes and providing a framework for policy-making which could serve as an alternative to both the marketplace (governed by motives of economic self-interest) and the state (dominated by imperious, largely unaccountable bureaucracies). This movement of thought was essentially liberal. Its goal was not to revive those forms of community which had stifled individuality in the past but rather to fashion new forms of community which would encourage a new individualism. Rather than repudiating rights, these corporatist liberals wanted to give new meaning to the term "rights," applying it to economic as well as political life. Liberal corporatism is therefore distinct from at least some versions of catholic corporatism which have been less sympathetic to individualism and rights; and liberal corporatism must certainly be distinguished from fascist and authoritarian corporatism.

Among the intellectuals who advocated reforms in this direction are the Webbs, the early Harold Laski, Leon Duguit, and John Dewey. These liberal corporatists generally described themselves as socialists; but the socialism they advocated was not simply state ownership of the means of production but rather a form of guild socialism which, if pursued to its logical extreme, demands the replacement of parliamentary/congressional-presidential political arrangements with a congress of economic interests. Trade associations and trade unions would become the fundamental political units of representation, and a general congress of interest groups would be divided along class lines. It is this aspect of corporatism which makes a study of the NRA indispensable to a study of New Deal partisanship; for if the NRA is a somewhat watered-down version of this form of corporatism, then there was an anti-party animus associated with the early New Deal.[4] Parties were institutions which organized elections within a parliamentary or congressional context. Parties are associated with territorial rather than functional representation. Indeed, parties could destroy the "logic" of functional representation by "artificially" dividing functionally undifferentiated units. For instance, parties might reinforce ethnic and religious differences by following those lines of cleavage in the polity and thus destroying the solidarity of a functional category like "steelworkers."

Two presuppositions generally associated with the corporatist world-view are worthy of note. The first is that people's interests are fundamentally defined by the economic role they play. Non-economic interests should be relativised. They are subjective rather than objective interests, and they should be consigned to the private sphere for satisfaction. The model here is the way liberals handled religious conflicts, and the scenario of religious toleration can be generalized to handle all non-economic issues.

---

[4]For an argument that there is a connection between this intellectual Tradition and the NRA, see Donald R. Brand, *Corporatism and the Rule of Law* (Ithaca: Cornell University Press, 1988), Part I.

Rationality is associated with economic interests, and a rational system of representation will therefore be structured along economic or functional lines. Philippe Schmitter's widely utilized definition of corporatism incorporates this presupposition in the very definition of corporatism:

Corporatism can be defined as a system of interest representation in which the constituent units are organized into a limited number of singular, compulsory, noncompetitive, hierarchically ordered and *functionally differentiated* categories, recognized or licensed (if not created) by the state and granted a deliberate representational monopoly within their respective categories in exchange for observing certain controls on their selection of leaders and articulation of demands and supports.[5]

A second presupposition is the potential reconciliation of economic conflicts of interests. Properly structured (i.e., corporatism) a regime could produce far more unity than these theorists had discovered under capitalist liberalism. Collectivising ownership alone might not eliminate the clashes of interest between managers and workers, but if combined with a guild structure to nurture solidaristic inclinations, the conflicts of interest between managers and workers will not be as intractable as the earlier clashes between capitalists and workers. Similarly, divisions between producers and consumers will prove to be more apparent than real. An economic congress can therefore act on the basis of consensus rather than majority rule. The potential veto power possessed by either unions or trade associations need not be a problem since an economic policy which serves the interests of both is discoverable. Bargaining and compromise will produce the requisite social unity. If consensus is possible, parties would appear to be superfluous.

The aspirations which lay behind the NRA shed important light on the status of partisanship in the New Deal, but the fate of the NRA also provides ample grounds for concluding that the New Deal devaluation of parties was inappropriate and based on an unworkable political psychology. The immediate reason for the demise of the NRA was, of course, that the Supreme Court declared the NIRA unconstitutional in *United States* v. *Schechter Poultry Corp.*[6] But historians have frequently noted that the NRA was in deep trouble before the Supreme Court stepped in and mercifully laid it to rest. The premise of the NRA was that industrial self-government would provide a framework capable of eliciting

[5]Philippe Schmitter, "Still the Century of Corporatism," in *Trends Toward Corporatist Intermediation*, ed. Philippe Schmitter and Gerhard Lehmbruch (Beverly Hills, Calif., 1979), 13. [emphasis mine]

[6]295 U.S. 495 (1935)

public-spirited and cooperative behavior from participants. These expectations proved overly sanguine. Many businesses, trade associations, and labor unions simply tried to maximize their own self-interest. Others attempted to act responsibly, but were forced by competitive pressures to quickly resume a more self-interested posture. The NRA soon degenerated into an orgy of self-interested factionalism and economic recovery was actually retarded. While the term "self-interested" is used to describe the behavior of the participants in the NRA drama, this term connotes more than simply economic interests. Differences of economic interests will only go so far in explaining the demise of the NRA. Critical actors in the process were driven by pride to act in ways which went contrary to their economic interests, and any explanation which ignored this fact would be incomplete.

As an example, take the struggle between business and labor. The NRA had envisioned that labor and business would cooperate in drafting and administering codes of fair trade competition. According to Section 7a of the NIRA, labor was to be accorded the right to organize and bargain collectively. The National Labor Board and, subsequently, the National Labor Relations Board, agencies established to implement Section 7a, concluded that this right entailed federally supervised labor elections in which the union winning a majority of the votes would be recognized as the legitimate bargaining partner, speaking for all of the workers in an industry. Businessmen often refused to grant this recognition. They drafted proposed codes without the input of labor and insisted on administering the codes through code authorities without formal labor representation. They resisted unionization even when it entailed the economic hardships associated with a prolonged strike or an economic boycott. Yet firms could function quite profitably after granting recognition and sharing power with labor unions, so it does not appear that the resistance of firms to the development of unions was motivated strictly by economic considerations. Businessmen were defending their managerial prerogatives and the *status* associated with those prerogatives. Firms were their property and property entailed the right to use it and control it. Unions were challenging not so much their economic interests as their rights and their status.

One cannot read a history of labor unions during this period without coming to a similar conclusion. Most of the strikes during this period concerned the implementation of Section 7a, not higher wages or shorter hours. Labor unions sought rights and recognition, and workers demanded respect more than immediate economic advantages. Workers sacrificed economic interests, and at times took extraordinary risks, for the sake of establishing and preserving their pride in themselves. Because they were driven by pride, they were at times less willing to compromise than they would have been had they been driven by economic consider- ations. Businessmen had attempted to establish company unions as an alternative to independent labor unions, and they demanded that these company unions be represented at the bargaining table in proportion to the votes they secured in labor elections. The American Federation of Labor rejected any such division of labor representation. They refused to sit at the same table with labor quislings and stooges of business, they refused to grant them any recognition of legitimacy. They preferred to risk everything to gain genuine representation, even though their interests might well have been advanced in a multiple representation scheme.[7] Perhaps they realized that pride-inspired conflicts are zero-sum, that there must be winners and losers, and that they had to deal a defeat to business if they were to advance their own claims for self- respect. The struggle for recognition doomed corporatism and its appeals for moderation and cooperation.

Social scientists who have rejected economic reductionism have always been skeptical of corporatism. If non-economic con- flicts cannot be dismissed as irrational, rendered moot through privatization, or reinterpreted as economic conflicts, then one could argue that a congress based on functional representation is at the least an inappropriate arena for resolving non-economic conflicts. Moreover, if the logic of corporatist representation sug- gests consensual decision-making on the presumption that com- mon interests do exist and can be recognized, then the use of such a decision-making procedure in handling zero-sum non-economic conflicts will lead to stalemate. Issues which might otherwise have been resolved may fester, become coupled with other issues, and eventually lead to a regime crisis. To provide resolution for non- economic conflicts, some form of majority rule or an approxima- tion to it (at the very least no veto power to groups) would seem to be necessary. The parliamentary institutions associated with tra- ditional liberalism were better structured to handle divisive issues.[8]

If one did not go beyond the considerations mentioned above, it would still seem plausible to have a division of labor between two congresses, one based on territorial representation and the other based on functional representation. Economic issues would be

[7]Brand, Chapter 10.

[8]Indeed traditional parliamentary structures arose out of the cultural struggle between liberals and defenders of the ancient regime, and thus they were in part designed to handle such a cultural conflict.

handled by the latter and non-economic issues by the former. Our analysis of the NRA suggests that any such scheme would quickly break down. The problem runs much deeper than the problem of borderline cases. The problem is that even issues which appear to be indisputably economic in fact involve far more complex considerations. Human pride is inextricably intertwined with economic interests; our interest in property is bound up with the demand for recognition. Even if economic conflicts are not intractable, this may make little difference if it is impossible to segregate economic and non-economic concerns.

The fact that liberal democracy appears to be alive and well in such small Western European nations as Sweden, Austria, Switzerland, and the Netherlands despite high degrees of corporatism in these nations, would appear to belie the dismal scenario mentioned above. These nations have experienced rates of economic growth comparable to, or even at times exceeding, the growth of the less corporatist large nations of Western Europe. Conflicts do not appear to be festering in these societies. They do not appear to be headed for a crisis of regime legitimacy. The experiences of these nations may nevertheless be the exception which proves the rule regarding the relationship between corporatism and liberal democracy. Sweden is a nation long noted for its cultural homogeneity. In small nations where it may be possible to speak of unity concerning fundamental values, where the most divisive issues faced are the relatively tractable conflicts of economic interests, and where there is little danger that economic issues will become vehicles for cultural conflicts because the latter are minimal to begin with, then corporatism and a consensual politics may well be feasible. It could nevertheless be argued that such conditions are atypical and that cultural homogeneity is unlikely to be preserved in the modern world.

THE NEW DEAL LEGACY

The New Deal attempt to universalize economics destabilized the American two party system. This instability was not immediately evident in part because the New Deal coalition was still winning Presidential elections as late as 1964 and in part because political scientists failed to see the signs of decay. Most political scientists were themselves New Deal liberals, sharing the belief that politics could essentially be reduced to economics, and they therefore tended to conceptualize parties as nothing more than interest aggregators. Contrary to the expectations of the New Dealers, however, interests proved difficult to aggregate and even successful bargaining did not necessarily arrive at the public interest. The legitimization the New Deal ideology provided to interest groups astutely pursuing their self-interest made it all the more difficult for political leaders to appeal for moderation. Sacrificing self-interest in the service of something higher became virtually unthinkable. Narrowly self-interested demands and obstructionism became increasingly familiar aspects of interest group politics. The standard diagnosis of the problem with the American political system became its vulnerability to stalemate, but political scientists were far more inclined to blame the Founders and their Constitution rather than Roosevelt and his New Deal.

The post-New Deal political stalemate had another, more visible and familiar aspect. The Democratic Party was the dominant party of the age, and liberals and moderates dominated the presidential selection process of the Democratic party. Presidents therefore tended to be relatively liberal. Congress, on the other hand, was dominated by southern conservative Democrats who had risen to powerful committee chairmanships through the seniority system. Conservative legislation faced an almost certain presidential veto. Liberal legislation, even when initiated by the President with all the advantages which that conveys, would often fail as conservative southern Democrats joined with conservative Republicans. This characteristic of our political system was not simply the predetermined consequence of impersonal societal forces. Political decisions made during the New Deal shaped the coalitions which solidified in its wake.

Southern conservatives acquired the power which they had in Congress in part because they could continue to identify with the Democratic party. Roosevelt made this possible by agreeing to keep reform of race relations off the political agenda in exchange for support for his New Deal economic reforms. The infamous symbol of this trade was Roosevelt's refusal to make an anti-lynching bill a priority of his administration in 1934, in effect thereby killing legislation that would have helped to secure the most fundamental of natural rights, due process of law, for black Americans living in the South. In exchange for this, Roosevelt asserted that he gained greater freedom to advance other aspects of his New Deal program, especially his economic initiatives. Roosevelt clearly subordinated the issue of race to the issue of economic recovery.

Some would argue that although the early New Deal emphasized economic recovery at the expense of justice, the second New Deal was more radical because it elevated a politics of interest to a politics of principle. One example of the new emphasis on principle during the second New Deal was Roosevelt's 1938 Democratic Party purge. Targeting those Democrats who had distinguished themselves by their opposition to New Deal initiatives, Roosevelt asserted that the Democratic Party had committed itself to a "liberal declaration of principles" in the 1936 Democratic platform and that there was no longer room in the party for those who were out of step with the New Deal. This invocation of principles might indicate an appeal to moral principles. Had the second New Deal in fact rejected the primacy of economics which we have discovered in the first New Deal? Had this second, more ideological New Deal restored the moral and political to their rightful preeminence over economics? A closer look at the purge of 1938 renders any such interpretation of the second New Deal dubious.

Roosevelt's treatment of racial segregation in the South provides critical insights into the status of moral principles during the second New Deal. While it is true that Roosevelt provided more support for an anti-lynching bill introduced in 1938 than he had for the anti-lynching bill of 1934, he still abandoned the bill to save his economic initiatives after a struggle ensued with Southerners in Congress. Furthermore, Roosevelt's 1938 Democratic party purge was not targeted against Southerners. His strategy had Western and Northern components as well; indeed, the only real success in the purge campaign was the unseating of John O'Connor, a New York Congressman who chaired the Rules Committee. Neither did it target those who defended racial segregation, as long as they had not stood in the way of the advancement of the economic agenda of the New Deal. Senator "Cotton Ed" Smith of South Carolina, one of the most notorious defenders of segregation, was one of the targets of the purge; but Roosevelt supported Smith's opponent, Governor Olin D. Johnson, because he was more likely to support the New Deal's economic agenda. Johnson was no more a defender of racial equality than "Cotton Ed" Smith was, and during the campaign he even accused Smith of once "voting to let a big buck nigger sit next to your wife or daughter on a train."[9] The "liberal declaration of principles" to which Roosevelt demanded adherence turned out to be not support for an equalitarian principle of justice but rather support for New Deal economic experimentation.

One possible explanation for Roosevelt's reluctance to embrace the cause of racial justice was that he was simply uncon-

[9]James MacGregor Burns, *Roosevelt, The Lion and the Fox*, (New York: Harcourt, Brace and Company, 1956), 364.

cerned about the fate of black Americans. The expansiveness of his sympathy for the downtrodden argues against such an assertion. Roosevelt was undoubtedly perfectly sincere when he told Mary Bethune, a leading black educator whom he had appointed to head the Office of Minority Affairs for the National Youth Administration, "People like you and me are fighting and must continue to fight for the day when a man will be regarded as a man regardless of his race or faith or country."[10] It is far more likely that Roosevelt believed he was working to establish racial justice by advancing the economic agenda of the New Deal. Liberals have often been susceptible to a variety of interrelated beliefs: that man is fundamentally an economic being, that poverty is the worst of evils, that poverty is the true cause of such evils as crime and racism, and that a combination of economic abundance and enlightenment will eliminate destructive forms of conflict. Middle and upper class reformers had always found the more openly-expressed racism of lower and working class whites more offensive than the more genteel racism of their own classes, and it was therefore plausible to them that poverty breeds racism. Such beliefs would certainly rationalize the tacit deal which Roosevelt struck with southern conservatives.

The naivete of the beliefs that racial conflicts were really just transposed economic conflicts and that racial tensions could be overcome by eliminating poverty should be readily apparent to anyone living in the 1990s. The development of a black middle class over the past twenty years has had little impact on racial tensions. As the economic condition of blacks has generally improved, race has become more rather than less salient electorally. Anyone who still believes that integration will accompany economic betterment should visit the nearest "integrated" college campus which recruits its student body, black and white, predominantly from the middle class. Racial separation, not integration, is the norm. An increasing number of black high school graduates are opting to go to traditional Negro colleges rather than cope with the hypocrisy and tensions of an integrated campus. Racial pride, in both its negative and positive manifestations, has reasserted itself.

Politics has followed suit. The easy-going politics of interest group bargaining and compromises, the form of politics which the New Deal had hoped it could produce, has given way to a more strident and conflicted politics. New Deal liberals may lament this

[10]Arthur Schlesinger Jr., *The Politics of Upheaval*, (Boston: Houghton Mifflin Company, 1960). 435.

fact, but we cannot simply wish away a powerful and enduring motive like pride just because it complicates political life. Nor need we despair. Racial warfare is not inevitable just because pride has become central to racial politics. Pride is not simply impervious to reason and it is not always associated with immoderation. The issue of pride was at the center of Frederick Douglass's statesmanship, yet Douglass remained devoted to the moderate cause of liberal constitutionalism. A proud man demands more than economic security—he demands justice and some recognition of his nobility. These claims are not inherently incompatible with a decent politics and they are more elevated than the claims of economic self-interest.

The emphasis which Roosevelt placed on economic growth and the widespread distribution of the fruits of economic growth contributed both to the breadth and the vulnerability of the New Deal coalition. As long as New Dealers could sustain the image of proficient economic managers, they could attract under their political banner an extraordinarily broad assortment of groups. But when economic growth slowed during the 1970s and the intellectual hegemony of Keynesian economics, the system of ideas which had become identified with the New Deal had been shattered, then the absence of a clear moral core led to a fragmentation of that coalition. A common standard of justice is the glue which holds a party together, and conflicts between working class whites and blacks—two of the groups most closely identified with the New Deal—over such issues as busing and the welfare state proved irreconcilable because there was no shared higher standard to appeal to. The belated attempt of John Rawls to supply a theory of justice which basically rationalized the post New-Deal order proved too little and too late.

It is interesting to speculate about the path American political history might have taken if Roosevelt had in fact built the Democratic party around a consistently equalitarian or democratic principle of justice. Certainly Roosevelt would have had little to lose by attempting such a realignment in the late 1930s. New Deal reformism was dead in Congress and could only have been revived by fundamental political change. If Roosevelt had applied the principle of equality to race relations, Southern conservatives would probably have seceded from the Democratic party, but they were obstructing Roosevelt from within the party in any case. Some southern conservatives undoubtedly would have joined the Republican party, but many southerners could never have joined the party they held responsible for the civil war and the defeat of the South and many others were sufficiently hostile to Wall Street to reject any alliance with the party identified with big business. It seems likely that the one party system of the South would have broken down earlier than it in fact did.

It is highly unlikely that there would have been dramatic progress toward achieving equality for black Americans. Greater progress than did in fact occur, however, was certainly feasible. An anti-lynching bill appealed to widely accepted American values, as George Gallup discovered in 1938 when an early public opinion survey revealed 57 percent of southerners and 72 percent of the nation favored such legislation.[11] In the long run, race relations might have evolved in a very different manner than they did. If race had been on the political agenda in the New Deal and even piecemeal progress had been made in achieving legal equality for blacks, then the courts might not have felt the need to intrude so forcefully later in the century. If relations between the races had been defined more by the political process and less by the legal process, then the debate concerning issues of race would not have been so pervasively formulated in legal terms. Formulating issues legalistically has a tendency to exacerbate some forms of conflict by encouraging immoderate formulation of demands in terms of rights and by holding out the possibility of producing a clear cut winner if the judges side with you. Busing as a policy would have been dead on arrival politically, but the goal of school desegregation in major urban centers was never achieved in any case, and the policy generated intense white backlash. Voting rights and the exercise of black political muscle would have been the focus of the civil rights movement; progress toward black equality would have been achieved less by the intervention of mostly white judges and more through black self-help. There is every reason to believe this would have been salutary.

It is also interesting to broaden the horizon beyond the issue of race and to speculate on the general consequences which the creation of a principled party of equality might have had for the Supreme Court. The "liberal" Warren Court was to an extraordinary extent shaped by its role in *Brown* v. *Board of Education*. I put liberal in quotes because *Brown* v. *Board of Education* was more concerned with equality than it was with liberty and it can be argued that this was true of many other major Warren Court decisions as well.[12] The problem of race put the problem of equality at the center of

[11]Harvard Sitkoff, *A New Deal for Blacks*, (New York: Oxford University Press, 1978), p. 291.

[12]Phillip B. Kurland, *Politics, the Constitution, and the Warren Court* (Chicago: The University of Chicago Press, 1970).

the Court's thinking during this era, and this represented a fundamental departure from the traditional focus of the Court on the issue of liberty.

As Tocqueville so brilliantly demonstrated in an analysis which is as relevant today as it was in the 1830s, liberty and equality are likely to be conflicting values in a democracy even if they can be theoretically reconciled. If equalitarianism had been advanced by a political party committed to an equalitarian principle of justice, would the Warren Court have retained the traditional focus on liberty even while redirecting it in unconventional directions? Undoubtedly a Court appointed by Roosevelt would have been particularly solicitous of the rights most valued by the democratic majority for whom Roosevelt spoke; but would a court still focused on liberty have abandoned the defense of property rights as thoroughly as the Warren Court did? Surely the actual record of the Warren Court in the area of property rights reflected its equalitarianism, its suspicion that property rights were fundamentally the rights of the wealthy. A court less influenced by equalitarianism might have articulated a more coherent version of liberalism, a version which did not draw an artificial line between economic rights and non-economic rights, and such a version of liberalism might have rallied liberals together under a common banner. The division of liberals into left and right liberals, the former committed to an expansive agenda of non-economic rights and the latter committed to an expansive conception of property rights, is one of the most important political facts of the latter half of the twentieth century.[13] Factionalism among liberals is likely to lead to the advancement of equalitarianism at the expense of liberty.

When Franklin Roosevelt chose the term liberal rather than the term progressive to describe his New Deal agenda he made the task of the political analyst considerably more difficult. It seems far more appropriate to describe Franklin Roosevelt as a democrat than as a liberal. The bond which Roosevelt established with the common man is unmistakable, and his New Deal agenda was designed to advance the interests of the many over the interests of the few. Roosevelt by nature was a modern day Jefferson, even though his representation of the common man was distorted by his emphasis on the economic at the expense of the political.

His record as a liberal is not nearly as noteworthy. When his New Deal agenda was threatened by the Supreme Court, he tried

---

[13]The most interesting exploration of the character of contemporary liberalism is Harvey C. Mansfield, Jr., *The Spirit of Liberalism*, (Cambridge: Harvard University Press, 1984).

to pack the Supreme Court. True liberals were horrified by this attack on the institution most closely identified with the protection of rights, and with the help of others, they were able to defeat Roosevelt's court packing scheme. This battle was not an aberration and it was not just a battle between Roosevelt and a set of cantankerous Justices defending an outmoded conception of property rights. The precedent which Roosevelt's court packing scheme would have established, if successful, would have affected the role of the Court even with a more prudent and sensible majority. Roosevelt's willingness to establish such a precedent reflected his general distrust of lawyers and legalism. For liberals, on the other hand, the rule of law is virtually sacrosanct because it is indispensable to a regime which respects rights. The conclusion that Roosevelt was fundamentally a democrat (small d) and not a liberal would also explain why Roosevelt could have tolerated the incarceration of Japanese-Americans during World War II, the most shocking violation of civil liberties in this country during the twentieth century.

If Roosevelt had been true to his democratic genius, he certainly could have gone far in reconstituting the Democratic Party upon an equalitarian principle of justice; and if he had done so, then the tensions which Tocqueville identified between liberty and equality might have been more clearly reflected in the partisan and institutional cleavages of American political life. The Supreme Court would not have been the only institution affected. The division between the parties might also have more clearly reflected the tension between equality and liberty. In Tocquevillian terms one might say that conventional political parties would more closely approximate the natural political parties which form in a liberal democracy. A party of equality would have called forth a party of liberty, which in turn would defend the justifiable inequalities which emerge under conditions of liberty. Indeed, a party of liberty might be thought of as the liberal surrogate for the aristocratic parties of earlier times, since liberty is sometimes conceived of not only as an end in itself but also as a means to the achievement of excellence, the end pursued by the natural aristocracy.

Such parties would be more clearly wedded to distinct principles of justice, and a division of parties along such lines could reasonably be expected to lead to more elevated political debates and to a more high-toned politics in general. The British have been widely admired for the quality of their political debates, and it is hard to believe that this characteristic of their political system is unrelated to the fact that their political parties have tended to divide either along democratic/aristocratic lines or democratic/

liberal lines. Parties respectively committed to equality and to liberty would embody partial principles of justice. Justice, therefore, would emerge more clearly as the central issue of American politics, and one has better grounds for hope that justice will emerge out of the conflict between two such parties than one does from any other imaginable political configuration. At the very least, the creation of a party system where parties divide over principles of justice should invigorate political parties, and almost all political scientists would agree that vigorous political parties are indispensable to the stability of liberal democracy.

CONCLUSION

We have been describing a road not taken in American politics. It has been the contention of this article that this road was not taken because Roosevelt did not truly embrace an equalitarian principle of justice and that he did not do so, fundamentally and unambiguously, because he believed that economics could displace politics. The New Deal was not the first time that an attempt had been made to replace the politically contentious search for justice with a consensus derived from economics. Ironically, the same aspiration inspired the liberals who opposed the New Deal in the name of laissez-faire capitalism. Indeed, one can find the origins of such a project in the writings of Locke, Montesquieu, Adam Smith, and other founders of the liberal tradition. The New Dealers simply radicalized and extended the work begun by others. Nevertheless, the radicalism of their project was its most serious defect. The most profound liberal theorists have been those who have seen the limits of any attempt to replace politics by economics, and the greatest liberal statesmen are those who have rescued liberal democracy from the destructive consequences that would follow from the systematic implementation of this ideal.

The Federalist, one of the greatest works in the liberal tradition, exemplifies this profounder dimension of liberalism. *The Federalist* does not suggest that all conflicts are fundamentally conflicts of economic interest even though they acknowledge that "the most common and durable source of factions has been the various and unequal distribution of property."[14] A common and durable source of factions is not necessarily the most important source of factions, and conflicts arising from differences of opinion and emotional attachments to leaders are treated with at least as much

---

[14]Clinton Rossiter, ed., *The Federalist Papers* (New York, 1961), No. 10, 79.

seriousness as conflicts arising from the unequal division of property.[15] According to the Federalists the causes of faction are "sown in the nature of man," and they therefore reject the possibility of rising above factious conflicts to achieve a transpolitical harmony. The "spirit of party and faction" will inevitably rear its head in "the necessary and ordinary operations of government." The "spirit of party and faction" is to be expected, but it is not to be given free reign. Our political institutions were designed to enhance the possibility that the moderate voice of reason would hold sway rather than the immoderate voice of passion.

The Founders understood all too well the obstacles which stood in the way of a politics based upon reason, but they did not share the hope of some that a surrogate for reason could be found among the passions. The radical claims that greed was a more tractable and decent passion than pride, that in the proper institutional context greed could be channeled in the service of the public good, and that greed guided by a narrow calculating rationality would therefore suffice as a psychological foundation for a liberal democratic regime, were dismissed. In *Federalist* No. 6 Hamilton examines and rejects the claim that "the spirit of commerce has a tendency to soften the manners of men." Commercial republics are as belligerent as any other regime. Commercial republics are more likely to fight wars to gain wealth, but as Hamilton asks rhetorically, "Is not the love of wealth as domineering and enterprising a passion as that of power or glory?" In short, the Federalists do not expect economics to displace politics, and they do not expect the passion most closely associated with economic life—greed—to replace the passion most closely associated with political life—pride.

Consistent with this evaluation of the importance of pride as a political passion, one finds an expectation of a more high-toned political life. There are numerous appeals to virtue in *The Federalist* notwithstanding the notable political realism of the work. In *Federalist* No. 51, one of the most important papers, Madison acknowledges that the goal or end of the new polity is lofty indeed: "Justice is the end of government."[16] Finally, *The Federalist* defends the proposed Constitution as a system admirably suited to infuse reason into public deliberations. By reason they do not seem to mean the rather narrow calculating capacity held in high esteem by economists, but rather something broader. According to the Federalists,

---

[15]My reading of *The Federalist* has been deeply influenced by David Epstein, *The Political Theory of the Federalists* (Chicago: The University of Chicago Press, 1984).
[16]Rossiter, ed., 324.

the world does not present itself to us as units of some homogeneous underlying matter, quantities of which can be compared and summed. Rather, reality is complex and heterogeneous, differentiated into species and genera which must be distinguished to facilitate categorization and judgment of events. Theoretical precision is probably beyond human reach, but this need not paralyze us practically; and the Federalists do not draw the conclusion that therefore reason should be redirected along new lines.[17] It is our fate to struggle to achieve clarity in a world which reveals itself imperfectly, but the clarity which we can achieve is nevertheless useful in moderating the passions. A reasonable legislature is one which is less likely to act unjustly and not simply one which is less likely to act inefficiently.

The political science of the Federalists was a political science which dealt seriously with man's longing for justice. By contrast, contemporary political science generally ignores the power of this motive. This is particularly the case in the study of political parties. Too often, political scientists have focused exclusively on the organizational dimensions of strong parties—the kinds of rules of the game which centralize power and allow leaders to discipline followers versus the kinds of rules of the game which decentralize power and encourage independence and revolts against leadership. The kinds of variables which are central to such an analysis are undoubtedly important, but there is an additional element which enters the picture in a liberal democracy where a party cannot rely exclusively upon coercion. In such a regime, the rules of the game which govern any party organization will only retain their legitimacy over the long run if they have some connection to a principle of justice. Without such a connection even the strongest organization can whither and die.

Broadly understood, even though the Framers were suspicious of political parties their constitutional framework is hospitable to principled political parties because it encourages respect for and concern about justice. By contrast, even though the New Deal seemed to accept the need for partisanship the constitutional refounding attempted by the New Deal was inhospitable to principled political parties *because* it tended to sever the connection between political parties and justice. Those who would like to reinvigorate American political parties should begin by returning to the American Founding.

[17]Ibid., 227–230.

POLITICAL PARTIES, THE CONSTITUTION, AND THE FUTURE OF AMERICAN POLITICS

Charles R. Kesler

THE UNITED STATES CONSTITUTION IS A PARTISAN DOCUMENT, though it says nothing of political parties. It is partisan above all because it stands for a particular kind of government, for republican government, which it undertakes to guarantee to the states.[1] But who or what guarantees that the national government itself shall remain republican? The Constitution's own "auxiliary precautions"—separation of powers and legislative checks and balances—are just that, auxiliary. In the final analysis, it is "We the People" who are, in *The Federalist*'s words, "the primary control on the government," and thus the essential guarantors of American republicanism.[2]

The problem, of course, is how to enforce this guarantee, given that "it is impossible for the people spontaneously and universally to move in concert towards their object."[3] In order to save themselves, therefore, the people must accept some informal, extra-constitutional authority, and consequent organization. This is the need that American political parties were invented to fill, first as emergency mechanisms and then as regular, though still

---

[1]In Article IV, section 4: "The United States shall guarantee to every State in this Union a Republican Form of Government, and shall protect each of them against invasion, and on Application of the Legislature, or of the Executive (when the Legislature cannot be convened) against domestic Violence."
[2]See Alexander Hamilton, James Madison, and John Jay, *The Federalist Papers*, ed. Clinton Rossiter (New York: New American Library, 1961), No. 51, 322.
[3]*The Federalist*, No. 40, 253.

informal, parts of our politics.[4] They were devised to preserve the Constitution against its enemies, to protect the Republic by encouraging good men to keep a jealous guard of it—by keeping a watchful eye on one another.

Loyalty to the Constitution was thus the historic touchstone of America's party politics. Whatever parties did, and in due course they did plenty—recruiting and nominating candidates at the local, state, and national levels; motivating voters to go to the polls; dividing up the spoils of office—they did ultimately in the name of guarding the Constitution. And though this reason could become a pretext for abuse of political power, it also provided the indispensable standards by which abuses could be judged. Serious partisan disputes were therefore constitutional disputes. So it was with Jefferson's Democratic-Republican opposition to the "monocrats" in 1800; Jackson's hostility to internal improvements and the "Money Power" in the 1820s and 1830s; Lincoln's refusal to allow the Constitution to become a pro-slavery document in the 1850s; the debate over social and economic regulation in the late 19th century, and so on.

In all these cases, American parties operated to restrain the passions of ambitious political men by forcing them to vie with other ambitious men in support of the Constitution. At the same time, parties harnessed such men's virtues and talents by connecting them to broader views of constitutional doctrine. The public benefited by being offered a choice between well-developed interpretations of these doctrines. A party *system*—in which more than one party could respectably and routinely contend for office—was able to emerge because the Constitution had room for several interpretations, though not for *every* interpretation, of its powers and principles.[5] Parties competed to prove their fidelity to the Constitution, each grudgingly conceding the legitimacy of the other(s), but insisting on its own superior credentials—and thus its right to define what was common ground, and what forbidden ground, in the public life.

In practice, these boundaries were set by the majority party; but the fight was always over who would get to set them—whose view of the Constitution would prevail. When the competing views

---

[4]For a fine overview of the justification and development of American parties, see James Ceaser, *Presidential Selection: Theory and Development* (Princeton: Princeton University Press, 1979).

[5]Roughly speaking, Americans could take either a more democratic or a more republican view of the democratic republic established by the Constitution. The former view emphasized popular sovereignty, the latter popular responsibility.

became sufficiently discordant, the American people faced a critical election whose consequences might include the overturn of the existing majority party, and the establishment of a new one. Such realigning elections are rare but revealing: they set the grounds of electoral competition for the next generation or two, and renew the nation's dedication to the moral and political goals of republicanism proclaimed in the Declaration of Independence and incorporated in the Constitution. Thus America's party system reflected the continuing vitality of the Constitution, and presupposed a healthy respect and even reverence for it.

Today, however, one seldom hears about the Constitution in connection with our political parties. Except for controversies over judicial and especially Supreme Court nominations—centering on abortion and the right to privacy—our political parties have little to say about the Constitution's relevance to their own functions. Partly this is because so many of the barriers the Constitution was once thought to raise to federal legislation have been removed or disregarded over the past 60 years. It has been a long time, for example, since the G.O.P. objected to a proposed new federal program not simply because it was spendthrift or imprudent, but because it was unconstitutional.

But the deeper reason why the Constitution's significance for our party system has declined is that the Constitution itself has been under running intellectual and political attack for about a hundred years. As a result, the Constitution no longer provides a clear *raison d'etre* for our parties. Deprived of their deepest ground of legitimacy, however, the parties have not prospered under the new dispensation; their public respectability has ebbed. Ross Perot's abortive presidential candidacy in 1992 was a sign of this, an ominous conjunction of disdain for political parties and barely suppressed impatience with the Constitution.

To be sure, that American political parties grew markedly weaker in the past few decades is well known, and the causes of the decline—e.g., a more educated and independent-minded electorate; television, direct mail, and the arts of the permanent campaign; the rise of the welfare state—have been extensively discussed.[6] There is no need to repeat those accounts here. What this essay contends is that beneath these various factors is another,

---

[6]For a lucid summary of this literature that also notes the ways in which parties were strengthened in the 1980s, see James Ceaser, "Political Parties—Declining, Stabilizing, or Resurging?" in Anthony King, ed., *The New American Political System*, 2nd version (Washington, D.C.: American Enterprise Institute Press, 1990), 87–137.

deeper cause, which has to do with the parties' disconnection from the Constitution and its principles. Whereas once the parties stood or tried to stand on the solid rock of the Constitution, now they struggle to gain a footing amid the sinking sand of a new generation of post-Constitutional doctrines.

What the future holds in store for American political parties will depend to a large extent on how they stand in regard to the Constitution. Our first order of business, then, is to examine how and why the older view of the Constitution and American political parties came to be transformed.

NATURAL RIGHTS AND ELECTIVE REPRESENTATION

Our most direct and authoritative access to the political principles of the American Founders is through the Declaration of Independence, which teaches that the ground of political right and obligation is human nature. By virtue of their being human, men possess equal and unalienable rights—natural rights—which "governments are instituted among men" to secure. The institution, alteration, or dissolution of a particular government is a choice that the governed must make wisely, if the decision is to be respectable and if it is to effect their real "safety and happiness." This choice belongs to the people, who are conservative, i.e., long-suffering; they seem disposed to heed the counsels of prudence. Indeed, insofar as it is not only their right but "it is their duty" to effect their safety and happiness, they are under obligation to follow what prudence "dictates."

But what are these "dictates"? They include the statement of causes, of reasons, given in the Declaration for the break with Great Britain and the decision for independence. The responsibility for assembling these reasons, and more important, for judging that George III's underlying intention was tyrannical, is taken squarely upon the shoulders of the Declaration's signers. They appeal to "the Supreme Judge of the Universe" for the "rectitude of their intentions," and pledge to each other their lives, fortunes, and "sacred Honour." The consciousness of their honor binds them together as they speak and act prudently on behalf of the people's right. In this manner, wisdom (of a few) and consent (of many) are brought together in what might be called the prototypical American party statement.

The Constitution attempts to preserve and extend this combination of wisdom and consent in two ways: by constitutionalizing wisdom through written restraints on government, the separation of powers, an independent judiciary, and other "inventions of prudence";[7] and by providing the American republic with offices whose mode of appointment, term, and distinctiveness make them suitable platforms for future statesmen. In Publius's words: "The aim of every political constitution is, or ought to be, first to obtain for rulers men who possess most wisdom to discern, and most virtue to pursue, the common good of the society; and in the next place, to take the most effectual precautions for keeping them virtuous. . . . " Under the Constitution, it is through elective representation that such rulers will be selected and, through the possibility of re-election, kept virtuous while in office. As Publius explains: "The elective mode of obtaining rulers is the characteristic policy of republican government."[8] Not every officer of the United States government is chosen by popular election, of course, but every one derives his powers "directly or indirectly from the great body of the people," and every major one is chosen or confirmed by some body (state legislatures, the Senate) responsible to an electorate.[9]

Through the application and modification of the elective principle, then, republican government is able to be good government, combining stability and energy with republican liberty.[10] Political parties effect a further modification of the elective principle, making it easier for candidates and voters to associate on the basis of common opinions and interests. The addition of political parties to the constitutional scheme required but one modification of the document's language and one further evolution in political practice. The single constitutional change needed to accommodate political parties was the Twelfth Amendment, which in effect transferred from the electoral college to political parties many of the deliberative functions integral to presidential selection. Then came the political change. After several decades, including a short period when national party competition had almost expired, the parties were revived and their deliberative and nominating functions were confided to national conventions rather than local grandees or party caucuses in the House of Representatives.

[7]*The Federalist*, No. 51, 322.
[8]*The Federalist*, No. 57, 350.
[9]*The Federalist*, No. 39, 241.
[10]See *The Federalist*, No. 37, 226–227, No. 62, 380–382, No. 63, 382–387, and No. 70, 423–428. The result is not simply the "form" of good government, protecting individual rights through an independent judiciary and so forth, but the substance of good government as well: the Constitution encourages office-holders and citizens to enact policies that serve the public good.

By these steps, parties were made consistent with the independence of the president and the general constitutional principle of
separation of powers. Though stripped of most of its deliberative
functions, the electoral college served (in this new arrangement)
to structure the party system, organizing it around state-by-state
competition for the presidency, which helped to keep the national
parties rooted in state and local organizations, and state and local
officials involved in national party affairs. What is more, the electoral college served to moderate party politics by encouraging parties to compete for votes across many different states containing
widely varying interests.

For these and other reasons, most Americans came to hold the
view that once political parties had been adapted to the Constitution's purposes, they would (and as a matter of fact, did)
strengthen republican government—adding a further barrier to
minority faction, and bolstering national opinion against the dangers of majority faction.

THE NEW VIEW OF RIGHTS

Over the course of the past century, however, a new and critical interpretation of the Constitution emerged that implied a
wholesale revision in the relation between political parties and the
Constitution. This critique was based on a new theory of rights
and representation, in many respects antithetical to the old.[11] Although there were important variations in the details of the critique—for example, between Woodrow Wilson's and Herbert
Croly's versions of it—its main elements were constant. They first
came to political prominence in the Progressive Era, began to be
institutionalized in the New Deal and Great Society, and live on in
the programs and decisions of today's administrative state and activist judiciary.

[11] It had antecendents, however, in certain aspects of the political thought of an-
tebellum America. Of particular interest is John C. Calhoun's rejection of the natural rights basis of American constitutionalism. He criticized the "great and
dangerous errors" arising from the "opinion that all men are born free and equal—
than which nothing can be more unfounded and false." Calhoun's doctrine proceeded to reject the role of political parties as guardians of the Constitution;
indeed, like Woodrow Wilson and later critics, he regarded parties as a means of
overcoming the Constitution's separation of powers and checks and balances. But
unlike them, Calhoun deplored this circumstance, arguing that parties delivered
the national government all the more surely into the hands of the unjust "numer-
ical majority." See John C. Calhoun, *A Disquisition on Government*, ed. C. Gordon
Post (Indianapolis: Bobbs-Merrill, 1953; orig. ed., 1853), 25–27, 44–45.

The new view of rights rejected the premise of traditional American republicanism, that men had rights from nature which it was the purpose of government to secure. Instead, it saw rights as products of historical development, the outcome of centuries and even millenia of political evolution. These rights were, accordingly, changeable, and if they were to remain relevant to modern times they would have to be adapted continually to new social and economic circumstances. This idea is familiar to us today in the notion of the "living Constitution," often invoked to justify far-reaching and unprecedented decisions by activist judges. But in its origins it was meant to apply to every branch of government; it was a theory of "the State."[12]

By making rights dependent on historical change, this theory may seem to open the door to moral relativism. Its formulators tried to shut that door, however, by regarding history as cumulatively or finally rational; there was an "end of history" that disclosed the final truth about man, which was that he is a being of infinite dignity, possessing a full panoply of rights that the state must protect for the sake of his full self-development or self-realization.[13] This doctrine derived from the political philosophy of Kant and Hegel, mixed with elements from the English historical school. Its American followers refused to accept Hegel's view that history ended in the rational state of constitutional monarchy, however, preferring to depict the end as a cooperative commonwealth of ever more equal citizens and ever more obliging government. Thus the "end of history" meant the end of any possible theoretical or practical challenges to equalitarian democracy, but not the end of democratization.

Further democratization was necessary in order to transform a regime based on natural rights into one that could secure real, evolving, social rights. The old view had held that rights were something natural or God-given, inhering in individual human beings, antecedent to the social contract. The new theory taught that rights emerged from the social contract, that they were defined by a bargain struck between the government and the governed, which bargain was subject to continual renegotiation as circumstances altered. In the traditional view, the contracting parties

---

[12]For a comprehensive discussion, see Woodrow Wilson, *The State: Elements of Historical and Practical Politics* (Boston: D. C. Heath & Co., 1895).

[13]See, e.g., Wilson, *The State*, 659–661 (secs. 1270–1274); Herbert Croly, *The Promise of American Life*, ed. Arthur M. Schlesinger, Jr. (Cambridge: Harvard University Press, 1965; orig. ed., 1909), 21–26, 409–454; John Dewey, *Liberalism and Social Action* (New York: Perigee Books, 1980; orig. ed., 1935), 3–9, 31–37, 88–93.

were individuals bearing rights, who set up government as their trustee and servant. In the new view, the contract is between the people and their rulers, or civil society and the state. The people come into being without an explicit act of choice; they have common historical, ethnic, linguistic, or religious roots, as in the 20th century (really, Wilsonian) doctrine of national self-determination. Moreover, they enter the contract bearing not rights but power (or freedom based on power); they get rights out of the balance of power between themselves and their government.[14]

As dangerous or precarious as that may sound, there was nothing to fear if history itself were progressive, if democracy were here to stay and monarchy, aristocracy, and tyranny were things of the past. Then it could be regarded as settled that henceforth the people would be the government—that was the meaning of democracy—and that they could be trusted not to abuse their power over themselves.[15] Accordingly, the real threat to democracy came not from demagoguery or tyranny of the majority, but from a tyranny that existed outside the public sphere, outside government —in civil society itself.[16] "Political tyranny was wiped out at Philadelphia on July 4, 1776," as F.D.R. put it in his 1936 Address Accepting the Democratic Nomination. But a new form of "economic tyranny" soon rose in its place:

The age of machinery, of railroads; of steam and electricity; the telegraph and the radio; mass production, mass distribution—all of these combined to bring forward a new civilization and with it a new problem for those who sought to remain free. For out of this modern civilization

[14]Woodrow Wilson's account of this may be found in *Constitutional Government in the United States* (Columbia: Columbia University Press, 1908), chs. 1–2. Cf. Franklin D. Roosevelt, "Campaign Address on Progressive Government at the Commonwealth Club, San Francisco, Calif., September 23, 1932," in *The Public Papers and Addresses of Franklin D. Roosevelt,* ed. Samuel I. Rosenman (New York: Random House, 1938), vol. 1, 742–756, at 743–749, and 753: "Government is a relation of give and take, a contract, perforce. . . . Under such a contract rulers were accorded power, and the people consented to that power on consideration that they be accorded certain rights" (753).

[15]See Wilson, *Constitutional Government in the United States,* 40; *The State,* 603 (sec. 1171); "The Study of Administration," in Arthur S. Link, ed., *The Papers of Woodrow Wilson* (Princeton: Princeton University Press, 1968), vol. 5, 359–380, at 365, 374–380.

[16]Thus many of the Constitution's safeguards against governmental and majority tyranny—most notably, the separation of powers—were thought by the Progressives to be obstacles to democracy. See Charles R. Kesler, "Separation of Powers and the Administrative State," in Gordon S. Jones and John Marini, eds., *The Imperial Congress: Crisis in the Separation of Powers* (New York: Pharos Books, 1988), 20–40.

economic royalists carved new dynasties. New kingdoms were built upon concentration of control over material things. . . . It was natural and perhaps human that the privileged princes of these economic dynasties, thirsting for power, reached out for control over Government itself. They created a new despotism and wrapped it in the robes of legal sanction. . . . The hours men and women worked, the wages they received, the conditions of their labor—these had passed beyond the control of the people, and were imposed by this new industrial dictatorship.[17]

In reality, then, only one form of political tyranny had been overcome in 1776, that of political royalists or monarchists. The divine right of kings had been toppled, but not the divine right of capital. To be sure, a measure of civil and religious liberty had been won in 1776 and secured by the Constitution in 1787; but the narrow and selfish doctrine of rights on which the Founding had been based was inadequate to support genuine, well-rounded, progressive human freedom. In F.D.R.'s words: "For too many of us the political equality we once had won was meaningless in the face of economic inequality."[18] The old political equality could not itself be sustained without the aid of the new economic equality. The old freedom was too formal; it masked a private system of domination by the rich, which soon extended to government.

The formal quality of the Founders' view of natural and civil rights was, in Roosevelt's interpretation, its undoing. For the rights to life, liberty, and the pursuit of happiness, while justifying limits on governmental power, left it largely up to individuals to govern their private economic appetites and to look after their economic needs—to anticipate periods of unemployment, to save for old age and medical emergencies, to extend charity to the unfortunate, and so forth. But these are precisely what most men cannot or should not be counted on to do, the New Dealers argued, particularly in the corporate and industrial age. For the modern industrial system and the rich who profit from it conspire to make these tasks difficult and unattractive; and besides, a certain insouciance or improvidence on the people's part blinds them to their long-term interest. Under these conditions, men cannot be held responsible for their own natures, for supplying the necessities of their natures. That is too daunting, too overwhelming a duty for

[17]Franklin D. Roosevelt, "Acceptance of the Renomination for the Presidency, Philadelphia, Pa., June 27, 1936," in *The Public Papers and Addresses of Franklin D. Roosevelt*, vol. 5, 230–236, at 232–233.

[18]Roosevelt, "Acceptance of the Renomination," 233; and cf. Dewey, *Liberalism and Social Action, passim.*

individual men, families, voluntary associations, or even state and local governments to perform. In Roosevelt's words, the economic royalists granted "that the Government could protect the citizen in his right to vote, but they denied that the Government could do anything to protect the citizen in his right to work and his right to live."[19] So the federal government must now turn to the protection of the right to work (i.e., to a job), and even to the right to a salubrious vacation from work; the right to social security; to medical care; to education; and so forth—to all the social and economic rights that are needed to make equality meaningful and freedom substantial.[20]

In other words, to quote one of F.D.R.'s favorite maxims, " 'necessitous men are not free men.' "[21] Necessity and freedom cannot coexist; freedom begins at the point at which man's necessities have been satisfied. By contrast, in the older view, freedom is the way in which man takes responsibility for himself while coming to grips with his necessities. Freedom is natural to man, but precisely because man's freedom is made possible (though not guaranteed) by nature, it is limited by nature. This allows man to be responsible for claiming his freedom through his own virtue, talent, and luck, without being ungrateful to nature and God for the potential that he is actualizing. For Roosevelt and the Progressives, however, freedom that is bounded by nature or dependent on nature is not real freedom, which is the work or creation of man in history. Hence the federal government must be redirected to provide for Americans' social and economic needs, must take care of our necessities in order that we may be free. The justification for this new mission comes from the re-definition of rights "in terms of a changing and growing social order," a re-definition away, that is, from nature.[22]

Herbert Croly was perhaps the most candid exponent of the new view. What it pointed to, he admitted, was a "radical transformation" of national policy and democratic principles from the "excessively individualized democracy" of the Founders to "a more highly socialized democracy." This, in turn, would require "the American state" to assume responsibility for "a morally and so-

[19]Roosevelt, "Acceptance of the Renomination," 233–234.

[20]Cf. the list of rights in Roosevelt's proposal for an "Economic Bill of Rights," in his 1944 Annual Message to Congress, *The Public Papers and Address of Franklin D. Roosevelt*, vol. 13, 32–44, at 41.

[21]See Roosevelt, "Acceptance of the Renomination," 233.

[22]Roosevelt, "Campaign Address on Progressive Government," 753.

cially desirable distribution of wealth."[23] The federal government would effect this redistribution through taxes and new experimental programs of social uplift and social engineering. Unlike the limited government established by the Constitution, this government, empowered to experiment on society, would be no strict observer of separation of powers or of the distinction between public and private. Neither positive constitutional rights nor natural rights would restrain it. For "if the chief purpose of a democratic political system is merely the preservation of such rights," Croly wrote dismissively, then it is nothing more than a glorification of the spirit of faction. Only "if these Constitutional and natural rights are considered a temporary philosophical or legal machinery, whereby a democratic society is to reach a higher moral and social consummation," can the promise of American life be realized.[24]

THE NEW VIEW OF REPRESENTATION

Supposing that the purpose of government is to bring about "a higher moral and social consummation," what does this imply for the function of political parties? In this scheme, clearly, parties do not work to preserve or perfect the Constitution, but rather to transcend it. They orient themselves not by the unchanging principles of its republicanism but by a vision of the future, a different and much better future than the Constitution or its Framers contemplated. They become vehicles for reaching, actually, approaching a promised land of democracy, which though constantly receding remains always alluring. They become conduits for what nowadays is called "leadership." The older understanding called for a system of elective representation designed to secure, and to exercise, men's inherent and unalienable rights; the new regards these rights, rooted in a retrograde view of human nature, as factious, and therefore regards elective representation as partial,

[23]Herbert Croly, *The Promise of American Life*, 23, 25. The Founders, too, were concerned that there should be a distribution of wealth conducive to democracy. But they saw this as a goal of prudent policy, not as the dictate of a radically new kind of right that impeached natural rights. They therefore sought to protect property rights, to encourage enterprise, and to enforce the obligation of contracts in order to provide a broad and stable middle-class basis for American democracy. Inheritance laws also played an important role. Cf. Alexis de Tocqueville, *Democracy in America*, trans. George Lawrence (New York: Doubleday, 1969), 51–55.

[24]Croly, *The Promise of American Life*, 79.

incomplete, subjective.[25] A just or complete representation cannot be based merely on subjective freedom, on the right of each voter or interest group to pursue its own interest.

Partisans of the old constitutionalism agreed, of course, that selfishness was not enough, but they looked to popular virtue, statesmanship, and parties incorporating constitutional principle to raise citizens' sights to the common good. For them, elective representation, as embodied in the Constitution, would "refine and enlarge the public views by passing them through the medium of a chosen body of citizens," distinguished by their wisdom, patriotism, and love of justice.[26] Accordingly, Publius predicted that the Senate would generally contain men "most distinguished by their abilities and virtue," and foresaw a "constant probability" and even a "moral certainty" that the president would be someone "pre-eminent for ability and virtue."[27] But the latter-day critics of the Constitution thought that both it and the political parties operating under its aegis were contaminated by the egoistic view of rights.

Therefore, new kinds of representation were needed to compensate for the excessive individualism of America's electoral system. These new forms of representation would serve the new view of rights, would give voice to qualities other than property, interest, virtue, ability, or even reason. Above all, the needs or private necessities of men would be heard. For so long as men were necessitous, they could not be free; so long as their desires were unmet, their reason would be unheeded: their reason could be sovereign only if their passions were satisfied. The new view of rights thus empowered the passions, demanding a minimal (but relative, therefore not so minimal) level of material welfare in order to make civil and religious rights worthwhile. The result was what we now call entitlements.

Entitlements are promises of material benefits made by government to broad classes of people whom it considers needy. These promises have in effect become a new social contract between the government and the governed. Their growing importance may be charted, roughly, by comparing the percentage of

---

[25]Cf. Croly: "It is in the nature of liberties and rights, abstractly considered, to be insubordinate and to conflict both with one another and, perhaps, with the common weal." If based on abstract rights, "democracy becomes an invitation to local, factional, and individual ambitions and purposes." *The Promise of American Life*, 79.

[26]*The Federalist*, No. 10, 82.

[27]*The Federalist*, No. 64, 391; No. 69, 414.

the federal budget devoted to "uncontrollable" social welfare spending versus the percentage devoted to defense, law enforcement, regulation of commerce, and other government activities characteristic of the old social contract.[28]

But what difference do entitlements make for political parties? Unlike natural rights, which point to elective representation— e.g., "no taxation without representation"—entitlement rights do not seem to need or to culminate in elective representation. They must be voted on in the beginning, of course, but their essence is to function as so many autonomous claims against electoral politics, as "trumps" that overrule political majorities. Future generations who might balk at the pricetag of these entitlements will be reminded that they have a duty to shell out the promised payments, not that they have a right to consent to taxes. For them, the operative principle will be "no representation without taxation"! Again, unlike the older political rights, entitlements require no spirited exertion to claim them, and hence no political parties to press such claims. Entitlements are spiritless. They go to the needy, i.e., strictly speaking, those who lack the wherewithal, even within themselves, to make a positive claim of any kind. If they could, if they claimed benefits as recognition for some contribution they make to the common good (freedom, virtue, wealth, etc.), then this would suggest that their needs do not in fact swallow up their rights. Their freedom would not be dependent on material well-being, after all. But entitlements find their appropriate political forum not in parties, legislatures, or executive offices but in bureaucracy.

Once they moved to the forefront of American politics, the new rights began to alter drastically our political system. To propagate entitlements across the country required in the first place an unprecedented centralization of administration in Washington, which was accomplished in the late 1960s and early 1970s. This, in turn, required a new and radical decentralization in the national legislature, particularly in the House of Representatives, in order to oversee the manifold federal programs now being implemented at the state and local level.[29] (These included vast new regulatory

[28]Entitlements and other "uncontrollable" spending surpassed discretionary federal spending for the first time in FY 1975, and have surpassed it ever since. The figures are collected in *The Economic and Budget Outlook: Fiscal Years 1993–1997* (Washington, D.C.: Congressional Budget Office, 1992), 118.

[29]See John Wettergreen, "Bureaucratizing the American Government," in Jones and Marini, eds., *The Imperial Congress*, 68–102; and John Marini, *The Politics of Budget Control: Congress, the Presidency, and the Growth of the Administrative State* (Washington, D.C.: Crane Russak, 1992).

efforts as well as social welfare activities.) The political effect of this was to make congressmen into ombudsmen, spending more time and money than ever on casework and constituent service in order to help their friends and supporters through the maze of federal programs. The electoral effect was to make congressmen so user-friendly that they seemed almost non-partisan; it became much harder to defeat incumbent congressmen.[30]

Members of the House thus came to enjoy a certain protection against the ebb and flow of partisan politics. Consequently, the House as a body became more insulated from the currents of national political opinion, and seemed to drop out of the pattern of electoral realignment. Four out of the last five presidents were Republicans—but Republicans have not captured the House in nearly 40 years. Perhaps political realignment is now impossible given the combined effects of the new view of rights and of the administrative state on American political parties.[31] Franklin Roosevelt seemed to envision something like this in 1932 when he announced portentously, "The day of enlightened administration has come."[32] If so, then the New Deal was meant to be the realignment to end all realignments. After it, there would be no questions of justice left in America that could not be solved by more of the same—entitlements, regulation, redistribution.[33]

THE PRESIDENT AND PARTY LEADERSHIP

Man does not live by administration alone, however, and before turning to the alternatives to elective representation that now confront and weaken our parties, let us glance at the presidency, still the focus of American party politics. As originally conceived, the presidency was to be an office above party. The president's statesmanship was to have been directed or shaped by the Constitution; but the "energy" of his office, compounded of its unity, duration, competent powers, and other qualities, also gave him a

[30]See Morris Fiorina, *Congress: Keystone of the Washington Establishment*, 2nd ed. (New Haven: Yale University Press, 1989).

[31]For speculation along these lines, see the interesting essays in Byron E. Shafer, ed., *The End of Realignment? Interpreting American Electoral Eras* (Madison: University of Wisconsin Press, 1991).

[32]Roosevelt, "Campaign Address on Progressive Government," 752.

[33]See Charles R. Kesler, "The Reagan Revolution and the Legacy of the New Deal: Obstacles to Party Realignment," in Dennis Mahoney and Peter W. Schramm, *The 1984 Election and the Future of American Politics* (Durham: Carolina Academic Press, 1987), 245–264; and the chapters by Sidney Milkis and Robert Eden in the present volume.

certain salutary freedom from the positive law.[34] The addition of political parties to the original constitutional scheme served to constrain presidents' independence somewhat, but could not overcome the constitutional character of the office. At the same time, parties multiplied presidential ties to Congress, and probably strengthened presidential influence over policy-making. At any rate, these tensions between the requirements of statesmanship and of party government became a normal part of the presidency by the mid-19th century.[35]

The modern tendency, however, is to attempt to resolve these tensions by reducing statesmanship to "leadership." The statesman as leader does not have to be magnanimous or to possess extraordinary prudence in order to make difficult choices about the common good; he has only to be in the lead, "out front" of the trends shaping his people's future. In this conception, the statesman is essentially a vessel for the Spirit of his Age. As such, his authority comes not from his character or the powers and duties of his office but from his connection to the historical trends coursing through his people, which means especially through their felt historical needs. This connection cannot run through a written, fixed Constitution, or even through political parties claiming to represent that Constitution's spirit, but must be through a new kind of party devoted to leadership, and necessarily culminating in a leader.[36]

The statesman is quintessentially a party leader, therefore, inasmuch as it is through a political party that he communicates with his followers and prepares them for the next stage in the march of progress. Parties are, then, no longer parts claiming to represent or speak for the whole people under the Constitution; parties represent the people's future to their present selves; and presidents, as party leaders, must use images and imaginative rhetoric to convey their "vision" of the people's future in order to inspire their party followers. What issues from this is a politics of imagination and passionate belief, not of "the cool and deliberate sense of the community."[37] Rather than parties devoted to constitutional

---

[34]See Harvey C. Mansfield, Jr., *Taming the Prince* (New York: The Free Press, 1989), chap. 10.

[35]On the general theme of statesmanship and political parties, see Harvey C. Mansfield's excellent *Statesmanship and Party Government: A Study of Burke and Bolingbroke* (Chicago: University of Chicago Press, 1965).

[36]Wilson, "Leaders of Men," in Link, ed., *The Papers of Woodrow Wilson*, vol. 6, 646–671; and *Constitutional Government in the United States*, chs. 3 and 8.

[37]*The Federalist*, No. 63, 384; and cf. No. 71, 432, where Publius emphasizes that presidents must have "courage and magnanimity enough" to resist the whims, passions, and momentary delusions of the people.

principle one gets parties addicted to post-constitutional enthus-iasms. It used to be enough for a president to preside over the government; now each administration wants to refound the coun-try, as can be gathered from the century's slogans—the New Free-dom, New Deal, New Frontier, Great Society, "New Covenant."

Yet the substance of these inspiring new visions of leadership is hard to distinguish from the uninspiring agenda of administra-tion that we have already discussed. It is essential to "the vision thing" to promise socio-economic advance, but this requires pro-grams that must be administered; and it is difficult for a president to be a leader and an administrator at the same time. The result is that leadership tends to crumble away into administration. We are left with "the education president," "the environmental presi-dent," "the civil rights president," and so forth; but like Humpty-Dumpty, the whole President of the United States cannot be put back together again. Besides, by trying to lead public opinion the president too often ends up following it—reacting to opinion polls, dancing to the tunes called by interest groups, etc. Political parties, which used to steady him amid the crosswinds of public opinion, now look to the president for leadership and their own sense of mission. Too often, they discover that the afflatus has left him.

CHALLENGES TO ELECTIVE REPRESENTATION

As the natural rights foundation of American government has eroded, the whole structure of our politics has tilted away from elective representation and party politics and towards new, non-elective and non-deliberative modes of representation. Of these, at least two deserve consideration here.

1. Bureaucratic Representation. The new view of rights criticizes political or elective representation of the sort ordained by the Constitution because it is too formal: it cannot overcome the so-cial and economic inequalities of American life. The self-interestedness of civil society, in other words, cannot be overcome by representing civil society in the government. Instead, "the American state" must rise above civil society; to do so, it must have the support of a class that can represent the common good. Hegel called this the "universal class" of civil servants or bureaucrats.[38] If the common good is to be secured, there must be at least one class

---

[38]G. W. F. Hegel, *Elements of the Philosophy of Right*, trans. H. B. Nisbet (Cam-bridge: Cambridge University Press, 1991), secs. 205, 289.

in the State that is unselfish, that has nothing but the common good as its object. Of course, this class must have a proper education and upbringing (lots of Hegel) in order to prepare and implement laws unselfishly. America never went so far as to build a bureaucratic class into the Constitution, but in the civil service system and in the formal and informal roles played by experts in the administrative agencies we do have a simulacrum of Hegel's system.

And in truth, to fulfill the promise of the new social and economic rights, to achieve "a morally and socially desirable distribution of wealth," something like this class is needed. For if civil society is a realm of irredeemably self-interested activity, then somehow the higher ethical order must be infused into it from outside, if justice is to be done.[39] In such a project, it would be foolish to ask the consent of the self-interested to the redistributive taxation or public-spirited regulation that must be applied to them. Here a notion of consent developed by Kant and Hegel comes to the rescue of democratic appearances: consent may be *presumed* from what a rational and moral being would agree to, without actually having to ask any particular human being for his approval.[40] Thus if a rational being could agree, e.g., to cost-of-living-adjustments for entitlement programs, it becomes unnecessary to ask actual taxpayers or their representatives to approve such increases. In fact, consent ceases to be a right and becomes a *duty*— on the part of taxpayers and other human beings, that is.[41]

These are cases, and there are many others in modern government, where unelected representatives wield power as if in the name of justice or wisdom alone, without any perceived need to get the actual consent of the governed. What might seem a dangerous arrogation of power is often defended on the grounds that for people at the bottom of the economic pyramid, deprived of their social and economic rights, bureaucratic representation is

---

[39]Strictly speaking, for Hegel the civil servants are an estate or part of civil society—its highest part. See Hegel, *Elements of the Philosophy of Right*, secs. 205, 294.

[40]See Immanuel Kant, "Perpetual Peace," in Lewis White Beck, ed., *Kant on History* (Indianapolis: Bobbs-Merrill, 1963), 92–97.

[41]Something like this doctrine stands behind the right of experts in federal agencies, e.g., the Environmental Protection Agency, to make detailed regulations on the basis of extremely broad laws. True, Congress may repeal laws and regulations of which it disapproves, and it is Congress's authority, not the agencies', that nominally lies behind the regulations. But the rules and regulations are *presumed* valid on the basis of the regulators' expertness and disinterestedness.

more representative, because more sympathetic and useful, than elective representation.[42]

Why bother then with political parties? At most, one needs interest groups (or coalitions of interest groups) to press for more benefits and to guard against abuse of power; but coalitions are not political parties, at least not in the constitutional sense spoken of here. (Indeed, the open secret of the "New Deal coalition" was that the Democratic party was on its way to becoming something quite different from a traditional political party.) The possibility of bureaucratic abuse of power does remind one of the utility of elected officials, who need and appreciate votes; and Congress and the Executive do keep an eye on the bureaucracy. But the other main watchdog on the agencies—the so-called public interest law firms and advocacy groups—operate more in the spirit of Hegel's universal class than of elected representatives. Their names tell the story: they belong to the "public-interest sector," not to the egoistic world of their fellow citizens.

2. *Racial-ethnic representation.* The principle of presumptive consent undercuts political parties from another direction, too. The formalism of natural and constitutional rights neglects race and ethnicity as much as class. Therefore, it is not surprising to see new claims for group rights based on race and ethnicity emerging out of this critique of the Constitution. The idea of individual rights is, from this viewpoint, both too universalistic and too particularistic. Too universalistic, because it abstracts from racial and other differences; too particularistic, because it takes account of innumerable subjective differences when tallying up the consent of millions of people. So it is more concrete, and more rational or objective, to try to represent men through some sort of groups, with large differences among them preserved but the small differences worn away. The modern American twist on this Hegelian idea is to use racial and ethnic groups rather than corporate or vocational ones.[43]

In the past, racial, ethnic, and religious minorities worked through political parties, advancing their interests by bargaining

---

[42]See, for example, Peter Woll, *American Bureaucracy* (New York: Norton, 1963), 138–141; cf. 175: "And the bureaucracy, which is actually a more representative body than Congress, combines essential democratic ingredients at the same time that it formulates important policy. Administrative agencies, removed from the electoral process, can take action without consulting Congress, and such action is as responsive to the demands and needs of the community as any that Congress could take. . . . "

[43]For Hegel's views on corporations, see *Elements of the Philosophy of Right,* secs. 250–255.

with other groups under the same party umbrella. By spreading their influence in party circles, they could leverage their strength in key districts and states far beyond their overall numbers. But today many of these groups follow a separatist path, desiring geographical concentration and isolation of their strength rather than its diffusion through a political party. Partly this is because the critique of the Constitution has rubbed off on the parties. That is, they are seen as racist or bourgeois (think of the battles inside and outside the 1968 Democratic National Convention), just like the rest of the power structure. Partly, too, the popularity of this new kind of virtual representation is due to the passion for authenticity that it feeds. It celebrates the notion (now enshrined in many "affirmative action gerrymanders" around the country) that blacks can only be authentically represented by a black, Latinos by a Latino, and so forth. In this respect, the basic argument for the new view of rights—that what really needs representing is men's historical desires or will, not their reason or interest—leads to the self-destruction of the very notion of human rights and of equal citizenship under law.

CONCLUSION

Allegiance to the Constitutution is still strong and deep among the American public, but discontent and even disgust with the operations of government seem to be growing. This disaffection extends to our political parties, too, which seem increasingly to be viewed as little more than factions. Perhaps this is why divided government has been the norm for the past 25 years. If neither party commands the firm support of a majority of Americans—if neither party can make a legitimate claim to represent the country's opinions, affections, and interests—then it makes sense to pit them against each other: to protect the Constitution from both of them.

To rescue the Constitution from its many critics will require both wisdom and political courage. The party that demonstrates these virtues first will help to preserve the Constitution, the country, and itself. If such an effort is not made, one can say for sure only that the American people's disgust with political parties will one day wear off on our political system, including the Constitution.

CONTRIBUTORS

Donald R. Brand is Assistant Professor of Political Science at Wilkes University.

Robert Eden is Professor of History and Politics at Hillsdale College.

William A. Galston is Professor at the School of Public Affairs, University of Maryland at College Park, and Senior Research Scholar at the University's Institute for Philosophy and Public Policy.

Michael A. Gillespie is Associate Professor of Political Science at Duke University.

Elaine Ciulla Kamarck is a Senior Fellow at the Progressive Policy Institute in Washington, D.C. and is a Visiting Assistant Professor at Barnard College.

Charles R. Kesler is Associate Professor of Government at Claremont McKenna College and Director of the Henry Salvatori Center for the Study of Freedom in the Modern World.

Michael J. Malbin is Professor of Political Science at the State University of New York at Albany and Director of the Center for Legislative Studies.

Harvey C. Mansfield, Jr., is the Frank G. Thomson Professor of Government at Harvard University.

Sidney M. Milkis is Assistant Professor of Politics at Brandeis University.

John J. Pitney, Jr. is Assistant Professor of Government at Claremont McKenna College.

Glen Thurow is the Graduate Dean and Professor of Politics at the University of Dallas.

EDITORS

Peter W. Schramm is Associate Professor of Political Science at Ashland University and Associate Director for Publications at the John M. Ashbrook Center for Public Affairs.

Bradford P. Wilson is Professor of Political Science at Ashland University and Deputy Director of the John M. Ashbrook Center for Public Affairs.

INDEX